# Which A levels?

The guide to choosing A levels
and other post-16 qualifications

## Alison Dixon

Honeyman Publishing

## Which A levels?

The guide to choosing A levels and other post-16 qualifications

© Alison Dixon

Eighth edition

Published by Honeyman Publishing 2014

ISBN 978-1-291-69755-1

Cover design by Andy Southan, Wordcraft Typesetting.

Typeset by Wordcraft Typesetting

Honeyman Publishing

honeymanpublishing@gmail..com

# Contents

## Acknowledgements

With thanks to
Andy Southan, Helen Evans and everyone who gave me quotes.

**Your post-16 options**

# THE NEXT TWO YEARS

When you complete your GCSEs, or equivalent, you must choose your next step. You might want to continue studying full time at school, or go to a different sixth form or college. You also have the option to continue your studies part time through an apprenticeship.

## Your choice of qualifications

Many people who decide to continue studying after GCSEs opt for A levels. This book provides detailed information on A levels, including descriptions of over 50 A level subjects and where each could lead. However, remember that there are alternative qualifications at the same level (level 3) such as BTEC or Cambridge Technicals. It is possible to combine these qualifications alongside A levels, so your choice of qualifications is wide.

## Tech levels

Technical level qualifications (tech levels) are for 16-year-old students who have a clear idea about the occupation they wish to pursue. They are vocational and equip students with the specialist knowledge they need for a specific recognised occupation, such as engineering, computing, accounting or hospitality.

## Raising the Participation Age

Besides continuing with full-time study after 16, your other options include apprenticeships or work or voluntary work that must include training. The training must be included in England because of legislation known as Raising the Participation Age or RPA. It means that any young person entering year 11 from September 2014 ( the academic year 2014-15) will have to stay in education and training until the end of the academic year they turn 18.

## Apprenticeships

Apprenticeships are available in many career areas. They offer structured training with an employer, leading to further qualifications. They generally fall into one of three categories:

- Intermediate Level Apprenticeships equivalent to GCSE level
- Advanced Level Apprenticeships equivalent to A level or BTEC National
- Higher Apprenticeships equivalent to a Level 4 qualification or higher.

Apprenticeships are open to anybody over 16 and there is no upper age limit so they are a realistic alternative to studying full time. You might even progress to higher education as part of, or after completing, an apprenticeship.

See www.apprenticeships.org.uk for details of the National Apprenticeship Service where you can search online for vacancies. In Wales you can search on www.careerswales.com.

## Work now, study later?

Some people decide to have a break in full-time education and then resume their studies as a mature student. Many students also consider a gap year between completing their sixth form study and going on to higher education. Gap years can consist of anything from work (paid or voluntary) or travel, or a mixture of both. In general, admissions officers in higher education are fine about gap years as they feel that students benefit from increased experience and maturity.

However, for some subjects, such as mathematics, where a break may affect progress, or for longer courses, such as medical studies, it is always advisable to check with admissions tutors for their advice.

## What to do next

The decision is yours and yours alone. Help and advice are available from your careers teacher or careers adviser in school or college and at careers centres.

You will need to consider all the alternatives and all the issues surrounding A levels and other post-16 options. Parents and friends can also offer advice, although they may not have the latest information.

To help you to decide, ask yourself some basic questions.

- Why am I interested in studying further?
- Would I benefit from further study?
- Would I learn better through a mixture of work and training?
- Do I really understand what is involved in further study?
- Do my teachers think I am right to continue in full-time education?
- Do I know what is available?
- What am I good at (including skills and knowledge outside the classroom)?
- What do I really enjoy?
- What would I do after further study? Go on to university or college, or into an apprenticeship/job that includes further training?
- Do I have any clear ideas about a career or the future?

# HIGHER EDUCATION

## What is it and how do I decide whether it is for me?

Higher education does not just mean going to university. Higher education courses can also be taken at a college of higher or further education or studied by distance learning (including via the internet) and can be part time as well as full time. You can study locally or in another part of the country. Your course might last anything from two to five years and could include work or study placements in the UK or worldwide.

## What are the benefits of higher education?

This is a difficult one as there are so many advantages to higher education—it depends on what you want to get out of it. You will be going somewhere new, studying a subject you like, or a new subject, in depth. You will be meeting a whole range of new people and will get the chance to do new things. You will be learning lots of useful skills for life in addition to what your course teaches you. It is also worth remembering that graduates can earn on average 20 to 25% more than non-graduates and this is higher with degrees in subjects such as engineering, maths and sciences. You will of course have to weigh up the financial implications as well.

## What courses are available?

*Degree courses:* these are courses that people automatically think about when they are thinking of higher education. They usually last three or four years, full time (longer if you are studying subjects such as medicine). They can also be studied part time, sometimes while working in a related job.

*HNC/HND courses:* Higher National Certificates (HNCs) or Diplomas (HNDs) are work-related qualifications, available in everything from accounting to film production. HNCs are the part-time equivalents of HNDs. Students often study HNCs part time over two years, while they are in employment.

HNDs take two years to complete on a full-time basis (or three years with a work placement). HNCs and HNDs can allow entry into the second or third year of a degree course.

*Foundation degrees:* these are qualifications designed with employers, and combine academic study with workplace learning. Some have been designed to tackle particular skills shortages. They last two years, full time (or they can be taken part time) and it's possible to progress to further or higher study or top up to a full degree. You may go straight into work after a foundation degree. You can search for foundation degree courses on the UCAS website.

## Art Foundation course

If you are thinking of studying art and design at university, you usually have to study an Art Foundation course at a college of further education or art school, then move on to your degree studies. Entry to college or art school depends far more on a strong portfolio (collection of artwork that you have produced) than specified grades for A levels or equivalent.

The degree that you take can have an impact on the careers that you can enter. Make sure that your choice of degree is appropriate for the career in which you are interested.

# A LEVELS

If you are considering taking A levels, think about some of these questions.

- Do I know the full range of options at 16+?
- Why do I want to do A levels?
- How demanding are A levels?
- How can I do well at them?
- What subjects should I study?
- Should I study at school or college?
- Have I taken advice from careers advisers, teachers, parents and friends?

## How are A levels structured?

The Government is currently looking at a new structure for A levels.The changes mean that the new A level will be linear, with all assessment at the end of two years of study. Although the AS level will be retained, it will be redesigned as a high quality stand-alone qualification rather than a means of progression to A2. The first of the new A levels will be introduced for teaching in schools from September 2015, with first exams being sat in 2017. At the time of writing, the subjects to be offered from 2015 are art and design, business studies, computing, economics, English (language, literature, language and literature), geography, history, psychology, sciences (physics, chemistry, biology) and sociology.

## Choosing your A level subjects

The two most important criteria for choosing subjects are:
- what you are likely to be good at
- what you are likely to enjoy.

You will find there are some subjects available that you won't have come across previously at school. Find out about them before you choose. The subjects listed in this book will be a good place to start.

Most higher education courses require certain A level grades (or alternative equivalent qualifications), and many specify the A level subjects and GCSE subjects that you should have. Think ahead to what you will be doing after A levels to help you choose the best subjects now. If you are not sure what career you will enter, try to choose a selection of subjects that will keep your options as open as possible.

Therefore, when making your choices you should consider:
- the subjects in which you are interested
- your abilities, aptitudes and skills
- how open you want to keep your career choice
- which A level subjects are available at your school or in local sixth forms and colleges.

## A level subject combinations

Some A levels cover common ground, for example, geography and environmental studies, or media studies and film studies. If the overlap is too great, some higher education institutions may not accept the combination. On the other hand, two complementary subjects may help a great deal in your studies. For example, doing physics without mathematics or another science would be difficult and is not generally recommended.

Some degree courses specify the A level subjects that you need. The following list shows the most popular degrees that often require specific A levels:

*biology*–biology and another science or maths

*chemistry*–chemistry and sometimes maths and/or another science

*dentistry*–chemistry and one or two other sciences

*engineering*–maths and physics (or maths and chemistry for chemical engineering)

*maths*–maths and possibly further maths

*medicine*–chemistry and usually one or two other sciences. The majority of medical schools require a full A level in chemistry.

Some require biology at A level. (For candidates without science subjects at A level or equivalent, it is possible to undertake an additional pre-medical year at some universities. The pre-medical year is a preliminary course in chemistry, physics and biology.)

**modern languages**–usually you will need the language at A level standard but requirements vary, especially for less common languages

**music**–music

**physics**–physics and maths

**veterinary science**–chemistry and one or two other sciences.

## Facilitating subjects

Some courses at universities require applicants to have studied certain subjects already, so you must be sure how your choices at school and college may close off certain subjects at university. A group of universities called the Russell Group has listed subjects that are usually considered by universities to be helpful and/or required at advanced level (e.g. A level) for particular courses. For more information see www.russellgroup.ac.uk.

These subjects are called 'facilitating' because choosing them at advanced level leaves open a wide range of options for university study. These facilitating subjects include maths and further maths, physics, biology, chemistry, history, geography, modern and classical languages and English literature.

## Advanced Extension Award (AEA)

The AEA is an examination designed to stretch the most able of A level students. It was available in 19 subjects but has now been withdrawn with the exception of the maths qualification, which will be available until 2015. It counts for points on the UCAS tariff.

# ALTERNATIVES TO A LEVELS

There is a range of qualifications that you could consider instead of, or in combination with, A levels. Some of these qualifications, such as BTEC National and Cambridge Technical qualifications, are widely available. Other programmes of learning included, such as the International Baccalaureate or Cambridge Pre-U, are offered by some institutions.

## BTEC National qualifications

These are specialist vocational qualifications valued by both employers and higher education. They focus on applied knowledge and understanding of a specialised area. BTEC National Diplomas are practical, work-related courses and are at level 3, the same level as A levels. You learn by completing projects and assignments that are based on realistic workplace situations, activities and demands. Students focus on a particular subject area and develop a range of specialist skills and knowledge. BTEC qualifications attract points on the UCAS tariff.

BTEC qualifications have recently been revised so the BTEC National Diploma is now known as the Edexcel BTEC Level 3 Extended Diploma, equivalent to three full A levels. It prepares students for direct entry into employment or for progression to higher education.

The subject areas below are those in which BTEC Level 3 National qualifications are available:

- aerospace engineering
- agriculture
- animal management
- applied law
- applied science
- art and design
- aviation operations
- beauty therapy sciences
- blacksmithing and metalworking
- business
- children's care, learning and development
- communications technology
- construction, building services engineering and civil engineering
- countryside management
- dental technology
- electrical/electronic engineering
- engineering
- fish management
- horticulture
- hospitality
- floristry
- forestry and arboriculture
- hairdressing
- health and social care
- horse management
- IT practitioners
- land-based technology
- manufacturing engineering
- mechanical engineering
- media
- music and music technology
- operations and maintnance engineering
- performing arts
- personal and business finance
- pharmacy services
- production arts
- public service
- retail
- sport
- sport and exercise studies
- travel and tourism
- uniformed public services
- vehicle technology.

To find out more about these and other subjects go to the Edexcel website: www.edexcel.org.uk.

## Cambridge Technicals

Cambridge Technicals are vocational qualifications at Level 2 and Level 3 for students aged 16+. They're designed with the workplace in mind and are an alternative to A Levels.

The qualifications allow for a high degree of flexibility with the choice of units that make up the qualifications, so students can specialise in the specific areas of the subject that interest them most. Students at both levels can progress to employment or further education. In addition, at Level 3, Cambridge Technicals attract UCAS points and can therefore enable progression to higher education as well.

They are available in these subject areas: art and design, business, health and social care, ICT, media and communication, performing arts, science and sport, leisure and recreation.

For further information go to the OCR website: www.ocr.org.uk.

## International Baccalaureate (IB)

The International Baccalaureate Diploma programme is equivalent to other post-16 qualifications, such as A levels. It normally takes two years and covers a broader range of subjects than A levels. You study six subjects, which include mathematics, your own language, a foreign language, a humanities subject, a science and an arts subject. You could take a second foreign language or science in place of the arts subject. The IB Diploma also includes an extended essay. The IB Diploma is accepted for university entry and attracts points on the UCAS tariff. To find out more see www.ibo.org.

## Cambridge Pre-U

The Cambridge Pre-U is an alternative to A levels. It aims to prepare students with the skills and knowledge they need to be successful in higher education and attracts UCAS points. It consists of a number of principal subjects plus the core Global Perspectives and Research (GPR) element.

The Cambridge Pre-U Diploma is awarded to those completing three principal subjects and the core GPR component. Up to two A levels may be substituted for the principal subjects. The Cambridge Pre-U GPR element can be taken as a freestanding package, and a separate qualification.

The Cambridge Pre-U Diploma is available in 25 principal subjects, certificated separately and assessed at the end of a two-year programme of study. One-year short courses are available in modern languages.

You can find out more at www.cie.org.uk.

## AQA Bacc

This consists of three A levels plus an AS in critical thinking, general studies, citizenship, science in society or world development. It also includes an Extended Project Qualification (EPQ) and core enrichment activities, which include work-related learning, community or voluntary work and personal development activities such as public speaking, first aid, photography, sport or performing arts. See www.aqa.org.uk for more information.

## Welsh Baccalaureate

The Welsh Baccalaureate Diploma is formed of two parts:

**Core** consists of the following components: essential skills; Wales, Europe and the world (which includes a language option); work-related education, personal and social education and an individual investigation.

**Options** consists of principal learning and a project together with other options such as GCSEs, AS/A levels and BTECs.

The Welsh Baccalaureate Diploma is available at foundation, intermediate and advanced level. The Advanced Diploma is accepted for entry into higher education and attracts UCAS points. For more information, visit www.welshbaccalaureate.org.uk.

## Scottish Highers and Advanced Highers

Available in Scotland, Highers are the qualifications normally needed for entry into university or college to study for degrees and Higher National courses (HNCs and HNDs).

Four or five Highers are normally taken in Scotland in the fifth and sixth year of secondary school or at a college of further education and are studied in considerable depth, involving coursework and final examinations. Advanced Highers are taken in the sixth year at school, or at college, and are aimed particularly at students who have passed Highers. They extend the skills and knowledge gained at Higher level and are additional qualifications that are useful for entry into higher education or the workplace. Universities express their entry requirements in terms of

Highers; entry profiles for Highers and Advanced Highers can be found on the UCAS website, www.ucas.com.

## Scottish Baccalaureate

There are four available in languages, science, expressive arts or social sciences. They consist of a group of relevant Higher and Advanced Higher qualifications depending on the area chosen. In addition there is an Interdisciplinary Project. This is an Advanced Higher Unit in which you apply your subject knowledge in realistic contexts. The idea of the Interdisciplinary Project is to help you develop and show evidence of initiative, responsibility and independent working. These are skills that will help you in higher education and in employment. Find out more at www.sqa.org.uk/baccalaureates.

# A level subjects

# Accounting

*Accountancy studies the money side of business and aims to answer questions such as: What profit has our business made? How does it compare with the previous year?*

*Can we afford to expand/take on more staff? The course stresses the importance of discipline in terms of accuracy and presentation, but leaves you to interpret financial positions. You will gain an understanding of the wider business environment, how financial control is vital to business success and how, without it, even profitable firms can fail. You will learn about the effects of economic, legal and technological change on accounting, and the social implications of accounting decisions.*

*An interest in business and GCSE maths will be an advantage and may be an entry requirement. You don't need a GCSE in accounting as the A/AS level can be started from scratch.*

## What do you study?

*The topics listed give an idea of what could be covered. The exact content of courses differs according to exam boards, so you will need to check with your school or college about the exact modules available to you.*

There are two main types of business accounting, both covered by A level. The first is financial accounting, which is mainly concerned with the current state of a company's accounts. Financial accountants undertake auditing (checking in detail) the financial records of companies and preparing annual accounts for HM Revenue & Customs and shareholders.

The second type is management accounting, which mainly deals with examining a company's accounts to help senior managers with forward planning and decision making.

As you progress through your course, you are often put in the role of financial adviser to the managers of a business. You are asked to recommend the actions that the business should take to improve its performance or to get out of financial trouble.

The AS is a general introduction and will be useful to anybody interested in business and finance. At A level students study management accounting and company accounts.

## Financial accounting

- *Accounting records*–how to keep records of a company's financial activity, including double-entry bookkeeping (every credit on one account must be matched by a debit on another), how to treat debts, creditors, investments and capital. The use of ICT in accounting.
- *Formal presentation of financial information*–
  trial balances, cash-flow statements, balance sheets, profit-and-loss accounts and published company accounts.
- *Stock valuation*–how to organise and present information about stock held by a business organisation.

## Management accounting

- *Budgeting and cash-flow forecasts*–predicting the company's financial future.
- *Break-even analysis*–assessing whether a business project can cover its costs and how much it must sell before making a profit.
- *Investment appraisal*–the pros and cons of investing money.
- *Overheads*–accounting for indirect costs that are not incurred in the actual product or a service (e.g. an IT system).
- *Analysing and interpreting accounts*–understanding what accounts can (and can't) tell you about the health and prospects of a business, and using ratios to analyse company performance.
- *Planning and decision*–making how decisions are made on the basis of financial information and how managers use this to plan ahead.

## Subject combinations

Popular A level combinations include business studies, economics, ICT, languages and law. However, make sure there isn't too much overlap with other subjects, especially business studies. If you are considering accountancy at degree level, some universities ask for mathematics or statistics at A level.

Accounting A level is not a requirement for accountancy courses, and while some courses find it a useful preparation others may not accept it. Check with higher education institutions.

GCSE maths is often required and sometimes English.

# Higher education options

## Degree-level study

You don't need an accountancy degree to qualify as an accountant so you could consider related subjects such as business studies, maths, economics, actuarial science or law. Quantity surveying is another option, as quantity surveyors are the accountants of the construction industry.

To qualify as a professional accountant after graduating, you must complete an initial stage of formal training, the foundation stage, followed by a three-year training contract while working and studying for professional exams. An accountancy degree exempts you from most of the foundation exams. Some degree subjects such as business economics, business information management and management science, also give exemptions. Check with professional accountancy bodies for a full list.

Many degrees are called accounting and finance, but have the same content as accounting or accountancy. Some degrees have an international perspective, including languages and a period of study or work abroad.

## Degree subject combinations

Accounting can be combined with many subjects. ICT, economics, law, marketing, business studies and psychology are popular, but if you reduce the proportion of accountancy in your degree you may not get all the professional exam exemptions.

## Other higher education qualifications

There are foundation degrees available in accounting, some including business management or administration. Accounting and related subjects such as business and management are available at HND/HNC. You will need to check to see if they give any exemptions from professional accountancy exams.

## Relevance to other subjects?

Your accounting A level is useful even if you don't intend to qualify as an accountant or work in business. The understanding you gain of business and finance is useful for degree courses in economics, law, ICT, marketing, administration or tourism.

## Important advice

If you are considering a year out between A levels and your degree, check with the institutions. Some prefer accountancy students not to take gap years, or ask that you get some relevant work experience. Make your plans clear on your UCAS application.

# Future careers

### ▷ After A levels

Higher Apprenticeships are available in accounting which combine work experience with university level study.

The ICAEW (Institute of Chartered Accountants in England and Wales) offers a training route with qualifications from the Association of Accounting Technicians (AAT). This is a fast-track route, which enables you to qualify as a chartered accountant in four years. Employers usually ask for between 240 and 320 UCAS points.

To qualify as a chartered accountant without a degree involves a four-year training contract with a firm of chartered accountants or with a company finance department. During this time you would take AAT and ICAEW exams. You then join graduate entrants to the profession as you move on to the professional training stage. The route to qualification with the other professional bodies is very similar.

You could consider qualifying as an accounting technician and may get some exemptions for the qualification because of your A level in accounting. The course is based on skills tests and simulations and training is offered by the AAT and the Association of Chartered Certified Accountants (ACCA).

If you don't plan to qualify as an accountant, there are opportunities for working in finance departments of many organisations. Such jobs involve arranging salaries, paying bills and issuing invoices. A management trainee scheme or apprenticeship would allow you to use your accounting skills and undertake further training.

You could consider working in banks or building societies, or becoming a financial adviser. Skills gained like numeracy, research and analysis, problem-solving, communication and computer skills will be useful in many jobs.

## ▷After a degree

### Working in accounting

These are the areas of accountancy open to graduates. The choice of professional body that you train with depends on the kind of work you want to do.

***Chartered accountants*** work in private practice mainly dealing with taxation and auditing. Chartered accountancy firms mainly operate as partners, so if you become a partner, you take a share of the profits rather than a salary. Private practice accountants usually qualify with the ICAEW.

***Certified accountants*** work as salaried employees in commerce or industry. In all but the smallest businesses, they have either a financial or management accountancy role. The professional body for this type of accountancy is the ACCA, but ICAEW and ACCA qualifications are interchangeable.

***Management accountants*** are more firmly oriented towards business, especially financial planning and strategy, and the use of IT for management information. They qualify with the Chartered Institute of Management Accountants (CIMA).

***Public finance accountants*** work within the Civil Service, NHS or local government. Public service has a very clear career structure but is a specialised form of accounting so it might be difficult to move into other areas. Public finance accountants qualify with the Chartered Institute of Public Finance and Accountancy (CIPFA).

***Accounting technicians*** work alongside professionally qualified accountants collecting financial information to assist them in making business decisions. Accounting technicians usually work in a support role within an accountancy firm or in the finance department of an organisation.

Depending on the route taken to qualify for the AAT and any experience gained, accounting technicians may undertake a range of roles, which will include:
- assisting with the preparation of accounts
- preparing the payroll
- dealing with invoices needing payment
- dealing with basic bookkeeping.

At a more senior level, they may be employed in audit work, both external and internal.

## Working outside accounting

Wherever you work, financial knowledge is valuable. You could consider a career in financial advice, financial analysis or in insurance or investment, assessing peoples needs and advising them on investments. A career in business management or consultancy would require you to have a clear understanding of how finances work and you could consider a graduate training scheme. Your skills would also be useful in jobs within HM Revenue & Customs.

## Sources of information

Association of Accounting Technicians (AAT)
www.aat.org.uk

Association of Chartered Certified Accountants (ACCA)
www.acca.org.uk

Chartered Institute of Management Accountants (CIMA)
www.cimaglobal.com

Chartered Institute of Public Finance and Accountancy(CIPFA)
www.cipfa.org.uk

Institute of Chartered Accountants in England and Wales (ICAEW)
www.icaew.com

Institute of Chartered Accountants in Scotland (ICAS)
www.icas.org.uk

---

*'I didn't want to end up with a huge debt, so I have taken the Higher Apprenticeship route. I like the fact that I can put all my learning into practice straight away but still end up with a degree level qualification.'*
Deirdre, aged 19, first year Higher Apprentice

---

# Ancient history

*Are you fascinated by the ancient world as portrayed in films like* Troy, Gladiator **and** *300?* **If you want to make sense of the world today, it's important to understand key events, individuals, movements and conflicts that have shaped history.**

*A study of ancient history covers all aspects of the classical world from Ancient Greece to the fall of the Roman Empire (from about the sixth century BC to AD 410). You look at how the political and military influence of city states and empires rose and fell and how their economy, culture and society changed. The subject involves all aspects of classical civilisation, including social factors (women, slavery and religion), artistic and literary factors (literature, sculpture and architecture), intellectual developments (philosophy and education) and economic aspects of the societies. The Roman Empire provides one example of a united Europe, something relevant today, and you will discover how these civilisations influenced the Western world and still do today.*

## What do you study?
*OCR is the only exam board currently offering this subject as part of its suite of classics qualifications and the official title is now classics: ancient history. The AQA classical civilisation specification offers options in ancient history.*

For AS you will study the following:

## Greek History from original sources
Greek history studied through the interpretation and evaluation of original sources:
- Athenian Democracy in the 5th century BC
- Delian League to Athenian Empire
- Politics and society of Ancient Sparta

## Roman History from original sources
Roman history studied through the interpretation and evaluation of original sources:
- Cicero and political life in late Republican Rome
- Augustus and the Principate
- Britain in the Roman Empire

A2 broadens your studies:

## Greek History: conflict and culture

A study of culture and conflict in the Greek World of the 5th century BC
- Greece and Persia 499-449 BC
- Greece in conflict 460-403 BC
- The culture of Athens 449-399 BC

## Roman History: the use and abuse of power

A study of the Roman World from the late Republic to the early empire
- The fall of the Roman Republic 81-31 BC
- The invention of Imperial Rome 31 BC-AD 96
- Ruling the Roman Empire AD 14-117

There is a GCSE in ancient history and also one in classical civilisation, which will be a useful preparation for the subject, although not essential.

Latin or Greek can provide valuable background to the ancient history A level. All texts are studied in English, so you don't need any knowledge of Latin or Greek. A good English GCSE is sometimes required for this course.

## Subject combinations

If you plan to take a degree in ancient history, an ancient history A level is the best preparation although not always required by universities. It is unlikely that you would be required to offer any other specific A level. If you wished to offer a classics A level combining elements of the other pathways (Latin, classical Greek or classical civilisation) this would also be acceptable. The combination of A level ancient history with Greek or Latin options could lead to a degree in subjects like politics, English, foreign languages and archaeology.

If you are taking ancient history with an archaeology degree in mind, it would be very useful to have a science subject at A level; you would be expected to have it at GCSE level. Occasionally a GCSE in a modern language is required, but otherwise any subject that demands similar research and essay-writing techniques will be useful. This would include subjects such as history, English, and government and politics.

# Higher education options

### Degree-level study

Ancient history degrees involve a first year spent developing general background knowledge about the subject, plus the basic skills needed to analyse and interpret historical data. You are not expected to have learned an ancient language at school but most courses allow you to learn Latin, Greek or even Egyptian or Sumerian. In the second and third year, courses include a broader range of topics, but may also allow you to specialise in a specific area such as Greek, Roman, Egyptian or near eastern ancient history. You may be able to go on study trips to areas or countries relevant to your chosen options.

### Degree subject combinations

Many students at university combine ancient history with a related subject such as archaeology, classical studies, Egyptology, Greek, Latin or medieval studies. It can be combined with other history specialisms such as medieval history, the history of ideas, or modern history. Each has a unique approach to the study of past societies and provides you with a wider perspective on your studies of ancient civilisations. Subjects that look at political, cultural, religious and economic factors in human societies work especially well with ancient history. These include religious studies, philosophy, politics, anthropology, economic and social history, history of art and modern languages.

### Other higher education qualifications

There are no ancient history foundation degrees but there are related subjects such as history, heritage and archaeology, management for the heritage sector and practical archaeology, giving you a mixture of practical and theoretical work.

### Relevance to other subjects?

Ancient history has a number of related areas. Archaeology can be an ideal progression from ancient history A level. Medieval history and medieval studies focus on the origins and development of societies between about AD 400 and 1500. Celtic civilisation, Welsh, Irish and Scottish history cover the languages and cultures of the peoples who have lived in the British Isles since before the arrival of the Romans and Anglo-Saxons. Classical civilisation courses are often similar to ancient history but have a specific focus on Greece and Rome, and include more study of literature, usually in translation.

Courses in classics, Latin and Greek cover similar ground, but the literary and historical sources are studied in the original so much more time is spent on language work.

## Important advice

Because A level ancient history is rarely a requirement for entry to an ancient history degree, choosing to study the subject demonstrates a genuine interest. This could play an important part in whether or not you are offered a place. Evidence of such interest can come from visiting sites of historic interest whenever you have the chance, getting involved in archaeological digs as a volunteer and reading as much as you can about the subject in your spare time.

# Future careers

## ▷ After A levels

As a student of A level ancient history, you will have gained skills in evaluating different types of evidence, placing them in context, and presenting them in a clear and balanced way. These are exactly the skills you need to work in areas such as management, sales and marketing. You might also want to consider jobs as a museum or library assistant.

## ▷ After a degree

### Working in ancient history

It is very unlikely that a degree in ancient history will lead to a career that will use your specialist knowledge to any great extent. For example, to teach the subject in schools you would need to be able to teach another subject as well, so you would need to consider a combined degree. Ancient history is clearly related to archaeology, but again there are specialist archaeology degrees, many of which involve an element of scientific analysis. To work as an archaeologist, therefore, you should aim either for a degree in archaeology or a combined degree in ancient history and archaeology. However, there could be opportunities in the heritage industry working in museums and other attractions.

### Working outside ancient history

The skills of an ancient historian - research, analysis and reasoning - are attractive to employers in many professions. Graduates in ancient history go on to careers in a wide range of areas including business, education and the media. Your research skills could also prove valuable for a career in law as an understanding of the systems of control used within classical civilisations (in particular, that of the Romans) is helpful in understanding the origins of our present-day legal system.

## Sources of information
Council for British Archaeology
www.archaeologyuk.org

www.creative-choices.co.uk

www.besthistorysites.net

> 'Ancient history helped to shape the world today; it's just as important as learning about the two world wars and the industrial revolution.'
> Jackie, aged 17, studying A levels in ancient history, politics and ICT

# Anthropology

*Anthropology is the study of mankind: where we came from, how we live differently in societies across the world, and how we interact with our environments. It looks at questions relating to human behaviour from biological, social and ecological perspectives. It examines the context of societies and societal change and makes cross-cultural comparisons.*

*Studying anthropology will help you to think critically about your own society. You will gain an understanding of your own society and also develop a broad knowledge about global politics, economic development, cultures and beliefs, and an insight into the realities of life in other regions of the world. Anthropology has several different disciplines within it such as cultural, archaeological, linguistic, and biological or physical anthropology. The latter deals with the social behaviour and biology of different people and includes the study of evolution.*

## What do you study?

### Being human: unity and diversity
- The body
- Ways of thinking and communicating
- Organising social relations
- Engaging with nature

### Becoming a person: identity and belonging
- Personhood
- Becoming a person
- Drawing boundaries and defining groups

At A2 you get to explore issues in a global as well as local context, and also to apply knowledge and understanding of anthropological principles to a small-scale investigation on an anthropological topic of your choice.

### Global and local: societies, environments and globalisation
- Approaches to globalisation
- Local and global processes: ethnographic perspectives

### Practising anthropology: methods and investigations
- Themes within anthropology
- Methods and investigations

### Subject combinations
Anthropology can have either a social sciences or scientific slant so combines well with many different A level subjects.

# Higher education options

### Degree-level study
There are many different ways to study anthropology to either BA or BSc level. Some universities teach biological and social anthropology as separate degrees, others don't distinguish between the two. There are also specialised courses like forensic anthropology, where human remains are analysed for either medical or legal purposes. Some university courses specialise in different regions of the world.

### Degree subject combinations
Anthropology is often taught together with another subject such as archaeology or a language but can be combined with many subjects.

### Other higher education qualifications
There are no foundation degrees or HNDS in anthropology.

### Important advice
Visit local and national museums to find out more about the different types of anthropology and help your applications. There are more and more television programmes covering this and related areas.

# Future careers

### ▷Into work after A levels
Employers will value your understanding of human social behaviour and society as well as your research skills. Career opportunities include working for the government, market research, human resources, the police or prison service as well as in social care.

### ▷After a degree
There are very few careers directly related to anthropology and they are likely to be in jobs such as lecturing or specialised research. However, anthropologists are creative and critical thinkers, who are well equipped for a variety of careers. Possibilities include education, government, advertising, charities, international organisations such as the World Health Organisation, museums and the media. Anthropology graduates also go into journalism; it's very useful for foreign correspondents and for marketing and PR.

## Sources of information

The Royal Anthropological Institute
www.therai.org.uk

Discover Anthropology
www.discoveranthropology.org.uk

> *'Anthropology really changes the way that you think about things. It challenges all your assumptions about the world.'*
> John, social anthropology degree student

# Archaeology

*Archaeology is the study of past societies through their material remains and environmental context. This includes artefacts, buildings, burials and landscapes. Methods of data collection and analysis include excavation, survey and artefact studies, utilising a range of scientific and theoretical approaches.*

## What do you study?

In archaeology A level, you study the techniques of modern archaeological research and its place in society and themes that are wide ranging in both time and geographical distribution. The units cover the archaeology of religion and ritual, archaeological skills and methods, world archaeology and archaeological investigation.

The periods you might study include prehistoric Britain (Neolithic to Iron Age), Ancient Egypt, the Roman world or the Maya. The course encourages you to develop your capacity for critical thinking and to see the relationships between different aspects of archaeology. In the final unit, you undertake your own archaeological investigation, a piece of coursework based on personal research and fieldwork. This investigation normally focuses on your local environment, using local resources and using the archaeological methodology learned elsewhere in the course. The course includes field trips to archaeological sites.

## Subject combinations

Archaeology combines well with many other subjects such as science, art, technology, geography, history, sociology, anthropology and religious studies. Sciences are especially useful if you intend to study archaeology at degree level and some universities require at least one A level in geography, environmental science, biology, history, chemistry, physics, mathematics, information technology or geology. Archaeological science courses may require one or two science subjects.

# Higher education options

## Degree-level study

There are a variety of courses on offer and most courses cover British and European archaeology - Stone Age, Bronze Age, Iron Age, Roman and medieval periods. If you want to do something more specialised like Egyptology or classical archaeology for example then the choices are more limited. Although most courses offer practical skills, there are some that specialise more in practical archaeology. Archaeological science concentrates on the application of science to archaeology with specialisms like forensic archaeology. All courses will offer some element of field work.

## Degree subject combinations
Many subjects are available to combine with archaeology. The most common are anthropology, ancient history, geography, classics and modern languages.

## Other higher education qualifications
There are some foundation degrees available in archaeology and in history, heritage and archaeology; also a crime scene and forensic science foundation degree which contains some elements of archaeological sciences.

## Important advice
See if you can visit an archaeological dig to see how it is done. Your local museum may know what is going on in your area.

# Future careers

## ▷After A levels
You will have excellent research and administration skills from your A level study which could prove useful in many jobs. There may be apprenticeships in museums, heritage or tourism where you can use your knowledge and skills. Look out for cultural and heritage apprenticeships in your area.

## ▷After a degree
## Working in archaeology
Archaeologists are employed in all sorts of places, not just on digs. They find work in national agencies, local authorities, museums, universities, planning consultancies and private practice, undertaking a wide variety of activities from field practice to laboratory work, information management to education, specialist research to artefact curation and display. Many students take a postgraduate course after their first degree to improve their job prospects. There are a variety of courses available including bioarchaeology, osteoarchaeology, environmental archaeology, field archaeology, forensic archaeology, heritage, landscape

archaeology, GIS (geographical information systems), maritime archaeology and museum studies.

## Working outside archaeology

A degree in archaeology can help with a number of careers including lecturing, the Civil Service, teaching, professional consultancy, media and the arts. Archaeology requires such a broad range of skills that its graduates are well equipped for many careers, and have developed the ability to inquire scientifically but also to see broad patterns of change. Many graduates find work in the heritage sector: museums, historical tourism and for organisations like English Heritage and the National Trust.

## Sources of information

Current Archaeology
www.archaeology.co.uk
has a directory of current digs in the UK, some of which will consider applications from 16 upwards.

Council for British Archaeology
www.archaeologyuk.org

---

*'Make sure you get some experience before you apply. There is always something locally. I went to my local library and they were very helpful'*
Dionne, 21 in final year of archaeology degree

---

# Art and design

*The visual world is a key aspect in many forms of communication. This course is for anyone who appreciates the visual world as it helps you develop an understanding of all things visual. You will learn traditional drawing and painting skills, new media techniques and also theoretical terms. You will be encouraged to look at a broad range of artists and to review your own work in relation to what you have studied. You will also learn to analyse your own work as a way of improving and developing it.*

## What do you study?

Painting and drawing are the core components of art and design A level and the new specifications will have a bigger emphasis on drawing.

You also study the following:

- how and why art works as a form of communication
- the forms and styles that such communication may take
- issues relating to light, colour, form, perspective and movement.

Options could include the following:

- **fine art**–traditional painting and drawing in oils, watercolour and other materials
- **three-dimensional design**–pottery and sculpture in clay, wood, stone and similar materials
- **textile design**–the design and creation of fabrics and clothing
- **graphic communication**–two-dimensional design for business, advertising and industry (company logos, trademarks and packaging etc), as a way of communicating information and a companys image, often using IT-based techniques
- **photography**–the creation and use of photographic images
- **film and video**–including directing and editing
- **critical and historical studies**–looking at a range of artists both from the past and in the contemporary art world to encourage you to develop a greater understanding of the subject and help you look more critically at your own work.

It is recommended, but not essential, to have studied GCSE art and design to take art and design A level.

Art and design A level work is mainly practical although written work may feature in some assignments. You learn through practice either working on your own or in a group under the guidance of the teacher. Practising your art and design skills is time consuming and you must be prepared to spend a lot of your own time in the studio. There will be coursework—a number of pieces to be completed during your studies—and practical exams, which involve supervised working over a set period of time. You will also go on visits to a range of art galleries and exhibitions to study art first hand.

### Subject combinations

If you want to move onto a practical art and design course at a higher level the usual route is an A level in art and design plus an Art Foundation course. For more academic higher education courses such as art history, you will need one or two more A levels. If you are considering architecture or landscape architecture, it would be useful although not essential to have maths or sciences to support your application. A level art and design may not be acceptable as an academic subject for entry to unrelated degree subjects, so you should always check with universities and colleges.

## Higher education options

### Degree-level study

The normal route to a degree in art and design is through a one-year Art Foundation course. This can be taken at local colleges of art, many further education colleges and several universities. The purpose of the Art Foundation course is to give you the opportunity to explore a greater range of media than is usually possible in schools and to help and support you in preparing a portfolio of work to support your degree course applications. It is designed to be diagnostic that is, enabling you to explore the breadth of your interests and abilities within art and design, helping you make decisions about your future direction within the subject. To get onto an Art Foundation course, you normally need to have at least one A level, preferably in art and design, or equivalent.

Your portfolio needs to be of a high standard, and your A level course is the best opportunity for building that up. Your portfolio will be reviewed at interview and needs to demonstrate your ability in:

- visualisation skills (e.g. drawing, photography, 3D work)
- research and investigative skills
- creative thinking and problem solving abilities
- the use of a range of materials and processes.

It should contain between 20 and 25 pieces of your recent art and design work.

Art and design degree courses range from courses in which you continue to work in a medium that you have already used, but more intensively, to specialist areas of art and design.

Courses can be grouped into four broad areas: fine art, graphic and lens-based media, fashion and textiles and 3D design. Under these umbrella titles each course offers particular specialisms covering such areas as jewellery and silversmithing, ceramics, animation, illustration, TV and theatre set design, interior design, industrial design, textiles and many others.

In some areas, such as furniture, jewellery, fashion or textiles, you will learn methods and use materials that are completely new to you. Alternatively, if your interest in art is on the critical and analytical side rather than the practical and creative, you could consider a degree course in history of art.

## Degree subject combinations

You can combine art and design with a wide range of other subjects, although this is more common on university courses rather than art college courses.

## Other higher education qualifications

Not to be confused with the one-year Art Foundation courses that prepare you for entry to higher education, foundation degrees are available in many specialist areas such as digital art and design, fine art, graphic communication, commercial fashion, 3D design, TV and film, interior design, garden and landscape design, web design and furniture making. They are a mixture of work-based experience and study.

HND and HNC courses are available in graphic design, games design, furniture design, product design and web design.

## Relevance to other subjects?

As art and design A level can include such a wide range of subjects, materials and techniques, you will find it a useful qualification for many other degree courses.

Degree-level study in photography, media or cultural studies, drama (including stage, costume and lighting design), advertising and architecture can benefit from the experience that you have gained through A level art and design.

## Important advice

If you want to find out more about studying art and/or design at a higher level, contact your local school of art and design and ask to go to a degree show, where you can see the sort of work that students produce. Degree shows are usually held in the summer term. Some art colleges run part-time classes (often on a Saturday) for A level students, and these can help you with portfolio building.

# Future careers

### ▷ After A levels

There aren't many jobs where you can use your artistic knowledge and ability straight after A level. There could be jobs as juniors in design companies, especially in multimedia design (websites, games or DVDs), and you might consider working in retail display or merchandising (which includes window dressing and designing point-of-sale materials), interior design and styling, model making and producing props for film or the stage. Working as a photographer's assistant or in printing, in art galleries, for art dealers or in specialist art shops would also be possibilities. Apprenticeships may be available.

### ▷ After a degree

### Working in art and design

Many art and design graduates do find work related to their degree either in the UK or abroad. It is easier for design graduates, although it depends on the specialism. Graduates have to be prepared to freelance and build up their career gradually through networking and contacts, or move into a related design discipline. Many courses offer training in self-employment including marketing and networking.

Fine art graduates who want to work as fine artists often have to supplement their earnings from art by teaching or other part-time work. Some graduates do further postgraduate study to learn additional specialist skills or crafts.

*Art therapists* help children or adults with disabilities, or who have suffered emotional or physical harm, to overcome their problems through work on artistic projects. This type of work requires further training at masters level.

***Conservation/restoration work*** could involve working in anything from paintings to books to furniture. Further training may be needed for this.

***Fashion and textile designers*** are employed by fashion companies, or work for themselves, creating fabric and clothes designs for organisations ranging from high-street stores to international designer fashion houses.

***Graphic designers*** work in a variety of settings, designing logos for companies or events, through to web or computer games design. They also work in publishing, creating the covers and page layouts of books, magazines and newspapers. Many work as freelancers.

***Product designers*** use their design skills in the creation of products from washing-up liquid bottles to chairs and cars. There are also specialist packaging designers.

***Theatre, film and television designers*** work creating lighting plans for the stage, costumes for period dramas on television, and complete film sets.

***Teachers*** need to undertake postgraduate training. There are a few postgraduate art teaching courses for primary schools but they are mainly for secondary teaching.

## Working outside art and design

The ability to communicate visually makes you a good candidate for a career in advertising, marketing and public relations (PR). There may be opportunities within the film or television industries, although this is a very competitive field. Another possibility is arts administration, where you might be responsible for the running of galleries, theatre companies and buildings, and other arts organisations.

## Sources of information

Chartered Society of Designers
www.csd.org.uk

www.creativeskillset.org

www.creative-choices.co.uk

---

'When you go into a design job you have to learn to work to a brief. You can be creative but you have to do what the customer wants.' Jane, graphic designer

---

# Biology

*Biology is the study of the structure and behaviour of all forms of life plant, animal and human. It covers a range of topics, from cell structure and microbiology, through human anatomy and health, to environmental problems, forensic science, ecology and biodiversity. You explore basic scientific principles and also look at how advances in science have raised other challenges for scientists, society and the economy as a whole for example, designer babies and carbon neutral fuel.*

## What do you study?

*The topics listed give an idea of what could be covered. The exact content of AS and A2 specifications differs according to exam boards, so you will need to check with your school or college about the exact modules available to you.*

- **The variety of living organisms**–biodiversity, taxonomy (the classification of organisms into groups and types), populations and ecosystems (how groups of organisms relate to each other and their environment).
- **Development**–tissues and organs, cell ultra-structure, protein synthesis, molecules.
- **Continuity of life**–genetics and reproduction, chromosomes, DNA (the molecule that determines an organisms characteristics), RNA, meiosis, mitosis, protein synthesis, inheritance, natural selection, evolution including environmental factors, mutations, principles of gene therapy.
- **Energy**–respiration (how energy is released from food), ATP (transports chemical energy within cells for metabolism), glycolysis, exercise and the body, photosynthesis (how plants obtain energy from sunlight, carbon dioxide and water), nutrition and metabolism.
- **Response and control**–perception of the external environment (through sense organs), interpretation (nervous system, brain), response (muscle action, control of the heart and ventilation, hormone release) adaptation to change and homeostasis (how an organism regulates its internal environment).
- **Transport and exchange**–how nutrients and waste materials are moved around animals, including the roles of the heart, blood vessels, liver, kidneys and excretion, transport of water and nutrients in plants.
- **Examination of current issues**– this could be stem cell research and its implications, applications of genetics, the ethics of animal

testing, populations and environment, climate change, or ecosystems and biochemistry.

There could also be options in human biology, forensic science, environmental biology or mammalian physiology and behaviour.

Each specification involves learning the practical, experimental and research skills needed by scientists.

A good grade in biology or a double subject science GCSE is usually required. You will need to work with data and understand the chemical processes within organisms, so good grades in GCSE mathematics and chemistry are also important.

## Subject combinations

If you are aiming for a science-based degree then mathematics, chemistry or physics are the best combinations. Chemistry is required for some biology degrees. It is possible to study biology without traditional science subjects and it combines well with psychology, sociology, PE, science in society, health and social care, and critical thinking. If you are considering physiotherapy then check the requirements as sometimes an additional science can help your application for this competitive subject.

# Higher education options

There is a huge range of courses in biology and related subjects like biochemistry. A level biology is required for many of these courses. It can also be required or preferred for degrees like medicine, dentistry or veterinary science.

## Degree-level study

Biology is a demanding scientific subject, so an analytical mind, competence in maths, laboratory skills and a good knowledge of chemistry and biology are all important. A typical biology degree will cover a range of topics in the first and second years, such as cell and molecular biology, microbiology, physiology and adaptation, and genes and DNA. You usually specialise in the third year. You might study topics such as plant biotechnology, animal biology, international health and disease, evolutionary biology, conservation ecology, microbiology and infectious disease cancer epidemiology, molecular and cellular biology or bioethics. Field trips will be an important part of the course, giving you the opportunity to study at locations elsewhere in the UK and sometimes abroad.

Whatever the degree title, the degree format is likely to be the same; a degree in marine biology, for example, will still cover the broad range of biology topics.

There are many specialist and applied biology degrees you could consider; look at degrees in anatomical sciences, aquatic biology, molecular biology and genetics, human embryology and developmental biology, ecology, environmental biology, exercise, nutrition and health, forensic biology, genetics, microbiology, molecular biology, neuroscience, parasitology, physiology, plant science, sports biology, zoology and biomedical sciences. Some courses in biomedical sciences include a professional training year.

## Degree subject combinations
Biology is available in combination with a wide range of subjects and popular combinations are biochemistry, chemistry, geography and psychology.

## Other higher education qualifications
Foundation degrees are available in biology and specialist areas such as environmental biology, life science laboratory technology, microbiology, marine biology and coastal zone management. There are also related courses in animal management and welfare, countryside management and veterinary nursing.

Biology HND and HNC courses emphasise the practical applications of biology for a career. Applied biology, applied bioscience, chemical biology and conservation biology are possible options at HND/HNC level. Some courses are more specialised, offering training for careers such as conservation and countryside management, horticulture and animal care.

## Relevance to other subjects?
Biology A level is a good preparation for many related subjects at a higher level, and in many cases is required or preferred at least to AS level. Examples include medicine, veterinary science, dentistry, nursing, physiotherapy, microbiology, biochemistry, biotechnology, pharmacy and pharmacology.

**Important advice**

If you are considering a biology-based degree, you will need to check that you have chosen the right A level subject choices, as many courses will ask for another science such as chemistry. If you are looking at a specialist degree in biology such as biomedical sciences, environmental or conservation biology, or forensic biology, make sure you research the content carefully, to make sure it is right for you.

# Future careers

## ▷After A levels

An A level in biology will give you a wide range of skills. Employers will like the fact that you are numerate, a clear logical thinker and a good researcher. Most biology-related jobs at this level require further training and apprenticeships may be available.

Related jobs could be a laboratory technician or assistant, working anywhere from a school or a university to a commercial research laboratory. Another possibility would be a dental technician (bridges, crowns etc), a dental surgery assistant or a pharmacy technician. The study of biology is a good preparation for work in the health service, and with care providers. You could enter part-time or full-time training at this level and possibly progress into nursing, paramedical careers or social work if you get the right qualifications. Your skills with numbers would be a good preparation for careers in the financial sector.

## ▷After a degree

### Working in biology

### Research

This can be 'pure' (not carried out with a view to its immediate use) or applied. Pure research is mostly based in universities and often starts with studying for a PhD (just over a quarter of biology graduates undertake further study of some kind including PhD, MSc or MRes courses). University research posts beyond PhD level are usually on short-term contracts and are quite competitive. Applied research is also carried out in universities, although much is done in the pharmaceutical, food, medical and agrochemical industries, where you would study aspects of biology related to the design and development of particular products. Further study could take you to Europe or the USA.

## Medicine

It is possibly for biology graduates to take a four-year graduate course to qualify in medicine. Entry is competitive and you may be required to have taken certain science A levels, even though you are a graduate. You will have to sit a selection test.

## Teaching

Another option where you can use your enthusiasm for your subject is to teach others. This could be in a primary or secondary school, college, university or teaching adults. There is a shortage of science teachers so there are incentives for training.

## Other work

There are opportunities for public sector work in the Civil Service, public health, medical and veterinary laboratory work, forensic science and the National Health Service (NHS). There is also environment-related work, including consultancy in the private or public sector, pollution monitoring, environmental impact assessment and conservation work.

## Working outside biology

Biology graduates have skills employers value such as the ability to think logically and being numerate and IT literate. Possibilities include finance, management and the IT industry.

## Sources of information

Biochemical Society
www.biochemistry.org

Society of Biology
www.societyofbiology.org

Institute of Biomedical Science
www.ibms.org

www.nuffieldfoundation.org/salters-nuffield-advanced-biology

www.biology4all.com

www.biology-careers.org

*'I want to do sports science, so biology will help me a lot with my future career'.* Muni, aged 17, taking biology, physical education and business

# Human biology

*Are you interested in how the human body works? Would you like a better working knowledge of your own body and how your lifestyle affects it? What about how humans interact with the environment and the research taking place in the fields of medicine, genetics and biotechnology?*

The human biology A level covers biological molecules; cells; enzymes; blood and circulation; the control of breathing and heartbeat; energy and exercise; disease-causing organisms; defence against disease; mitosis, meiosis and the cell cycle; DNA and protein synthesis; genetic engineering; heart disease and cancer; diagnosis of disease; and drugs used to control and treat disease. You then go on to genetics and variation; photosynthesis and respiration; natural selection and evolution; sexual reproduction; the development of the foetus; growth; the digestive system; diet; transport of respiratory gases; the nervous system; muscles; homeostasis; senescence; and a study of ecosystems and the environment. Practical assignments are an important part of the course.

A level human biology is useful for a wide range of careers, including healthcare, sports and leisure, and complementary therapies. The course will help you to develop essential skills and knowledge of biological principles as they relate to human beings. If you are considering a degree in medicine, veterinary medicine or biology check to see if it is accepted. Sometimes biology is preferred as it is a broader course and some biology specifications cover human biology.

# Business studies

*A level business studies helps you to understand all about business today, both in the UK and internationally, using examples based on real business problems. The course helps you to understand the process by which a business makes its decisions by looking at the businesss aims, the information it needs and the constraints under which it operates. You may have the opportunity to research into business problems and areas in which you are particularly interested.*

## What do you study?

*The topics listed give an idea of what could be covered. The exact content of AS and A2 specifications differs according to exam boards, so you will need to check with your school or college about the exact modules available to you. There is also and an applied business A level available, the applied A level is more vocational and concentrates on the practical side of business.*

- *Managing a business*–recruiting and managing staff, how to make your business successful and increase your profits, how to market your business and operations management, which includes technology and how to give your customers a great service.
- *The business environment*–planning and developing your business from your first idea to starting and developing your business including financial matters.
- *Managing change*–the impact of economic, political, cultural and technological changes on your business and working in a global economy.
- *Strategic management*–effective strategies to improve your business and profits, have great employee relations and to make your business competitive.
- *International business*–how global businesses work and marketing businesses abroad.
- *Business functions*–accounting and finance, product development, advertising, pricing, business ratios, and profits and losses.

It is not essential to have studied the subject at GCSE in order to study A level business studies. Some of the course will involve figure work, so even though you won't need any advanced maths, GCSE maths could be useful and learning how to use a calculator is definitely important. There will be visits to local, national and even international businesses and you may undertake some work shadowing.

## Subject combinations

An A level in business studies is not essential for the study of the subject at a higher level, and you should always check that universities will consider it for entrance to business courses. Some universities may not accept economics and business studies as two separate A levels. This is because they find the areas of study are too similar. Some universities specify a broad skill set so prefer a combination of different subjects. This could mean that if you are offering maths and science they will prefer a humanities subject as your third A level. You will need to research this before you apply, whatever course you are considering. Some degrees in business may specify certain subjects at A level. An A level in maths is required for a few degree courses, especially those entitled management science. GCSE maths is nearly always specified for degree-level study.

Apart from that, business studies can be combined with almost any other A level subject. Modern languages are a good combination as learning a language can give you a great insight into a culture and from there how business works in that country.

# Higher education options

## Degree-level study

You will find there are hundreds of degree courses in business studies and in related subjects, such as marketing and human resources. Many are very popular, attracting large numbers of applicants, although entry requirements vary widely.

The first degree to consider is a general business studies degree. This is likely to be multidisciplinary covering a broad range of subjects such as accounting, banking, finance, economics, management, marketing and entrepreneurship. You will also find more specialised degrees such as business administration.

There are then degrees where you would specialise in one business function such as marketing, information technology or human resources. Some of these specialist degrees can exempt you from professional exams in, for example, accountancy or marketing.

Another choice of degree would be one that focuses on one type of business or industry, such as retail, hospitality, tourism or music management. There are degrees in entrepreneurship and business enterprise if you want to start your own business.

Some courses have an international slant with links to other countries such as the USA and Australia. You will also find courses in Chinese business management and international management in Japan and Korea as well as Latin American business management.

## Degree subject combinations

Business studies can be combined with almost anything, but one of the most popular subjects is a modern language as this gives you added value with employers. Important business languages are French, German, Mandarin/Cantonese, Spanish, Polish, Russian, Arabic, Portuguese, Japanese and Korean. On these courses, you are likely to spend part of your course gaining work experience with a business in another country. This might be anywhere in the world and can provide a valuable insight into the way business is conducted in that country.

Other subjects such as psychology, politics, sociology and law can complement business studies by adding to your understanding of the environment in which business must function, as well as the people it employs. You will also find business studies included in many engineering degrees, or you may study engineering specifically from a management perspective.

## Other higher education qualifications

Foundation degrees are available in business and business management and in specialist management areas such as finance and law, business IT and in specialised areas such as culinary skills and kitchen management, beauty and spa management, cruise industry management, equine business, events management, golf management, adventure and extreme sports management, tourism, music business and wine business management.

HND and HNC business studies courses are extremely popular and course titles include business and finance, business and marketing, and business and human resources. Courses are modular and offer a wide choice of options according to the institution.

There are also specialist courses available including e-business, the music industry and countryside management.

## Relevance to other subjects?

Business studies A level provides a good starting point for a degree in accountancy, financial services or management. Even if you do not wish to go on to take a business-related course you will have a good understanding of the business world, which could well prove useful to you in the future, especially if you go on to study subjects such as economics, law, media studies or politics.

## Important advice

It is important to look closely at the contents of each business studies course that you are considering. You will find that some courses require a higher level of maths than others. Some courses are very competitive.

To give yourself the edge over other applicants you should try to get as much relevant work experience as you can. This can range from a weekend retail job to working in an office during holidays. This experience can help you to make good contacts, which could be useful later on if you wanted, for example, work experience on your degree course.

# Future careers

### ▷After A levels

A level business studies gives you an idea of the range of careers available in business and shows employers that you have some relevant knowledge and interest. You could consider jobs in administration, accounts or trainee management. Retail companies such as super-markets and department stores often recruit A level trainees or higher apprentices, as do some banks, building societies, insurance, IT, law and finance companies. As a trainee or apprentice, you could study professional qualifications or, possibly, work towards a degree.

### ▷After a degree

### Working in business

Business studies graduates enter a wide range of jobs, depending on the emphasis of their degree.

*Administration—within a public or private organisation.* This could include buying business IT and other equipment, creating a good working environment through facilities management, administering staff salaries, car fleets or business travel. In a small business you could well be doing all of this and more.

*Advertising*—working on behalf of clients to develop advertising campaigns for products from toothpaste to banking services.

*Financial services*–assessing the needs of individuals or companies in terms of investment, insurance, savings plans and pensions. You may be self-employed as a financial adviser or work for an organisation such as a bank, building society or investment company. You could also train to be an accountant. About 21% of business studies graduates go into a financial role.

*Human resources*–recruiting and training staff.

*Management*–this could be in general management in a particular sector such as retail, or hotel and catering.

*Marketing*–identifying the potential market for a product or service and devising the most effective way of selling it.

*Teaching or lecturing*–in schools or colleges. With the increasing popularity of business studies A level and higher courses, there is an increasing demand for good teachers.

## Working outside business

A business or management degree is very useful in almost any area of work, as you learn how organisations work and grow. Areas such as health, education and charities all value people with business skills and experience, and there is a wide range of opportunities available.

## Sources of information

www.bized.co.uk

www.thetimes100.co.uk

'Business has opened my eyes to the financial world and, increasingly, I have become interested in reading newspapers and tracking the business world.' Morton, aged 18, A levels in business studies, German and politics

# Economics and business

Economics and business A level combines elements of economics and business and is designed so that you will develop an understanding of economic and business theories and be able to apply them to a range of real-world issues. You will also learn how to make decisions using economic and business information, and how to appreciate economic and business issues from the perspectives of everybody involved including customers, managers, creditors, shareholders and employees. You learn how to analyse, explain and evaluate the strengths and weaknesses of the market economy in a wider context, including in international business.

The specification has an emphasis on international business and entrepreneurship.

# Chemistry

*Everything in the world around you is made from chemicals: the food you eat, the air you breathe, your own body, your mobile phone, the plants and streets around you. Chemistry encompasses the environment, with pollution control, recycling and the development of biodiesel. In industry you will find it in the development of new foodstuffs, synthetic materials and medicines. In fact anyone studying chemistry has a difficult career choice because there are now so many career paths available.*

## What do you study?

*The topics listed give an idea of what could be covered. The exact content of AS and A2 specifications differs according to exam boards, so you will need to check with your school or college about the exact modules available to you.*

- **Structure and bonding**–the structure of the atom, how atoms are joined together to make molecules, the periodic table, what happens when the bonds break and reform.
- **Physical chemistry**–what determines whether a possible chemical reaction actually takes place (energetics) and how quickly it happens (kinetics), the properties of gases, liquids and solids, and electrochemistry.
- **Organic chemistry**–the chemistry of carbon compounds, the variety and complexity that has allowed life to evolve (it is this connection with the chemistry of living organisms that gives this branch of chemistry its name).
- **Inorganic chemistry**–the chemistry of all the other elements and the ways that their properties are related to their position in the periodic table.

At A level you apply the chemistry you learn to industrial and medical applications and consider the environmental and social impact of chemistry.

There may also be options to study, for example, biochemistry, environmental chemistry or materials chemistry. Some courses have an emphasis on applied chemistry and how it is used in everyday life.

A level chemistry builds on and develops what you learned at GCSE, so you should have chemistry or science and additional science at grade C or above before starting the course. You will need to be confident in handling numbers, as chemistry uses many quantitative methods, so you should have GCSE mathematics at grade C or higher.

Chemistry is a practical subject so you will carry out your own experiments. The practicals give you real-life experience of what you are studying and teach you essential skills. You will also be involved in investigations that allow you to get into a topic in more detail than is possible in the usual laboratory work, and the investigative skills you learn doing this will be assessed. Most class work takes the form of information and notes presented by the teacher, discussion and examples to work through. This will be supported by presentations showing industrial processes and computer programs simulating experiments and processes that cannot be carried out in the school or college laboratory. You may go on industrial visits to see how chemistry is used in practice.

## Subject combinations

Chemistry is an essential subject for some degree courses such as chemistry, chemical engineering, biochemistry, medicine, dentistry, pharmacy, pharmacology and veterinary science where it will need to be combined with maths or other science subjects. Combined with biology, it is very useful for any biology-related courses.

Studying chemistry can provide valuable support for a wide range of other subjects including physics, geology, environmental science and geography. It is a well-respected academic subject, regarded well by universities, so there is no reason why you couldnt combine chemistry with subjects such as economics, business studies, languages or any other.

# Higher education options

A good pass in A level chemistry is nearly always required to study chemistry at degree level.

## Degree-level study

As well as courses simply called chemistry, there are many other closely related courses such as applied chemistry, biochemistry, chemistry for medicines development, chemistry for drugs development, medicinal chemistry and marine chemistry. You might wish to look at subjects that don't have chemistry in the title such as natural science, pharmaceutical science or cosmetic science.

Many courses offer an industrial year as part of the course. You will find courses linked to universities in places such as Australia, Japan, Europe and the USA, offering a period of study overseas. Try to find out as much as you possibly can about the courses that interest you, and make sure you understand exactly what you'll be letting yourself in for.

## Degree subject combinations

If you do not want to specialise in chemistry alone, you can combine it with other science subjects such as toxicology, analytical chemistry, nanotechnology, pharmacology or forensic science. There are also specially designed degree programmes combining chemistry with non-science subjects, for example, modern languages, IT, law and management. Languages will be important if you will be studying or working in a non-English speaking country as part of your course.

## Other higher education qualifications

Foundation degrees are available in applied chemistry, analytical and forensic science and chemical and pharmaceutical science. These are linked to degree courses if you wish to continue studying after the initial foundation degree. HNC and HND courses in a wide range of chemistry-related subjects are available. In institutions also offering degree courses, you can often transfer to the second or third year of the degree course after completing an HND.

## Relevance to other subjects?

A related subject to investigate is chemical engineering. This looks at the development, design and operation of industrial chemical processes, such as the manufacture of synthetic fabrics, plastics and metal alloys. You would need to be taking maths and physics with your chemistry A level to get into this. Chemical engineering can also be combined with other subjects such an energy engineering or management.

Pharmacy is another option and A levels should include chemistry and two others from biology, maths or physics.

## Important advice

Chemistry is such a huge subject that no degree course can cover it all. If you aren't sure which type of chemistry you want to specialise in then take a straight chemistry course to get a good grounding in the subject. You can then specialise later on, either in the later stages of a degree or at masters level. This allows you to keep your options open.

A number of companies are willing to sponsor students through degree courses in chemistry and chemical engineering. University chemistry departments will have details of these companies.

# Future careers

## ▷After A levels

Chemistry A level is highly regarded by employers and the knowledge and skills you will have gained will help you in virtually any career. However, if you wish to work within professional chemistry you will need to obtain some extra qualifications first, or your options may be limited. This could be via a full-time degree or by doing a Higher Apprenticeship which will include professional level qualifications and/or an HNC or foundation degree. Other jobs that would use your knowledge of chemistry include laboratory technician, pharmacy technician, dental, veterinary, or healthcare assistant but you will need further training for all these.

## ▷After a degree

### Working in chemistry

Most chemistry graduates obtain work as professional chemists or in related areas. However, chemistry is a very large and highly developed subject, so you can only cover a small part of it in a degree course. This is why about 35% of chemistry graduates stay on after their degree to do research and/or further academic study for higher level qualifications.

There are many career options for the professional chemist, including the following:
- *research and development*—chemists work to develop processes for making new products such as plastics, drugs, fuel, pesticides, fertilisers, dyes and foods
- *production*—chemists are involved in planning the manufacture of products and in monitoring quality
- *support*—some chemists are employed to support research and production activities by searching technical papers for information and in writing patent specifications. They may also be involved in the selling and marketing of chemical products and in advising customers
- *technical writing and journalism*—there are opportunities in writing technical articles for scientific publications and journals, editing science books or websites, or writing more popular scientific articles for newspapers and magazines
- *Civil Service and local government*—chemists employed by government bodies monitor and advise on the safety of

foodstuffs, water and environmental pollution, and chemical safety

- **forensic science**—chemists are employed by forensic science laboratories examining evidence relating to crimes
- **teaching**—chemistry is a shortage subject and there are incentives to train.

## Working outside chemistry

A degree in chemistry is useful in many jobs not directly related to chemistry because chemistry graduates are numerate, have problem-solving, investigative and analytical skills, and good IT and communication skills, which will all have been developed during degree-level study.

Business and finance is a popular area and approximately 11% of chemistry graduates go into this type of work. Chemistry graduates are also employed by local government, the Civil Service and in many areas of industry and business including marketing, sales and advertising; arts, design and sport; and social and welfare professions.

## Sources of information

Royal Society of Chemistry
www.rsc.org

Futuremorph
www.futuremorph.org

www.geoset.info

www.whynotchemeng.com

'To survive into the next century we need to develop imaginative new sustainable technologies including new sources of energy, new efficient materials, recyclable devices and clever new molecular-based medical solutions. Legions of humanitarian contributions to society have come from the chemistry-based sciences from penicillin to sewage treatment, from shampoo to anaesthetics and from paints to liquid crystal displays. There can thus be little doubt that the chemical sciences promise to make similarly revolutionary and beneficial contributions to the way we shall live in the 21st century. If the future is in anyone's hands it is in the hands of the next generation of ingenious young chemists.'
Professor Sir Harry Kroto, Nobel Laureate in chemistry

# Citizenship studies

*What is a good citizen? How does our national identity develop? Why do so many people not vote? What rights do you have if you are stopped and searched by the police? How can you become involved and make a difference in your local community? If you have an interest in society, politics, community and equality then you'll enjoy citizenship studies. You study subjects such as justice, power, and law and order. Citizenship studies draws on aspects of geography, history and religious education and includes elements of economics and politics.*

*Being a good and active citizen involves responsibilities as well as rights and the course looks at these rights and responsibilities, how society works, and how to participate in the democratic process. You will be asked to look at issues from different points of view, learn how to advocate, negotiate, plan, make decisions and take action on citizenship issues. You will learn how to work with others as well as using problem-solving and critical approaches to the issues. A central theme running through the subject will be how individuals can influence the decision-making process at a local and national level.*

## What do you study?

*AQA is currently the only exam board offering this specification at AS/A level.*

- **What is the definition of a citizen?** What does it mean to be a British citizen in a diverse society? Prejudice and stereotyping; discrimination and disadvantage–how can government policy influence these?
- **Rights and responsibilities.** How they work in society, including information about the Human Rights Act, the Data Protection Act and the Freedom of Information Act.
- **Who can make a difference?** What is power and who holds it in the UK? How is the power of the media controlled? The different types of government, European, national and local, and how they have an impact on our lives. What is the democratic process and how can citizens bring about change both individually and together? How can citizens successfully campaign and how does this impact on political decision making?
- **Active citizenship.** You will be required to become an active citizen yourself and take part in a range of citizenship activities to demonstrate your knowledge and how you can bring about change while working alone or with others. You will complete an active citizenship profile as part of your course.

- *Crime, justice and punishment.* How crime is defined and how the criminal justice system works, including the role of the police and the courts. What is justice? Who makes decisions? How a jury works and what happens in miscarriages of justice. Sentences and the types of sentences available, and how they relate to different age groups.
- *Politics, power and participation.* Who speaks on our behalf? How we choose who represents us, how they are held to account and how they represent us.
- *How is the UK governed?* The power of Parliament, political parties and the prime minister. The impact of the EU and other international organisations, such as the UN and NATO. The global village and how citizens can have an impact.
- *Human rights.* How they are protected in the UK. Universal human rights, human rights abuses and what citizens can do to change things.
- *Global issues.* Conflict and how it can be resolved.
- *Trade and environmental issues.* The world economic system, globalisation, fair trade, poverty and industrialisation. How can citizens make a difference?

You don't need citizenship studies GCSE to take the AS/A level.

## Subject combinations

Citizenship studies combines well with government and politics, sociology, law, philosophy, business studies and economics. It will help you in any subject where you have to present or analyse reasoned arguments. World development could also be a good choice if you have an interest in global citizenship.

# Higher education options

## Degree-level study

There are no degrees in citizenship but you will find the issues covered in other courses such as sociology, politics, human rights and social policy.

## Other higher education qualifications

There are no foundation degrees or HNDS/HNCs in citizenship.

### Relevance to other subjects?
You could look at courses in police and community studies, youth and community development, public administration and social welfare.

### Important advice
You will need to show some involvement in aspects of citizenship to prove you have an understanding of what these courses involve. This could mean getting involved with the school council, attending meetings on local issues, voluntary work, or sitting in the public gallery at council meetings. If you have already become involved and made a difference to your community then make sure this is included in your personal statement.

# Future careers

### ▷ After A levels
You might consider any sort of work in your local community, which could include the local authority or paid work with voluntary organisations. You will have an understanding of how courts work so could look at opportunities there as well as with organisations such as the police, Civil Service or the National Health Service.

### ▷ After a degree
Courses with an emphasis on citizenship could lead to careers in the public and volunteering sectors, including community and youth work, outreach and advocacy, charities, local or national government. You might also wish to pursue a career in law, working for campaigning organisations, social movements or in political lobbying.

There is a PGCE in citizenship education. This is part of the secondary curriculum, so there is a demand for specialist citizenship teachers. Citizenship is also included in primary level teaching training.

You will have developed skills to communicate and articulate different views, advocate, negotiate, plan and make decisions. You will have been taught to select, interpret, analyse and evaluate information, to construct reasoned and coherent arguments, propose alternative solutions and form conclusions. In addition you will be able to work with others, using problem-solving and critical approaches to the issues, problems and events.

You could consider postgraduate study to become a social worker or in law. With all these skills you will have a wide range of options including human resources and marketing.

## Sources of information

The Citizenship Foundation
www.citizenshipfoundation.org.uk

Citizen X
www.bbc.co.uk/schools/citizenx

---

'Citizenship has given me an insight into the justice system as well as politics. I now have an increased knowledge and confidence to talk or debate about these things and other current affairs.' Omar, aged 18, taking A levels in business, law and citizenship

---

# Classical civilisation

*The study of classical civilisations allows students to look at many aspects of the classical world which are significant in the development of the modern world. The classical civilisation A level is designed for students with an interest in classical studies, but who do not necessarily want to learn Latin or ancient/classical Greek. The period covered is Greek and Roman civilisation, from about 1500 BC to about AD 450. The specification covers all aspects of classical civilisation. It can cover a wide choice of topics including architecture, archaeology, art, history, politics, literature and philosophy.*

## What do you study?

*The topics listed give an idea of what could be covered. The exact content of AS and A2 specifications differ according to exam boards, so you will need to check with your school or college about the exact modules available to you.*

OCR offers this subject as part of its suite of classics qualifications and the official title is now classics: classical civilisation. Topics you might study include:

- **the Homeric epics**–the Iliad and the Odyssey
- **Greek tragedy in its context**–plays dramatising the frailty of human success and its dependence on fortune by Aeschylus, Sophocles, Euripides; Greek comedy such as Aristophanes and Menander
- **ancient philosophy**–values and politics, especially Plato's Republic
- **Greek historians**
- **Virgil and the world of the hero**
- **Greek history**–conflict and culture
- **Roman society and thought**–through a study of Roman literature (Plinys Letters and examples of satire from Horace, Petronius and Juvenal Virgils Aeneid) and its context
- **Roman history**–the use and abuse of power
- **Roman Britain**–life in the outpost of the Empire
- **archaeology**–looking at important sites and what they tell us about the civilisation
- **archaeological methodology**–the principles and practices
- **Roman architecture and town planning**
- **Art and architecture in the Greek world**
- **Greek history from original sources**–historical texts by Thucydides, Herodotus and Plutarch

- *city life in Roman Italy*–the cities of Pompeii, Herculaneum and Ostia in their social, cultural, political and historical contexts
- *Athenian democracy*
- *Athenian vase painting*
- *Athenian imperialism*
- *Socrates and Athens*
- *Aristophanes and Athens*
- *the life and times of Cicero*
- *the Persian wars*
- *Augustus and the foundation of the Principate*
- *Alexander*
- *Tiberius and Claudius*
- *The Second Punic War*
- *Archaeology*–Mycenae and the classical world.

You might also study themes such as women in Athens and Rome. You will be encouraged to make comparisons between the classical world and the world of today. The exact topics you study will be chosen by your institution. You do not need any previous experience of studying the ancient world or its languages in order to study classical civilisation A level.

You do not need classical civilisation GCSE to study the subject at A level.

You study translations of the literature of ancient Greece and Rome and descriptive works on topics such as art and architecture. Most of the work is essay based, and you will need to do additional reading beyond the prescribed lists. You might visit relevant places such as Bath, the Ashmolean Museum in Oxford and the British Museum in London or go to see some classical plays. There may be the opportunity to go on a study trip to Greece or Rome.

Knowledge of ancient Greek and Latin is not required but some students become interested in these languages and some schools and colleges may be able to offer the languages from scratch. The OCR classics specification offers this language option if available within your institution.

## Subject combinations
Some classics degrees require an A level in Latin or ancient Greek, and others will accept a modern language as evidence of your language skills and learning ability.

Classical civilisation can be combined with most other A level subjects, particularly those where essay writing and textual analysis are involved. Examples of these are English, communication and culture, drama and theatre studies, history of art, media studies, government and politics, history, history of art, religious studies and philosophy as well as a study of the classical languages.

It is a useful A level for archaeology degrees (although may need to be combined with a science subject at A level for some courses). Anthropology, art, government and politics, geography and history are also popular combinations.

# Higher education options

## Degree-level study

At degree level, you may have the option of starting a classical language if you have not done so already. Some degrees with the title classical civilisation or classical studies require you to spend some time on language work, while on others it is an option. Many of these degrees are open to students who have not taken classical civilisation or any classics subject at A level. However, an A level in a classical subject does demonstrate an interest in and commitment to the subject. In contrast, degrees called classics, Latin or ancient Greek all involve the study of one or both languages. You may be able to start one of the languages (although not usually both) from scratch at university.

Degrees in classical civilisation cover a broad range of topics (look also for classical studies, classical past, or ancient world studies in course titles). They include the philosophy, art, literature, religion, history, drama, science and archaeology of ancient Greece and Rome.

The classical civilisation A level would be a good preparation for a degree in archaeology and there are some specialist courses in classical archaeology. Classical civilisation is often a preferred A level for ancient history degrees.

For information on degrees in classics, Latin and ancient Greek, see the entry for Greek (classical)/Latin.)

## Degree subject combinations

Classical civilisation or classical studies form a part of many combined degree and modular degree programmes, which may include related subjects such as ancient history, classical languages, Greek and Roman civilisation, Byzantine studies, classical literature and archaeology. You will also find combinations with a wide range of related humanities or social science subjects, which require similar techniques of research and analysis of evidence. Possibilities include modern history, English, religious studies, philosophy, politics and history of art.

## Other higher education qualifications
There are no foundation degrees in classical civilisation, but related subjects available include history, heritage and archaeology, and archaeology. There are no HND or HNC courses in classical civilisation.

## Relevance to other subjects?
A level classical civilisation is worth considering, even if you are not thinking of continuing it beyond A level. The ancient world has helped to shape the culture and civilisation of Europe, its languages, literature, history, art and political structures. Classical civilisation is a good introduction to that world, and so is a useful A level qualification for many humanities degrees. Subjects such as English, history, history of art, drama, religious studies, modern languages and philosophy all benefit from a knowledge and understanding of classical civilisations.

## Important advice
Your chances of being accepted onto a higher education course in classical civilisation or a related subject will be improved if you can get some first-hand knowledge of the subject. You can get this by visiting museums and sites of historical importance, going on archaeological digs or excavations, reading related material in your spare time and generally being as active in your interest as you possibly can. Remember that you may have to pay something towards going on an archaeological dig.

# Future careers

### ▷After A levels
An A level in classical civilisation would provide you with a respected qualification for a wide range of careers. Even if there are few jobs that could immediately make use of what you have learned, the skills developed while studying the subject will be useful to you. These skills would include the ability to do research, analyse what you have found, reach an understanding about the people and society that you are studying, and argue your point, both in writing and verbally. There are

some related jobs in museums and heritage sites and possibly apprenticeships.

## ▷ After a degree

### Working in classical civilisation

It is unlikely that a degree in classical civilisation will lead to a career that will use your special knowledge to any great extent, unless you decide to become a teacher or lecturer. Classical civilisation is related to archaeology but remember that there are specialist archaeology degrees, many of which involve an element of scientific analysis, so to become an archaeologist you should aim for a degree in archaeology. Some opportunities may be available in museum work, exhibition design, galleries, libraries, heritage management or archive work, but you will be in competition with graduates in ancient history or archaeology. Postgraduate study in a subject like museum information or archive studies could be an option to make you more marketable.

### Working outside classical civilisation

Don't let the limited opportunities for using classical kno
wledge put you off a degree in classical civilisation. The skills in critical thinking, persuasive writing and self-expression provided by a classical civilisation degree are transferable to a wide range of careers. There would be opportunities in research, administration, media, the Civil Service, law, accountancy, computing, and business.

### Sources of information

Council for British Archaeology
www.archaeologyuk.org

www.classicspage.com

www.creative-choices.co.uk for heritage careers

---

'Knowledge of our classical heritage is invaluable to anyone trying to understand culture in the 21st century.' Malcom, taking a degree in history with A levels in classical civilisation, government and politics and history

---

# Communication and culture

*Communication and culture is all about how we communicate in today's world and you start by looking at your own forms of communication within your culture. The emphasis is very much on contemporary culture and how we relate to it and fit in with it.*

*Have you got a mobile phone or MP3 player? Are they important to you and why? Do these cultural objects tell us anything about ourselves and the way we relate to others? Do people communicate in a different way using Facebook, texting or tweeting? Does repeated use of social media increase or decrease your self-esteem? How do people behave and react to the virtual world? Does our spoken and body language change according to which group of people we are with? Is Banksy a genius or a criminal?*

*All these are forms of communication and shape our lives and our identities. This course will help you to develop your own communication skills and a sense of your own identity in the world. You will also look at our modern culture and topics such as the cult of celebrity and body modification.*

## What do you study?

*AQA is the only exam board currently offering communication and culture.*

What do we mean by communication? You look at how you communicate and how this gives you a sense of who you are.

In looking at how you communicate, you investigate the importance of non-verbal communication: the impact that your body language can have in conveying information about yourself and how you can use this to your advantage.

This links closely with group identity: how do we change ourselves to fit into various groups in society, how do we manipulate group situations and develop leadership skills, and how is this significant in shaping our identity?

Identity is a key word throughout the course and links closely with an examination of the nature of culture. What is it that defines us, not just as an individual but as a member of a particular cultural group?

You will examine the nature of culture and the reasons why different values are placed on different cultural products and practices; for example: is skateboarding better than rugby?

You then develop understanding of these ideas by preparing a portfolio of investigations, case studies, explorations and a presentation on 'My

Culture: who am I in context? exploring personal and cultural identity'. Your presentation should be both audio and visual so could be a website, podcast or short film, for example.

## Subject combinations

Since communication is so central to our everyday lives, the course naturally links with aspects of other subjects like English language, English literature, media, film studies, languages, psychology, art, photography, health and social care, ICT, business studies, government and politics, photography, sociology or theatre studies.

# Higher education options

The content of communication studies degrees can vary, covering a wide range of disciplines including psychology, linguistics, sociology, new media, new media broadcasting, culture and creative industries, and media production. Some degrees include placements in the communications industry.

## Degree-level study

Communications degrees are usually broad-based academic degree programmes aimed at those who are interested in communications or the media, but who don't want to specialise yet. You will find many degrees in media communications and culture, and also cultural studies.

## Degree subject combinations

Communication studies combines with many subjects and you could look at closely related areas such as journalism, media studies and new media. You could also consider combining the subject with languages, business, sociology, information technology or psychology.

## Other higher education qualifications

There are some communications-related foundation degrees such as business, management and communications and communication at work. There are many related foundation degrees including broadcast media, creative digital media, digital media and marketing, digital media and television production, digital media technologies, interactive media development, journalism and practical media, media (moving image and audio), media practice, media production, social media, television production and web design and development.

HNDs and HNCs could include creative media and production, media and communication, and creative media production (journalism).

## Relevance to other subjects?

Communication studies courses contain some aspects of media studies, cultural studies, psychology, sociology and English language, so have a look at these courses and compare their contents.

## Important advice

Think about which aspect of communications studies interests you and examine the courses carefully. Think about what you want out of a course and don't be afraid to ask admissions tutors about destinations of graduates.

If you are considering a career in the media/communications industry, any relevant work experience can help you to build up a portfolio that could prove useful in the future.

# Future careers

## ▷After A levels

The communication and culture A level will give you skills in communication and the ability to examine and analyse issues. These skills could help you in a wide range of careers such as business, administration, media, sales, retail and ICT.

## ▷After a degree

### Working in communications

A communication studies degree can be relevant for career opportunities in areas such as public relations, advertising, marketing, arts administration, broadcast and print journalism, broadcasting, communications consultancy, internet communications, media production, publishing, arts management, advertising, new media technologies and communication therapy. For some of these careers additional study and training are required. (See also careers after English and media courses.)

### Working outside communications

You will have gained presentation, communication and analytical skills, which can be useful in whichever field you are aiming for, so you could look at careers in management and administration in a wide range of business areas. Your communication skills could be useful in jobs such as personnel or human resources, social work, counselling and teaching. Careers such as librarianship and information management are also possibilities.

## Sources of information

Creative Skillset

www.creativeskillset.org

www.communicationandculture.co.uk

> 'My degree was so vocational. It teaches you all about different forms of communication and how to get your message across. It has set me up for my current job and future career.' Graham, press officer with a degree in communication studies

# Computer science

*Computers are an essential feature of 21st century life, controlling daily activities such as transport, medicine, banking and retailing. This course aims to encourage you to develop an understanding of the main principles of solving problems using computers programming in a range of languages and of the range of applications of computers and the effects of their use. You will develop an understanding of the organisation of computer systems, including software, data, hardware, communications and networks. You will also acquire the skills necessary to apply this understanding to developing computer-based solutions to problems.*

*See also ICT A level which is about the applied use of software and applications.*

## What do you study?

*The topics listed give an idea of what could be covered. The exact content of AS and A2 specifications differ according to exam boards, so you will need to check with your school or college about the exact modules available to you.*

- *Hardware*–the computer and its peripherals.
- *Software and systems*–the software life-cycle, from identification of requirements and problem analysis, through design and implementation, to improvement and eventually obsolescence; hardware use and design.
- *Operating systems and programming*–why operating systems are necessary and how they work.
- *Software engineering*–different types of programs available for different purposes. Designing solutions to particular problems, how procedural programs are structured, the types of data and data structures, the common facilities of procedural languages, how to write maintainable programs, and how to test and run solutions. Programming languages such as Pascal, PHP, VB.6, VB.Net, C#, Java, Python or C.
- *Data*–the presentation, structure and management of data, files and processing; database design, data security, SQL.
- *Communication and networking*–communication methods, serial data transmission, parallel data transmission, handshaking, protocol, baseband, broadband, local area networks (LAN), wide area networks (WAN), which include the web, wireless networking, Wi-Fi and Bluetooth.
- *Implications*–the impact of computing on individuals, organisations, the economy and society. Copyright and protection of data.

- **The internet and its uses**–the structure of the internet, the role of packet switching World Wide Web (WWW) and routers. The differences between the internet, the web and an intranet.
- **Web design**–web page construction, html and style sheets.

There are also software development and testing exercises and practical projects.

You do not need a GCSE in computer science or ICT to study computer science at A level, but if you do this will help you with your studies. You would be expected to have some experience and interest in using computers. You don't have to be a brilliant mathematician for this course but success in GCSE maths is advised as it can show an aptitude for the more technical side of computing. English will also be very useful.

## Subject combinations

A level mathematics and sometimes further maths is a requirement for some computer science degrees, and physics is an essential preparation for some of the more hardware-orientated courses, so you may want to consider these.

Even if you do not plan to go onto a computer science degree, you will find that computer science is a valuable A level in combination with many others. It could be taken alongside A levels suitable for careers in medicine, law, business, politics or any type of science. Your ability to manipulate and manage information in a logical manner will prove invaluable when it comes to project work, note taking, essay writing and revision in any other subject.

# Higher education options

Computer science A level is not always essential for entry to computer-related courses at a higher level, although mathematics and science subjects are sometimes required.

## Degree-level study

There is a huge variety of computer-related degree courses. You should never read too much into a course title without checking but, in general, courses called computer science are more likely to have a theoretical bias. You may find yourself looking into the formal and mathematical foundations of computing, as well as learning how to design and write complex programs in high-level and low-level languages. Courses called computer studies are more likely to focus on the applications of computing. Courses simply called computing can fall into either category. Course titles are changing all the time as the industry develops, and you will find courses in computer science (digital media and games) and network computing. You could also look at software engineering and the increasing numbers of courses in cyber security and computer forensics, which is currently a skills shortage area.

In addition, there are engineering-focused courses dealing with, for example, intelligent systems and robotics, cybertronics, computer systems engineering and network engineering. There are also specialised degrees in artificial intelligence. In this field, computers are used to do the complex things normally associated with human intelligence, such as planning, making decisions, understanding language, and recognising places and people. Many degrees are sandwich courses, in which you spend some time in industry, with placements abroad often available.

## Degree subject combinations

Many students combine computer science with business studies or management, either as separate subjects or on a course specially designed to bring the two together (as in degrees called business computing, or business information systems, for example). Mathematics is the most widely available combination, closely followed by statistics, business studies/accounting, psychology, physics and languages.

## Other higher education qualifications

Foundation degrees are available in computing, applied computing and in related areas such as computer networking, system support, computing (information systems), computer engineering, interactive multimedia, internet systems, business computing, computer aided design and 3D animation, computer software development, mobile applications development, development for the interactive industries (video game/ application design), digital media technologies, computer systems support, network engineering security and systems administration and web design.

HND and HNC courses are available with different specialisations, for example programming, network management or creative media production (computer game animation). You will also find courses in computer science, computing, computing forensics and security, computer networking and internet technology, software engineering, mobile computing and network and computing.

## Relevance to other subjects?

You will find your understanding of computing useful whatever you study, and in some subjects it will be extremely relevant. It is especially important for business courses and all science and engineering courses that involve computers for control, data collection and statistical analysis of results.

## Important advice

Some prospectuses give quite detailed information on the computing facilities provided, but it is also a good idea to attend open days, to find out first-hand what is available. It is also useful to find out what happens to graduates from courses in which you are interested, so that you can see if this is the direction you want to take.

# Future careers

## ▷After A levels

Having studied computer science at A level, you will be a valuable asset to any employer. There will be some apprenticeships and trainee jobs available in the computing industry but your skills and knowledge could prove useful in many business, financial and technical careers.

## ▷After a degree

## Working in computing

Depending on your area of specialisation at degree level, you will find a great deal of choice in potential careers. The British Computer Society estimated that there was a shortfall of 100,000 people in 2013. However, many entrants require some further training either whilst working or via a masters degree.

The main areas of work open to a graduate are as follows:

- *Account manager*—acts as the interface between ICT and the users or customer, advising on the best solutions for different types of application
- *Software engineer*—specifies, develops, documents and maintains computer software programs in order to meet client or employer needs

- **Database administrator**–responsible for the usage, accuracy, efficiency, security, maintenance and development of computerised databases
- **Applications developer**–writes and modifies programs to enable a computer to carry out specific tasks, such as stock control or payroll, typically for technical, commercial and business users
- **Systems operator (technical support)**–takes the specification for the requirements of a computer system and designs the system including hardware, software, communications, installation, testing and maintenance
- **Systems developer**–sets up the computer operating systems and standard software services essential to the operation of any computer
- **Information technology consultant**–gives independent and objective advice on how best to use information technology to solve business problems. The work includes analysing problems, making recommendations and implementing new systems
- **Computer virus expert**–works in a virus lab, identifying, unravelling and fixing computer viruses. A thorough knowledge of programming and applications is required
- **Network engineer**–responsible for the management of a computer network. This will include software installation and configuration, upgrades, diagnostics and troubleshooting
- **Information security specialist/cyber security specialist**–ensures that a companys infrastructure and systems receive an appropriate level of protection from external and internal security threats
- **Teacher**–computer science is a shortage subject so there are scholarships available for teacher training courses.

## Working outside computing

Computing graduates working outside the computing industry or specialist IT departments can put their skills and knowledge to work in business, administration or finance. All businesses need a good knowledge and understanding of computers among their general management staff. As a computing graduate you could consider management training schemes in many different organisations.

## Sources of information

BCS, The Chartered Institute for IT
www.bcs.org

e-skills UK
www.e-skills.com

www.bigambition.co.uk/

---

*'I have enjoyed my course so far, it's exactly what I thought it would be. Make sure your course is accredited by BCS, The Chartered Institute for IT, as it gives you a bit more street cred.'* Barbara, on BSc computer science

# Creative writing

*This A level is for anyone who would like to try their hand at creative writing but is equally useful for anyone interested in improving their creative and critical thinking and communication skills. Creative writing encourages the development of skills that are essential for further study and a range of professional careers. It complements the study of English language/literature as well as developing skills that can be used in the real world.*

## What do you study?

The course will teach you to:

- write regularly in a range of forms and genres in order to explore writing styles and develop technical control
- read widely and critically, developing your writing skills by widening your experience of reading
- share work-in-progress with others, respond productively to feedback and develop drafting and editing skills.

*Writing on demand*—many professional writers write to order, with tight deadlines and tight focus. The A level provides the opportunity to write to a specific professional brief, showing appropriate writing skills, in limited time. This could be a blog, marketing pitch, reviews or article.

*Exploring creative writing*—reading and writing in prose fiction, prose non-fiction, poetry and script. Involves regular reading and writing assignments to develop your expertise as a writer. You build a portfolio that includes examples across all four forms. You start to identify your strongest work.

*From reading to writing*—reading widely is an essential part of the development of the creative writer. You learn to recognise the learning that can be gained from reading the work of others, analyse the authorial craft of other writers through a programme of reading and class discussion, learn how to apply your learning to your own work through your own independent writing practice.

*The writing portfolio*—this unit offers ample opportunity for independent study and you develop your own programme of reading and writing, alongside assignments set in class. You will ultimately choose one form in which to specialise for coursework, from prose fiction, prose non-fiction, poetry and script.

**Subject combinations**

There is some overlap in the skills required for English literature, English language, and English language and literature. However, creative writing is a distinct discipline that complements but does not replicate English studies. Creative writing A level can be studied alongside English literature, English language or English language and literature.

# Future careers

Creative writing may lead onto careers in areas such as journalism, fiction writing, commercial writing (copywriting) and writing for the web.

**Sources of information**

www.creative-choices.co.uk

# Critical thinking

*Do you believe everything you see on TV or find on the web? Do you think that all politicians are telling the whole truth? What are the arguments for and against euthanasia? Can you argue your point of view calmly, sensibly and logically? Or do you get all emotional and start shouting instead?*

*Critical thinking is different from other subjects at A level because it is less about learning material and more about developing and applying explanatory, analytical and evaluative skills. It is skills-based rather than content-based. The skills you develop in critical thinking can help you to do well in your other A level subjects.*

*You learn to analyse and evaluate ideas and arguments and how to construct clear, logical and coherent lines of reasoning. A good critical thinking student will have an interest in developing skills for devising logical, coherent arguments and will want to improve their analytical skills useful in subjects as diverse as English literature, history, psychology and chemistry. You should want to make your mind up about the plausibility of various styles of argument and enjoy engaging in reasoned discussion.*

*The course will help you to develop your communication skills and you will be able to influence people with sound reasoning, but at the same time listen to and value their views. It will help you to use and analyse information from different sources and become a problem solver who can make reasoned decisions, based on evidence.*

## What do you study?

*The topics listed give an idea of what could be covered. The exact content of AS and A2 specifications differs according to exam boards, so you will need to check with your school or college about the exact modules available to you.*

You start with an introduction to the concepts, principles and techniques that underlie critical thinking, and then expand their application to a range of contexts. You need to be able to identify the difference between argument and explanation, the different types of reasoning used to construct an argument and how conclusions are reached. You may learn how to use statistics to back up your arguments.

You will learn how to recognise the language of reasoning, be able to analyse other peoples arguments, spot the assumptions and flaws in their reasoning, and evaluate the strength and effectiveness of reasoned arguments. You will discuss and debate topical issues, construct your own arguments with logic and clarity, and learn transferable thinking skills that will help you with your other subjects.

You then go on to apply your critical skills to the evaluation of beliefs, knowledge claims and hypotheses, and develop skills of logic and decision making.

At the end of the course you should be able to express your opinions about the things that are important to you; question, consider and argue against views that oppose your own; and learn how to use calm, persuasive argument to express those views clearly.

The course is mainly skills-based, and you will undertake a range of class-based activities. You will look at various sources including books, newspapers, magazines, radio, television, advertising materials and the web. You may look at other data such as statistics and the way that they are interpreted and used. You will take part in debates and discuss a wide range of topical issues, which could be national, international or local issues, such as speed cameras, building on the green belt or extending airports. The course encourages you to reflect on things. It teaches you how to observe your feelings on a subject (are you being emotional or logical?) and to try to understand the feelings of others, even if you don't necessarily agree with them. It's about argument, but reasoned argument so you don't start shouting and getting emotional!

### Subject combinations

Critical thinking is a suitable option alongside many A levels or vocational qualifications. It can go with science subjects equally as well as with humanities or arts subjects. It can also form part of the AQA Baccalaureate.

# Higher education options

Critical thinking skills are of great benefit for a wide range of degrees and HND/ HNC courses including law, social science, journalism, medicine, business, accounting and engineering. Critical thinking is taught in many courses as an essential skill. Many university and college departments recognise that students who have studied critical thinking possess the reasoning skills necessary to succeed in higher education.

University courses that involve analysis and evaluation of data or arguments particularly value A level critical thinking. However, when researching courses you will need to check with higher education institutions to see if it will be counted as part of any offers made. Some universities will accept it as a useful fourth A level, whereas others will include it as part of their main offer.

Don't forget that many universities now set entrance tests that assess your critical thinking skills, so taking the AS or A could be very helpful.

## Relevance to other subjects?

Critical thinking skills will be extremely useful to you whatever subject you study and will go on being useful throughout your career.

## Important advice

Get involved in a debating group or start studying the ways that the same news story is reported by different types of newspapers, TV channels or on the web.

# Future careers

## ▷ After A levels

Critical thinking skills will be useful for many careers including business and finance, management, retail and IT in fact, any jobs where you need to analyse information, make reasoned decisions or influence people.

## ▷ After a degree

Critical thinking will teach you how to evaluate and analyse information, weigh up evidence and communicate complex ideas effectively. Graduate recruiters often test critical thinking skills in their selection procedures. Critical thinking can provide an excellent foundation for a number of popular careers whatever your degree subject, including business, marketing, human resource management, law, public admin-istration, teaching, uniformed services, journalism and the media. To be able to apply advanced critical thinking skills in the workplace is an advantage in any career or profession that involves difficult decision making or the resolution of dilemmas.

# Dance

*Dance A level is designed to meet the needs of students who wish to study dance in depth. On this course you will gain experience of choreography and performance, and you will be encouraged to think critically about dance. You don't have to be a wonderful dancer but you do need to be motivated and fairly fit. The course encourages participation and the developing of skills in order to choreograph, rehearse and perform your own work. You don't need any prior qualifications to take dance A level and your experience of dance need not have taken place at school.*

## What do you study?

*Dance A level is offered by the AQA board.*

Core areas you will explore include dance technique, the art of choreography, anatomy, health and fitness, the history of dance and the analysis of professional works.

For AS you will study the dancer as a performer, the process and craft of choreography, and the significance of dances. You will create a solo choreography and perform in a duet or a trio.

For A2 you will study a chosen area of dance from modern dance, ballet or jazz dance, and one set work in depth. You will create a group dance (in which you do not perform) and perform a solo related to what you have studied.

- **Performance**—how to create and perform your own solo dances as well as performing from notated scores. You will use your skills in choreography when creating your own pieces. For the A2 you will gain the knowledge and skills required to choreograph for a group and you will prepare and present a group work for performance.
- **Choreography**—how dances are written down (notation) and the different types of notation used. You will be required to study only one form of notation, which you will use throughout the course in performance and appreciation. You will also study important choreographers and their work.
- **Dance analysis and appreciation**—how to analyse, for example, how a dance is created and look at it critically to increase your enjoyment of what you see. You look at how professional dance works and study professional dancers.
- **Basic anatomy and physiology**—in relation to dancing; this includes safeguarding your own health when dancing.

Throughout the course you will be analysing and evaluating your dance.

In order to follow this course you may be required to have GCSE dance or experience in dance outside school.

You will participate in practical dance and choreography classes. Theoretical study will involve watching professional works and discussing them. Notation lessons will involve both practical and theory work. You will take part in workshops including dance technique, choreography, anatomy, dance notation and dance analysis. Your course may include visits to local and national dance performances, and workshops with visiting dance companies.

You will be assessed through a combination of performance and choreography, coursework and exams. Much of the theory is taught through practice even the anatomy and physiology of dance.

### Subject combinations
Drama and music are obvious choices, but you could consider media studies, film studies or other subjects such as English language, literature, psychology, biology, human biology and sports science. Some people take AS level dance as a contrast to more classroom-based subjects. Some dance degrees prefer A levels offering writing skills, such as English or history, especially if there is an academic element to the course.

### Further education options
Some further education colleges run dance foundation courses. The course content for these courses varies considerably but usually includes an emphasis on dance technique with some choreography and dance appreciation. They may include GCSEs, A levels or BTEC performing arts courses. It is also worth remembering that many vocational dance courses take students from the age of 16.

# Higher education options

### Degree-level study
If you want to become a professional dancer, the most common route is to undertake training at a specialist dance school or college. Entrance requirements vary and competition for places is very strong. Most of the courses last three years and some lead to a degree, although they are mostly Diplomas. You do not necessarily need a degree to become a dancer so it is worth considering all your options.

Some colleges of higher education and universities also offer degrees in dance. These vary in their content and course titles include dance, dance studies and dance performance. Besides practical dance tutoring, these courses have an academic content, covering areas such as the physiology of movement, dance analysis, dance history and the sociology of dance. Some are not intended as courses for professional performers but more of a general education for those who want to be dance teachers, company administrators, education officers or to work in a related area. You will need to look at the content carefully to find out which course is suitable for you. You might want to consider a performing arts course or a specialist dance area, for example contemporary dance, dance theatre performance, urban dance, choreography or community dance. Your choice will depend on how much further dance training or performing you want to do and whether you want to specialise in a particular area, for example musical theatre.

## Degree subject combinations
Apart from the more obvious combinations such as music, drama, education or movement studies, there are some less obvious combinations such as law, criminology and maths.

## Other higher education qualifications
Foundation degrees are available in dance, performing arts, community dance practice, contemporary dance, dance and theatre arts, dance teaching, dance theatre performance, performance (dance), performing arts (acting, dance and creative technologies), professional dance and drama, professional dance practice, teaching dance (in the private sector) and theatre arts (dance).

There are HNDs and HNCs in dance, performing arts, professional stage dance and dance artists. Sometimes you are able to transfer onto a performing degree course after completion of the HND.

## Relevance to other subjects?
Depending on your A level choice you could consider degrees in arts and entertainment management, theatre studies, community arts, teaching, stage and technical theatre management, PE, English literature, media studies, communication studies and music.

## Important advice
Make sure you do your research into the right type of degree for you.

How much performing do you want? Do you want to study other subjects? What facilities are there? It is important to make the right choice of degree in this area.

You might think it won't happen to you but dancers are prone to injury. So if you are considering a career in dance or the performing arts it is always worth choosing some academic subjects at A level, just in case you ever need to retrain or if you need to work between dance jobs.

# Future careers

## ▷After A levels

It will be difficult to get a dance-related job after A levels, but you will have knowledge of the performing arts, anatomy and physiology as well as study and team-working skills. You could work in the health and fitness or leisure sector, either in administration or as a leisure centre assistant, or train to become a personal trainer. You might find work within the performing arts sector, such as front-of-house or box office work.

## ▷After a degree

### Working in dance

If you don't become a professional dancer, there is related work in the fields of choreography, dance therapy, dance teaching and arts administration. For some of these careers you will need to undertake further training, such as a PGCE in dance for teaching in state schools, and postgraduate courses for dance therapy and dance movement therapy.

There are postgraduate courses specialising in dance including performance, dance science, community dance leadership, global dance and choreography.

### Working outside dance

If you have studied an academic dance degree, you will be able to compete with graduates for jobs where graduates are accepted with any subject. This could include anything from the Armed Forces to jobs in business, IT, finance and administration. You could consider jobs connected with the performing arts in some way, such as arts administration, marketing, theatre management or community arts work. As you will have a good understanding of health and fitness, you may wish to consider jobs in fitness centres, gyms, personal training or working in health promotion in jobs such as a healthy lifestyles officer. You might consider also working in paramedical or complementary medicine by becoming a physiotherapist, osteopath, Alexander Technique teacher or reflexologist, although you would have to be prepared to undertake further training for all of these.

## Sources of information

Council for Dance Education and Training
www.cdet.org.uk

Dance UK
www.danceuk.org

National Association of Teachers of Dancing
www.natd.org.uk

National Resource Centre for Dance
www.surrey.ac.uk/NRCD

www.young-dancers.org

www.dancing-times.co.uk

*'If dance is what you really want to do, go for it, so you won't regret it later. Remember that dancing is 95% mental so a positive mindset is a must.'* Jess, studying for a dance Diploma

# Design and technology (food technology)

*Do you understand how and why food is labelled? Where does the meat come from in a ready meal? What are smart foods? What is a BMI and what constitutes a healthy diet? What are the health benefits of free-range versus factory-farmed chickens? Design and technology (food technology) will help you to answer these questions and find out more about this growing area of work where there is currently a skills shortage.*

## What do you study?

*The topics listed give an idea of what could be covered. The exact content of AS and A2 specifications differ according to exam boards, so you will need to check with your school or college about the exact modules available to you.*

You will find out about the use of food technology in all aspects of food production, from small one-off organic products through to mass-produced items. You will study a variety of food issues including production techniques, sampling, testing, marketing and the design of new food products. The course covers the social, scientific, economic and technological facts, principles and experience in industrial food production; and the impact and effect of market forces on consumers, manufacturers, producers and suppliers.

The topics studied include:
- **understanding food science**–the properties of the main food components and the effect of processing on them. How products are manipulated and combined in manufacture and processing, including food additives and all the stages in new product development
- **design and market influences**–the food industry, consideration of environmental, technological and socio-economic factors in the development of new food products. Trends in new food production, concept development, market research, prototype designs, packaging, testing, launching and evaluating new products
- **the relationship between diet and health**–nutritional principles, dietary planning, BMI, health promotion, lifestyle and how it is influenced by social, cultural and economic factors
- **environmental factors influencing food choices**–organic food and sources of energy
- **food hygiene and safety legislation**–including food labelling.

Practical work is a part of the course in the form of investigations and product analysis. You will need to be able to plan appropriate schemes of work together with the technological processes necessary to achieve them, and to have the ability to develop and produce solutions to any problems encountered. There will be design-and-make exercises where you will be able to demonstrate your skills and you will also learn the skills involved in analysing existing products. You may visit food manufacturers to observe the production processes.

## Subject combinations

If you are considering higher education in food technology, food science, food manufacture, nutrition or dietetics, one or more sciences are usually required, so chemistry and/or biology are recommended. For courses geared more towards the manufacturing process and engineering, you will need maths and physics A levels or equivalent. For careers in catering and hospitality management, or travel and tourism, business studies or modern languages would be helpful.

# Higher education options

## Degree-level study

Food is fuel, so of course it's fundamentally important to the wellbeing of every living human being. The scientific study of food takes a multi-disciplinary approach, integrating the basic sciences (biology, chemistry and mathematics) and examining them within the context of the modern food industry. You'll cover a range of contemporary topics including food safety, security, nutrition and wellness, sustainability, and related ethical and socio-economic issues. The safety of food and its assurance, together with the official and industrial control of food, are also covered.

There is a wide variety of courses available including food technology, food science and technology, food and consumer science, food design and nutrition, public health nutrition, food, nutrition and health, human nutrition and dietetics, food product design, food management and marketing and food production management. There are also specialised courses in areas like sports biomedicine and nutrition. Many courses have a sandwich period involving work experience in the UK or abroad. There is currently a shortage of suitably qualified food technology graduates.

If you want to become a registered dietician or nutritionist you will need to study for a degree in nutrition and dietetics. This will mean at least two sciences at A level. You will also find public health nutrition degrees, which might be worth considering for a more community-focused career.

## Degree subject combinations

You will see from the degrees above that many food technology degrees can be combined with elements of business, management and marketing.

## Other higher education qualifications

There are a number of foundation degrees available including food manufacture, food studies, food and consumer management, food chain technology, food industry with management, food manufacturing management, food science and technology, food, nutrition and health, baking technology management, and sustainable food production. This reflects the shortage status of this subject.

HND and HNC courses are available in human nutrition, food management, food marketing, hospitality and food management, and food technology, and will give a mixture of practical experience and theory.

## Relevance to other subjects?

You could consider related areas such as hospitality and catering, or travel and tourism. In addition, you will have gained a good knowledge of manufacturing and business functions so could consider business and marketing-related courses.

## Important advice

Many food technology and nutrition courses will ask for sciences at A level so check that you have the right subjects to progress in your chosen course. There is such a wide variety of food science/technology courses available that you will need to research the content thoroughly to make sure you are choosing the right course.

# Future careers

## ▷After A levels

With A level food technology you would be able to work for food manufacturers, in hospitality and catering, or in food retail such as supermarket management. You will have good problem-solving skills and knowledge of how business works so you could consider a wide range of jobs in business and administration. Your scientific skills could be used in investigative and analytical work, for example, in laboratories in the food industry, hospitals or in public health. Your knowledge of consumers could prove useful in consumer advice or other jobs working with the public. Nottingham Trent University offers Higher Apprenticeships in food science technology combining practical training with a foundation degree.

## ▷After a degree

### Working in food technology

The industry is facing a staffing crisis a shortage of food science graduates is causing a massive skills gap. There are still one in six of the sectors 1,700 or so vacancies requiring a food science degree left unfilled (2013 figures). Therefore graduates will have excellent career prospects in the food industry in areas relating to new product development, quality assurance, food retail and marketing and food law. In addition, there could be related jobs in food writing or journalism as well as marketing, sales and management. You could also consider teaching, training or lecturing. Teaching food technology is a shortage area so there is a demand for suitably qualified teachers.

### Working outside food technology

You will have a good insight into industry from a business and scientific point of view as well as good problem-solving and teamwork skills. There are related jobs such as the food retail industry, and hospitality and catering. Your knowledge of the manufacturing process could be equally useful in careers in business and management.

## Sources of information

British Dietetic Association
www.bda.uk.com

Institute of Food Science & Technology
www.ifst.org

www.chillededucation.org

British Nutrition Foundation
www.nutrition.org.uk

Nutrition Society
www.nutritionsociety.org

Improve (Food and Drink Skills Council)
www.improveltd.co.uk

www.careersinfoodanddrink.co.uk

> 'After graduating I had a choice of jobs. You have the choice of working in this country or abroad.' Julie-Anne, HND food technology, junior trainee

# Home economics (food, nutrition and health)

This A level overlaps with many topics from the food technology A level. You will study properties of food; design, development and production of food; advances in the food industry; consumer studies and consumer protection. Topics include nutrition and diet, food production, health and lifestyle, and the management of resources such as food, finances and energy to meet individual and family needs. You will also gain a thorough knowledge of resources, food provision, selection and purchase of food and household goods, food preparation and cooking equipment, food safety and hygiene.

# Design and technology (product design)

*Everything that has been made has been designed. You will learn what makes for good design and how design affects society and the environment. Central to the subject is the design process, which will teach you how to tackle real-life problems in a practical way. You will get involved in the design and manufacture of your own products as well as learning about how this process operates in industry.*

*You must be able to communicate your ideas and will have the opportunity to use a wide range of graphic techniques, from traditional drawing methods to computer-aided design (CAD). You will learn to consider the materials and manufacture of a product in its design and will work with wood, metals, paper, card, plastics and some textiles, using your imagination and creativity to produce quality products. You will learn to evaluate your own work and the work of others.*

## What do you study?

*The topics listed give an idea of what could be covered. The exact content of AS and A2 specifications differ according to exam boards, so you will need to check with your school or college about the exact modules available to you.*

In the first year, you learn and develop skills in design and production, gaining an understanding of the properties of a broad range of materials. You will carry out coursework assignments, evaluate existing products and assess how they could be improved. You will consider broader issues such as the environmental sustainability of products and their manufacture, as well as health and safety issues. You will look at how CAD and computer-aided manufacture (CAM) have influenced the production process and about other factors such as ergonomics and anthropometrics (different sizes of people), inclusive design and consumer safety. An important consideration will be the lifecycle of products, their manufacture, use and final disposal.

In the second year, your knowledge of materials, manufacture and design is developed further. You will complete a design project as coursework, and in some specifications carry out a marketing presentation to assess the commercial potential of your product. You will need to be able to plan appropriate schemes of work together with the processes necessary to achieve them. An important aspect of your work will be how to produce solutions to design problems. Again there are broader issues to take into consideration, such as health and safety as an element of design activity. You will also look at the use of natural resources, materials utilisation, conservation, waste disposal, pollution, recycling and the moral, economic, social and environmental responsibilities of the designer.

## Subject combinations

Design and technology (product design) combines well with other subjects. If you are interested in engineering, it would be a good idea to consider A levels in maths and physics. For architecture and product design courses, a creative and analytical mix is often considered desirable, such as a combination with maths, physics, ICT or art. It could be combined also with BTEC Nationals in engineering, although you would have to check that there is no major overlap with your school or college's specification for these subjects.

# Higher education options

## Degree-level study

Popular courses include product design, product design and technology, industrial product design, sustainable product design and 3D design. Courses have strong links with industry and many include sandwich placements. Some courses get students to partner with commercial companies to work on a specific brief. Product design degrees usually include related subjects such as management, business and innovation. The design-focused courses will ask for a portfolio of practical work as part of the application process.

Product design degrees have different focuses and specialisms. Examples include: product design engineering, transport product design and sports product design. In addition you might consider degrees in architecture or architectural design technology although you would need to check with institutions for their exact entry requirements. There are also some related degrees such as special effects and model making.

## Degree subject combinations

Product design tends to be offered in combination with relevant subjects such as business, management and innovation.

## Other higher education qualifications

Foundation degrees are available in product design, and product design and development and sustainable design and construction. There are also more engineering-focused degrees such as electrical or electronic manufacturing engineering, engineering design and development, and engineering design. There are HNDs and HNCs available in design technologies, product design and 3D design.

## Relevance to other subjects?

Combined with relevant subjects, design and technology (product design) can lead to engineering, architecture, design and art courses.

## Important advice

You will find a wide range of product-design related courses available so you will need to spend some time investigating them. You will be developing a portfolio as part of your course, but don't forget that any work you do outside your coursework may be a useful addition to your portfolio when you apply.

# Future careers

## ▷After A levels

It may be possible to go into Advanced Level Apprenticeships or Higher Apprenticeships in design, engineering, construction or manufacturing. There could be technician-level jobs in CAD or engineering. Further training will be necessary for all jobs at this level and some Advanced Level Apprenticeships and Higher Apprenticeships can lead to degree level study.

## ▷After a degree

### Working in product design

Product designers work in many business areas including consumer electronics, sports equipment, medical products and the automotive industry. Many product designers work directly for large and small businesses while others work for independent consultancies both in the UK and abroad. The skills learned in a product design degree make many other careers a possibility, and of course you could start your own business. Teaching is another option, as design and technology is a shortage area. You would need to undertake a PGCE for this and there may be financial incentives to study.

### Working outside product design

Good problem-solving, creative and analytical skills can lead into many other careers such as management, and business and finance.

## Sources of information

Chartered Institute of Architectural Technologists
www.ciat.org.uk

www.creative-choices.co.uk

Design Council
www.designcouncil.org.uk

Institution of Engineering Designers
www.ied.org.uk

www.design-technology.info

---

*'You need the ability to use both sides of your brain—creative and logical.'*
Sasha, industrial designer

---

# Design and technology (systems and control)

*This course is about designing and making things using electrical, mechanical and electronic systems and understanding the relationship between design, materials, manufacture and marketing.*

*Think about how cars are now manufactured by robots and other automated systems. What about the manufacture of food and clothes? How about how heating, air conditioning and security systems are all designed and controlled? All these control systems have become an essential part of our lives.*

*You will learn about the processes of how products are designed and manufactured. During the course you will investigate, analyse and evaluate a broad range of products to create your own original solutions and then design and manufacture models, prototypes, products and systems.*

*Electronics and computers play a large part in the control of many systems and this forms a significant part of the course. It will include robotics and control systems (including electronics, computer control and a range of other technical areas such as structural and mechanical systems).You will design and make a system that does a job for you; this could be anything from a system that regulates the temperature or humidity in a greenhouse to something that might make life easier for a disabled person, like a keyboard that will control gadgets around their house.*

## What do you study?

*The topics listed give an idea of what could be covered. The exact content of AS and A2 specifications differ according to exam boards, so you will need to check with your school or college about the exact modules available to you.*

At AS you will have the opportunity to learn through practical activities while producing solutions to control- and systems-based problems. You will learn the basics about the control-system process. You will study the materials and components and how they are used, and how cost and availability can influence your work. You will then demonstrate your ability to design, make, test and evaluate products by producing your own products.

At A2 level you will go on to see how industrial processes work and how engineers and designers overcome problems within commercial constraints. The specification gives you the opportunity to study the subject in more detail including, for example, computer simulation and its use to replicate an environment, product or system; industrial production; methods of harnessing alternative energy sources, energy transmission and storage. You will then manufacture a single prototype, system or product involving substantial designing and making.

The whole specification gives you the chance to apply all the skills you have learned. You learn principles of design, research techniques and problem-solving strategies, and learn how you can think creatively and originally to get your designs to work for you.

It would be helpful to have studied a design technology subject at GCSE but this is not essential. You would be expected to have good GCSEs in maths and English and possibly a science.

Lessons are a mixture of designing and modelling, theory and practical work on projects. You will be expected to undertake personal research in groups and present findings to other students. You will need to support your studies with your own background reading.

The subject is examined by written papers and coursework where you will design and manufacture a product and show proof of how you carried this out by means of a design folder. Examples of projects for systems and control could include a car alarm system, a roving robot, a foot-operated keyboard for the disabled, a wheelchair lift or rainfall meter.

You will visit trade shows and companies using systems and control technology processes, such as automated warehouses or car manufacturers.

### Subject combinations

Systems and control technology combines well with many subjects. If you are interested in engineering, it would be a good idea to consider A levels in maths and physics. For architecture and product design courses, a creative and analytical mix is often considered desirable, such as a combination with maths, physics, ICT or art. Systems and control technology could be combined with electronics A level or BTEC National qualifications in manufacturing or engineering, although you would have to check that there is no major overlap with your school or colleges specification for these subjects.

# Higher education options

### Degree-level study

When combined with other related AS or A level subjects, systems and control technology can lead to a wide range of higher education courses. You could consider courses in systems engineering (specialising in robotics, sustainability or instrumentation), computer systems engineering and product design engineering. You could also consider electronic engineering courses, which will include systems and control work and some offer specialisms such as electrical engineering with renewable energy systems. Software engineering courses could include systems and control elements, as could the more traditional engineering degrees of engineering or mechanical engineering.

Many courses are likely to include a sandwich placement; the design-focused courses will ask for a portfolio of practical work when you apply. Courses tend to be either BSc, BEng or MEng. You must check with institutions for their exact entry requirements. Some degrees may offer a foundation year for those without the exact required entry qualifications.

## Degree subject combinations

Systems engineering degrees are usually combined with electronics and other engineering subjects. You will also find combinations with business management.

## Other higher education qualifications

There are no foundation degrees entitled design and technology (systems and control), but plenty that are relevant to the subject. Look at engineering, engineering electrical systems, and refrigeration and air conditioning engineering, as well as electronic systems and control, electro technical industries, engineering (design and manufacture), mechanical design and manufacture, product design and development, and technology (mechanical, manufacture, electrical/electronic).

Related HNDs and HNCs are available in engineering systems, electronic and computer technology, instrumentation and control engineering and product design.

## Relevance to other subjects?

Combined with relevant subjects, the study of systems and control can lead to a wide range of engineering, manufacturing and design courses.

## Important advice

If you are considering future study in systems and control technology, such as systems engineering, you must make sure that you make the right choice of A levels. Some courses will require maths, physics or science in addition to your design and technology (systems and control) A level.

Don't forget that in control work there is a big emphasis on software engineering because of the embedded system nature of controllers so you must be interested in this and prepared to study it.

There is such a wide range of design and engineering courses available that you will need to spend some time investigating them. You will be developing a portfolio as part of your course, but don't forget that the work you do outside your coursework may be a useful addition to your portfolio when you apply.

# Future careers

### ▷After A levels
Depending on your subject choices it may be possible to enter a Higher Apprenticeship in engineering, construction or manufacturing. There could be technician-level jobs in manufacturing processes or engineering. This would involve part-time study, which could eventually lead to a degree.

### ▷After a degree

### Working in systems and control technology
Systems and control technology is a discipline at the core of many engineering disciplines. These include electrical, mechanical, aerospace, and chemical process engineering, manufacturing, automation and robotics. A degree in systems and control technology or a related subject will provide a sound foundation if you wish to pursue a career in designing, building and operating large-scale engineering systems, including those for railways, power generation and distribution, air traffic control, and oil and gas exploration and production.

There will be opportunities to travel abroad on short- or long-term projects. With a thorough knowledge of engineering systems and processes you could also consider careers in management or sales within the industry.

Teaching is another option, as design and technology is a shortage area. You would need to undertake a specialist PGCE for this and there may be financial incentives to study.

### Working outside systems and control technology
Good problem-solving, creative and analytical skills can lead into many other careers such as management and business and finance.

## Sources of information

Institute of Measurement and Control
www.instmc.org.uk

Institution of Engineering and Technology
www.theiet.org

www.apprentices.co.uk (details of engineering apprenticeships)

www.design-technology.info

---

*'It's not just knowing about engineering systems, it's being able to work commercially as well. That was the beauty of my degree.'* Joel, MEng in systems engineering, working for BAE

# Drama and theatre studies

*If you enjoy or participate in the performing arts then this course is for you. The skills gained from this course are a good preparation for the performing arts as well as being transferable to other areas of work. As well as the practical part of the course, you study the origins, aims and techniques of theatre, and gain an ability to view performances with a critical eye.*

## What do you study?

*The topics listed give an idea of what could be covered. The exact content of AS and A2 specifications differ according to exam boards, so you will need to check with your school or college about the exact modules available to you.*

Exam boards vary in the amount of performing involved but all courses contain elements of the following:

- **live performance**—how to devise your own performance with other students, which will give everyone the opportunity to try all aspects of organising and producing a piece of theatre
- **theatre texts**—(as pieces meant for performance) how they are translated into a stage performance; how creative opportunities are presented by this process; how effectively they communicate the feelings and ideas that they contain
- **set and costume design**—how these may be used to communicate ideas and add to the overall effectiveness of the performance
- **stage lighting and sound**—lighting and sound management skills; their importance in the creation of mood and atmosphere, use of special effects
- **masks and puppets**—the skills behind their use in theatre directing
- **theatre practitioners**—includes playwrights, directors, designers and theatre companies: playwrights from Shakespeare, Aristophanes and Marlowe to more contemporary playwrights like Ibsen, Buchner, OCasey, Littlewood and April De Angelis; directors such as Steven Berkoff, John Godber, Peter Hall, Katie Mitchell, Max Stafford Clark and Deborah Warner; designers such as Edward Gordon Craig, Ralph Koltai, John Napier, Julie Taymor and Anthony Ward; theatre companies such as Compliciti, Forced Entertainment, Frantic Assembly, Kneehigh and Shared Experience.

It is not essential to have studied the subject at GCSE in order to take the A level but you do need good grades in English and a genuine interest in the theatre.

There is also an A level available in performing arts, which includes options in dance, drama and music in its specifications.

Depending on the specification, you are encouraged to experience and gain skills in a number of areas, including direction, performance, design (set, lighting, costume, props and sound) and rehearsal. In addition there may be small group projects and some individual research for assignments. You will see live theatre performances, which will give you a means of comparison between theatre styles, playwrights, companies and periods. You create original drama presentations in which your theatre studies group is entirely responsible for all aspects developing an original idea, producing, designing and performing it.

## Subject combinations

English and drama and theatre studies is a popular combination. Some theatre studies courses at a higher level require A level in English in addition to, or instead of, a performance-based one. You mustn't make the mistake of assuming that the work you do on set texts in A level drama and theatre studies is exactly the same as that done on set texts in English or modern languages. In drama and theatre studies, you study the texts as a starting point and foundation for producing a performance rather than as literature. Drama and theatre studies is a subject in its own right, and not a variant of English literature. Other popular combinations are sociology, history, media studies, psychology and religious studies.

# Higher education options

An A level in drama and theatre studies is not essential to study at degree level.

## Degree-level study

Theatre and drama-related degree courses come in many forms with different titles. Your choice of course will depend on your areas of interest. For example, how much practical work do you want in comparison to theory? Do you want technical training in lighting, sound, stage management, costume or set design? Drama or theatre arts degrees tend to provide the most general grounding in all aspects of theatre skills and theory. You have the opportunity to choose options in later years in areas such as playwriting, design and physical theatre.

You might want to specialise and choose a course focusing on a particular aspect of theatre, for example technical theatre, theatre production or stage management.

Many traditional drama schools offer BA courses as well as Diplomas so you must research your choice of course carefully. Auditions will be an essential part of the selection process, especially for the drama schools. You have to be persistent and it may be worth reapplying if you are turned down the first time. You may be accepted later on, so waiting and getting more experience may pay dividends.

## Degree subject combinations

You can combine a theatre or drama course with related subjects such as English, music, media studies and modern languages. Some courses offer flexibility in your studies. For example, you could study a module in new theatre writing, followed by performance practice, followed by directing, while being assessed on each as you go.

## Other higher education qualifications

There are a numerous foundation degrees leading to degree-level study or employment; examples include acting performance, actor training (for theatre and media performance), artistic make-up and special effects, arts and entertainment management (audio and music production),circus arts, community dance practice, costume construction for stage and screen, costume for performance, creative industries (drama), creative industries (performing arts), creative music production and business, dance theatre performance, drama practitioners, drama, performance and arts management, electronic music production, fashion, theatrical and media hair and make-up, hair design and make up for theatre, TV and film, media make-up, music (performance and production),music business and management, music composition for film and media, music industry entrepreneurship, music performance (heavy metal), music performance (popular music), music performance, music production, music production and artist development, music production and performance, musical theatre, performance (dance), performance (physical theatre), performing arts (acting, dance and creative technologies), performing arts technologies, popular music, professional acting, professional dance and drama, sound and music for new media, sound, lighting and live event technology, stage management and technical theatre, theatre arts (prop making and special effects) and theatre media performance.

Examples of HNDs and HNCs available include performing arts, technical theatre, musical theatre and theatrical, media and special effects make-up.

## Relevance to other subjects

Theatre is a form of communication and expression that looks at human beings and how they behave in different situations. You will find a broad range of related subjects for which the drama and theatre studies A level will provide a good background. These include psychology, history, sociology, politics and classical civilisation. Your ability to analyse and extract information from the written word would be a valuable skill in the study of any subject that requires work on texts, such as English, modern languages, cultural studies, media studies and philosophy.

## Important advice

Courses involving practical performance or direction work will require an audition, where you may have to act, sing, direct or dance. In addition you will be judged according to how much performance experience you have and how much live theatre you have seen. You should try to gain as much practical experience as possible, by taking part in productions at school or college and joining local drama groups. For courses that involve a large design or technical element, you may be required to show evidence of your practical experience. This can be in the form of photographs or drawings of productions for which you have designed sets, lighting, costumes, etc.

# Future careers

## ▷ After A levels

An A level in drama and theatre studies will not automatically get you a career in the theatre but then neither will a degree course, although the degree route into the profession is becoming more common. Acting is a competitive and crowded profession. It is virtually impossible to perform without an Equity membership card (Equity being the union responsible for professional actors and performers), yet it is almost impossible to get an Equity card without having been offered professional work as a performer. You can get round this in two ways. Firstly by gaining further training at one of the accredited drama schools and thereby getting a provisional (temporary and basic level) Equity card. Secondly, by getting involved in a semi-professional or amateur production, and persuading a director or agent to come along. If they are impressed with you, they may be able to help you get work.

If you are interested in technical theatre or the business admin side of theatre work, there may be some apprenticeships available with A levels or equivalent.

You could gain relevant experience and training in drama-related careers by working in a theatre as a box-office assistant or usher, or volunteer working on community, youth or amateur theatre projects.

## ▷ After a degree

### Working in drama and theatre

The professional theatre is full of people looking for their next employment opportunity, and it can be difficult to get work. If you have determination and a realistic understanding of the difficulties involved, it is possible to break into the industry.

- *Actor*–usually self-employed but may have an agent to search out and negotiate contracts. Actors move between the various media, theatre, film, television and radio, and can often make the most money by doing commercials, voiceovers and training films.
- *Costume designer or costume and wardrobe*–this involves the design and creation or hiring and buying of costumes for a play, and keeping tabs on a theatres stock of costumes.
- *Designer*–some work on sets, others on sets and costumes and even lighting designs. Most have further training in the design field and are freelance.
- *Director*–responsible for choosing the actors; with the designer and lighting designer, working out the look of the piece. In rehearsals, the director works on the overall shape of the scenes, as well as perfecting the actors performances.
- *Drama therapist*–a career where you use drama to help the recovery of people with emotional or mental health issues. Specialist training is required in addition to your drama qualification.
- *Education officer*–employed by many theatres to work with schools and colleges and arrange educational trips to the theatre.

- *Marketing manager*—finds a way to get 'bums on seats'. May work with a press manager to deal with publicity.
- *Sound or lighting technician*—often employed by a theatre on a full-time basis. Works with visiting designers and directors on the aural and visual environment of a play.
- *Stage manager*—responsible for running the production in rehearsal and performance. Tasks range from photocopying the script to managing the stage crew, and telling actors and lighting technicians when they are to go on or switch on.

## Working outside drama and theatre

Any career that demands confident verbal and physical communication skills is one that a graduate of a performance-based degree would enjoy. A good example is sales and marketing. Your skills could also be used in human resources work, conference organising (including lighting, sound and direction), museum and other exhibition work, and advertising, where an awareness of the importance of visual image and design in the communication of an idea is vital.

## Sources of information

Equity
www.equity.org.uk

Get into theatre
www.getintotheatre.org

Drama UK (which has a list of drama schools)
www.dramauk.co.uk

> *'The subject gives you confidence, whatever you decide to do later on.'*
> Judith, taking A levels in drama and theatre studies, English literature and business

# Economics

*Economists are interested in all aspects of life, not only in the more obvious issues such as consumer spending, inflation, house prices, unemployment, wages and international trade but also in environmental pollution, how firms compete, living standards, how we behave as consumers, taxation, poverty, health, education and much more. All aspects of economic theory are applied to the real world to what determines growth, unemployment, inflation, the balance of payments, the gap between wealth and poverty, and society.*

*The study of economics will broaden your understanding of the business world and encourage you to evaluate the consequences of business and government decisions. Economics is useful to anyone wanting to go into business and finance since it is included as a core subject in the examinations of all the professional bodies including law, banking, marketing and accountancy.*

*Note that there is also an A level in economics and business, described at the end of the business studies A level entry.*

## What do you study?

*The topics listed give an idea of the range of issues that are covered in an A level economics course. The exact content of courses differs according to exam boards, so you will need to check with your school or college about the exact modules available to you.*

The course concentrates on: the workings of the market economy, the causes of breakdown in the market economy (such as mismanagement, crime, pollution and waste), threats to consumers from monopoly power etc., and the national and international economy.

For the AS you start by looking at different economic markets and at the national economy. At A2 there are extended courses that analyse the UK and international economy, transport economics, the economics of work and leisure, and the wider economy on a global scale.

In most A level courses, you study the main issues of the day and then use your knowledge and applied skills to investigate and understand the underlying causes, explanations and consequences. The topics covered range from those dealing with the economy as a whole (macroeconomics) to those dealing with individual parts of the economy (microeconomics):

- *inflation*–why does the Government have an inflation rate target and how does it affect us?
- *pensions*–can a future government afford to pay them?
- *the environment*–can pollution effectively be controlled?

- *the international situation*—why is there a gulf between rich and poor nations?
- *house prices*—why do house prices rise and fall?
- *the EU*—should Britain be in it?
- *competition between companies*—why is this good for customers?
- *wages*—what affects students wages in part-time employment?
- *privatisation*—is a service better if it is privatised?
- *the low-cost airline revolution*—has it benefited consumers?
- *immigration*—does it help the economy?
- *should the government intervene in the economy?*
- *unemployment*—the big debate; how to reduce it?
- *globalisation*—how are we affected by the Chinese and Indian economies?

It is not essential to have studied economics at GCSE in order to take the A level. You need to have a good understanding of maths, so a GCSE maths at grade A*-C is usually preferred.

You must take an interest in current affairs, read a quality newspaper and get involved in discussion and argument. You will be required to carry out research on your own, and need to be able to evaluate the merits of alternative arguments.

## Subject combinations

Economics combines well with a wide variety of other A level subjects and popular subjects are maths, English, history, government and politics, geography, philosophy and modern languages. If you have chosen business studies as one of your A levels it may overlap with economics, and some higher education institutions may not accept it. If you want to study economics at degree level, think about combining it with A level mathematics as this is requested or preferred by some universities. Some like you to have further maths A level but it is important to check this. Maths could really help your application as economics is such a popular course and will also help you on your degree. Check this with the universities you are interested in.

# Higher education options

No previous study of economics is required for most university courses although it is preferred by some. If your school or college does not offer economics at A level then business studies is considered as an alternative by some universities but it is vital to check with each institution.

## Degree-level study

Economics courses typically begin with a broad-based first year when you study economics along with other social sciences. In this first year mathematics and/or statistics are often compulsory subjects, especially for students who have not done them at A level. IT and languages may also be available at this stage. In the later years of the course, you can specialise through your choice of options, which could include forecasting and planning, public finance, or monetary theory, although some topics such as econometrics (mathematical economics), international trade, and labour economics are sometimes compulsory. You may also get the opportunity to study abroad.

Universities often specialise in different aspects of economics, so you should look at course outlines very carefully to decide exactly which areas you would like to study.

Related course titles to look out for include financial economics, applied economics, international economics and business economics.

## Degree subject combinations

You may choose to specialise in economics and there are related combinations available in finance, econometrics, economic history, international business, management, banking and statistics. However, there is also a whole range of other subjects available such as politics, accounting, geography, international development, sociology and modern languages.

## Other higher education qualifications

There are no pure economics foundation degrees but there are a few using applied knowledge: these include business and enterprise and business and finance.

Economics topics feature in many HND and HNC courses such as business studies, accounting and marketing and some have options in economic development.

## Relevance to other subjects?

Many students decide on a degree course in a related subject area such as business studies, finance, marketing, management science and international relations. In all these courses the study of economics is included, so your A level in economics would prove helpful. The development of your analytical skills also makes economics a good A level for law degrees.

## Important advice

Some degrees in economics and business studies are run as sandwich courses, where part of the course is spent on a work placement. When you apply for these courses you may be considered on your suitability for employment as well as your academic ability. Try to get some work experience in a related area such as banking, finance or accountancy before you apply.

# Future careers

## ▷ After A levels

An economics A level is useful for a lot of jobs after A levels. You will possess transferable skills in research, analysis and evaluation of written and numerical economic data, communication and working with others. You could consider the Civil Service or retail and business companies training or apprenticeship schemes. It is also useful in the financial world and is a good entry qualification for jobs in the City or banking.

## ▷ After a degree

## Working in economics

The majority of graduates get employment in banking and finance, business management or computing. A numerate degree with problem-solving skills is very marketable to employers. If you are considering working in economics you will need to consider postgraduate study. For graduates with non-economics degrees there are postgraduate conversion courses in economics.

However, there are many types of work in which you can use and apply your degree.

- **Government Economic Service**—advising government departments on economic policy.
- **Economic analysis and advice**—relating to share, currency or bond markets or the profiling of industries or different economies. The most prominent jobs are in the City, but more economists work for large companies, advising on their products and markets.

- *International work*–for example, for multinational companies or institutions such as the European Union or International Monetary Fund.
- *Economics or financial journalism*
- *Teaching or lecturing*–in school and colleges. You will need a postgraduate teaching qualification ( PGCE).

## Working outside economics

Knowledge of the economy and the logical, numerical and analytical skills that you gain through studying economics are valuable for many careers, such as banking, finance or accountancy. There are management training opportunities in large companies and organisations, including the Civil Service, and some openings in the financial departments of companies and local authorities. Careers in buying, marketing and selling, law and insurance are also popular.

## Sources of information

Government Economic Service
www.civilservice.gov.uk/networks/ges/

www.whystudyeconomics.ac.uk

www.economist.com

---

*'Get some work experience; it will really help you. You learn more about the work and whether it would suit you. You'll find out about the organisation and they will find out about you; it can be a great foot in the door!'* Parmjit, economics graduate, working in banking

# Electronics

*Electronics touches every part of our lives from TVs, mobile phones, cars and our heating control systems right through to transport and defence systems. Electronics is all about practical problem solving and creativity. This course will help you to understand engineering principles and their applications, and gain skills and knowledge of the industry and the many routes available into careers and further or higher education. You will need a good grasp of maths to undertake this course.*

## What do you study?

At AS you study all the key components that go into electronic design such as capacitors, diodes, transducers, logic gates, amplifiers etc. You will see how electronics is a major part of the many modern electronics systems you find in everyday life. The course reflects up-to-date practice, encourages a safe approach to using electronic systems, and promotes an awareness of the social, economic and cultural impact of electronics. Computing, such as the use of CAD systems, is also a feature of the course.

You'll have a first-year project, to design and make an electronic solution to a real-life problem. At A2 you'll step up a level to topics like microprocessors, robotics and communications systems. This will help you to decide which area of electronics really interests you. Again you'll have a practical project so you can get to grips with a solution that you can see really working. Practical skills are assessed in both AS and A2.

## Subject combinations

Mathematics, physics and ICT A levels would go well and be useful for applications for engineering courses; design and technology would also be helpful, either product design or systems and control specifications.

# Higher education options

## Degree-level study

Don't just research electronic engineering as there are degrees in related disciplines such as computer systems engineering, communications engineering or software engineering. There are also specialist courses such as medical electronics. Most courses will be for a BEng or MEng degree. MEng courses are for the most able students who want a route into fast-track management. Many courses have the opportunity for a sandwich year or industrial placement in the UK and sometimes abroad.

## Degree subject combinations

Electronic engineering can be combined with other branches of engineering such as electrical, and also with subjects such as computer science, languages and business management as well as sciences such as physics.

## Other higher education qualifications

There are foundation degrees in electronic and electrical engineering, marine electrical and electronics, electronics and communications and electrical technology as well as in general engineering and other branches of engineering such as civil engineering. There are HNDS/HNCs in electrical and electronic engineering.

## Relevance to other subjects?

Electronics A level gives you useful transferable skills so you could consider many other courses. You will need to check that you have the right A level subject combination for entry maths may be required, for example. Possible degree subjects might include cybernetics, mechatronics and robotics, disaster management, fire safety engineering and computer games.

## Important advice

Please note that A level maths and often A level physics (or equivalent) are required for electronics degree courses, although some institutions offer foundation courses in these subjects if you do not have them at A level. Some electronics specifications overlap slightly with physics and design and technology (systems and control), so check with your school or college.

# Future careers

### ▷ After A levels

Many electronics students progress to higher level study but there are technician level jobs at this level, which offer training combining work experience with further study, often through an Advanced Level Apprenticeship. Higher Apprenticeships offer the opportunity to study up to HNC, HND or degree level.

Typical jobs you might enter as a trainee or apprentice are:

- ***draftsperson/CAD operator***–drafting plans and documents, using computer technology
- ***estimator***–working out how much it will cost to design and make a product
- ***quality assurance technician***–making sure that the product meets the specified quality standards
- ***inspector***–making sure that everything is running as it should
- ***planner–scheduling everyone elses work***
- ***laboratory technician***–helping with research and testing, sometimes at supervisory level
- ***technician***–helping to develop new ideas and working with other departments in your organisation.

## ▷After a degree

### Working in electronics

Areas where electronic engineers are recruited include communications, power suppliers, defence, computing and medical electronics.

Most electronics graduates enter graduate trainee schemes with companies. These are the areas of work you could consider:

- **design, development and research engineering**
- **production engineering**
- **control engineering**
- **quality assurance engineering**
- **sales and marketing positions**
- **management.**

Once in employment as a trainee, you will undertake professional training towards registration as an incorporated or a chartered engineer. Many companies offer sponsorship for engineering degrees so you would be working for them while you are studying, including during vacations. Working outside electronics Your degree will provide you with good problem-solving skills as well as a good scientific and maths grounding, so you could consider trainee schemes in many areas including accountancy, banking and retail.

## Sources of information

The Institution of Engineering and Technology
www.theiet.org

The Institute of Physics and Engineering in Medicine
www.ipem.ac.uk

www.howstuffworks.com

'If you want to travel, then the sky's the limit in this career.' Peter, electronics engineer

# English language

*The study of English language at A level gives you the skills to analyse and evaluate written and spoken English and will improve your communication skills. Language is essential to our daily lives: it helps us to understand who we are, and what others might think of us; it is also a way to express thoughts and feelings; it even shapes our view of the world. If you study English language at A level, you develop your knowledge and understanding of the ways in which the English language can help us to communicate, how and why it is used differently by different speakers and by the same speaker in different situations and how it has changed over time and is still changing today. Think about the new words or phrases that didn't exist a few years ago such as staycation and selfie.*

## What do you study?

*The topics listed give an idea of what could be covered. The exact content of AS and A2 specifications differs according to exam boards, so you will need to check with your school or college about the exact modules available to you.*

English language looks at the following:

- **a detailed study of the language**–grammar, sentence and word structure, phonology (the sound of words and how they are formed), and typography (studying, for example, the layout and typeface of newspapers)
- **parsing**–how to unpick a sentence into basic constituents; language development, variation and change through the ages from early-modern English (Middle Ages) to the present day
- **the different theories whose research underpins attitudes**–for example, there are three different theories as to how children acquire language and you will have a chance to see how these theories fit in with the latest thinking
- **the social aspects of language**–dialects and the difference between male and female language use
- **the difference between speech and writing**–the theories behind this; you will study various types of media including newspapers and adverts
- **language variation**–how language has changed over time, how individuals speak English differently, through accent and dialect, and how we all vary the language we use according to the situation that we are in or to whom we are talking
- **the future of English**–does EastEnders improve the quality of English throughout the UK? What is estuary English? How is

language evolving with the introduction of new words? Has English been affected by different migrant communities in the UK?

- *language and representation*—the philosophy of language, e.g. gender and politics. This will cover political correctness, including slang, jargon and taboo language, and occupational usage such as in teaching, building or journalism
- *writing for specific genres, audiences and purposes*—you will demonstrate your skill in writing and explore the techniques of a variety of genres in order to produce effective texts for specific genres, audiences and purposes.

Most students who take English language A level will have done both English language and literature at GCSE. Good grades are necessary in order to study at A level.

You must read widely beyond the textbooks and develop a keen ear for eavesdropping on other peoples conversations or listening intently to conversations that you have. This latter skill is particularly useful in the part of the course that deals with the spoken word.

You will look at newspapers, advertisements, pamphlets and other marketing material, as well as conventional literature such as poetry, plays and novels. You will get the opportunity to write your own texts. The options are wide ranging, giving you the chance to focus on a topic of particular interest. An example could be looking at features from local or national newspapers or carrying out your own research in an aspect of language that interests you.

N.B. There is also an A level in English language and literature (see the end of the English literature entry for more details) and an A level in creative writing (see earlier entry).

## Subject combinations

If you are thinking of going on to study English language at a higher level, a modern language would be a good subject to combine with A level English. It means that you have a basis for comparison with what you read. If you are thinking of studying linguistics, a modern or classical language (or even two) is almost essential. Subjects that combine well with and support English include history, philosophy, sociology, psychology and media studies. If you are considering an English literature degree, you should look at English language and literature A level or English literature at A level, as English language A level alone may not be accepted.

# Higher education options

An A level in English language is often (although not always) required for degree courses in the subject.

## Degree-level study

In practice, an English language degree is often a degree in English language and linguistics. This means that you study linguistics in general and the linguistics of English in particular.

English language degrees will give you a strong understanding of the fundamentals of the English language and the necessary skills to carry out independent research. It also provides you with the knowledge of the historical development of English language as well as the essential understanding of the correlation between language and identity, language variation and language attitudes, language and ideologies, and the role of language in social relations and practices.

You will study the structure and use of geographical, social and historical varieties of English; data collection and analysis; critical skills in examining how language and discourses are represented in the world around us; awareness of language choices we make and the importance of the cultural, literary and historical contexts in which various discourses and texts are produced, as well as essential research and presentation skills, and project work.

Many courses give you the opportunity to apply what you have learned through practical projects focusing on presentation skills and writing for a particular brief, for example writing a press release, speaking to camera or organising a formal business meeting.

There are degrees available combining English language and literature and specialising in creative writing. Both English language and literature can be studied for a BEd degree, in which you study education and gain a teaching qualification alongside your English work. There are also courses and options on degrees in teaching English as a foreign language (TEFL) or teaching English as a second language (TESOL).

## Degree subject combinations

English language can be combined with many subjects. A combination with English is useful for any subject that requires an ability to understand how language can be used to communicate images, thoughts, emotions and a sense of the society in which the text was written. The most widely available combinations are communication, history, modern languages and sociology. A degree in international business English offers the opportunity to study business English with another language.

## Other higher education qualifications

There are some foundation degrees where English language could be useful including media writing with production, media practice, social media, journalism, printing, digital media and creative writing.

There are HND and HNC courses available in journalism and practical journalism. There are also pre-entry courses for journalism, which require good A levels or equivalent and sitting the National Council for the Training of Journalists (NCTJ) entrance test.

## Relevance to other subjects?

The study of English language at A level develops skills that will help you in subjects at a higher level. Among these are history, media studies, film studies, drama and linguistics. More applied courses such as creative writing, teaching and journalism are worth investigating.

## Important advice

Start taking an interest in English language in its written and spoken form. Look closely at newspaper headlines in different newspapers. Start listening more closely to conversations to hear how people really communicate. Think about the way that you communicate with your friends. How much slang do you use? Do you talk in text speak?

# Future careers

## ▷ After A levels

Studying for A level English language gives you plenty of practice in communicating in both speech and writing, which is an essential skill valued by many employers. You could consider a wide range of administration jobs. It might be useful to gain extra skills in administration, IT or secretarial studies and you could consider taking a full- or part-time course at college. You will find that some companies offer training schemes and apprenticeships, there is now an Advanced Level Apprenticeship in journalism. Other possible job areas include retail, marketing and sales.

## ▷After a degree

### Working in English language

Studying English language and linguistics equips you with skills that are relevant to a wide range of careers. There are many professions that require specific linguistic expertise, for example, publishing, journalism, public relations, advertising copywriting and technical authorship. You could also consider teaching in the UK and abroad, although you might have to do some further training. The ability to think linguistically is of great value to computer programmers and communications experts. English language and linguistics graduates are seen by employers as literate, numerate and articulate; studying English fosters skills in analysing and summarising data, arguing effectively and with supporting evidence, thinking logically, strategically and critically, working both independently and as part of a team, meeting deadlines and using computer technology.

Some English language graduates undertake further study in related subjects like creative writing or speech therapy.

*See also the entries on English literature and creative writing.*

### Working outside English language

You will have learned excellent communication skills on your course and a good understanding of the way that different people communicate. These skills can be useful in many types of work and you could consider careers in sales, the media, law, IT, accountancy and finance, management, personnel, retail and administration. For some of these careers there are postgraduate diplomas available such as publishing, information science, management and marketing.

### Sources of information

Professional Publishers Association
www.ppa.co.uk

www.bl.uk/soundsfamiliar

National Council for the Training of Journalists (NCTJ)
www.nctj.com

---

'You usually speak without thinking much about it, but this course helps you to listen and really understand what different people are saying and to really understand what they mean.' Jeanie, taking A levels in English language, law and business

---

# English literature

*You need to love reading to study this course but it's not just reading for the sake of it. This course develops your ability to discuss ideas, argue points of view and understand how literature affects and reflects our lives.*

*You study a range of works of literature written at any time between the end of the 14th century and the present day. You will study prose, poetry and drama and examine the techniques writers use to build characters, create atmosphere, drama or tension, and develop themes and ideas. You will learn to read in a way that will help you to evaluate not just the set texts but any piece of writing, learning how to communicate your own response to the texts in the form of essays. You will learn to develop and express your own opinions. You'll be able to read types of literature youve never read before or look at familiar pieces in a new, more analytical way.*

*N.B. There is also an A level in English language and literature (see the end of this entry for more details) and an A level in creative writing (see earlier entry).*

## What do you study?

*The exact content of courses differs according to exam boards, so you will need to check with your school or college about the exact modules available to you.*

The revised A level recommends a minimum of eight texts, which must include three pre-1900 works including a Shakespeare play, and a post-2000 work.

Recent contemporary set books have been by authors like Maya Angelou, Brian Moore, Carol Ann Duffy, Sebastian Faulks, Angela Carter and Owen Sheers. You must study at least some Shakespeare. Some specifications allow you to study on the basis of periods, such as 'World War I literature' or 'poetry and prose 1800-1945' or cover a whole genre such as a study of tragedy. You might also study thematically, which will enable you to compare works written from a similar perspective at very different periods, so for 'love through the ages', for example, you would look at the consequences of love in Shakespeare's *Romeo and Juliet*, Browning's *Dramatic Monologues* (19th century) and *Enduring Love* by Ian McEwan (late 20th century).

Most students who take English literature A level will have done both English language and literature at GCSE. Good GCSE grades are necessary in order to study the subject at A level.

A level English literature involves a lot of reading. This could be set texts and, in some specifications, extracts from texts. You will need to know the texts inside out if you are to do well. You should read around your texts, i.e. read other texts that are related in some way to those you are studying, whether in terms of the themes covered, when they were written or because they were written by the same author. When you study plays for English literature, it is important to remember that they were originally meant to be performed so that must be taken into account in your reading and interpretation.

You will usually take part in readings of the texts you are studying in class. Sometimes you are assessed on how much and how well you take part in this. You must take every opportunity to go to the theatre and to watch films and plays of literature on TV, at the cinema or on DVD. Don't wait for a trip to be organised, try to see as many productions and performances as you can (and not just of your set plays!).

## Subject combinations

English literature combines well with most subjects and popular combinations include history, philosophy, media studies, sociology, psychology, religious studies, drama and theatre studies, and modern languages. If you are thinking of studying linguistics, a modern or classical language is very useful. Don't forget there is a need for literate scientists so English literature could go well with sciences.

# Higher education options

An A level in English literature is often (although not always) required for degree courses in the subject.

## Degree-level study

English literature degrees are flexible and wide ranging. They cover not only traditional areas (like Shakespeare or Dickens) but broader fields such as American literature, creative writing, postcolonial literature and developments in literary theory. Courses could include topics such as crime fiction, literature and addiction, women writers, writing in multicultural Britain, the literature of food or children's literature. Some courses include popular fiction, song lyrics or film.

Some degrees will include the study of Old English language and literature (also known as Anglo-Saxon). This is very different from modern English and is learned as a foreign language. Other courses have a particular emphasis and can include, for example, study in North America, creative writing or English literature with English language. Both

English language and literature can be studied for a BEd degree or as a BA with qualified teacher status (QTS), where you study education and gain a teaching qualification alongside your English work.

## Degree subject combinations

English literature combines with related subjects, like journalism, media studies and new media publishing and specialisms within English literature, such as American literature. Other popular combinations are history, modern and classical languages, and sociology, as well as more unusual ones including criminology, biology and IT.

## Other higher education qualifications

There are no pure English literature foundation degrees but there are related degrees such as English and history, applied English, history with literature, English studies, media and journalism.

There are no English literature HNDs or HNCs but look at courses like media and communication and journalism. There are journalism courses, run by the National Council for the Training of Journalists (NCTJ), which require good A levels or equivalent.

## Relevance to other subjects?

The English literature A level develops skills that make a good background for many subjects at a higher level including history, sociology, religious studies, media studies, film studies, drama and linguistics. Consider courses in American, cultural or communication studies and creative writing.

## Important advice

If you apply for an English literature degree one of the most common interview questions is: 'What have you read apart from your set texts?' You should try to get into the habit of reading as much as possible in your spare time. Sunday newspapers contain book review sections, which will help you keep in touch with new books and writers. You could also read the *Times Literary Supplement* or *London Review of Books*—available online or in your local library.

# Future careers

## ▷After A levels

A level English literature develops communication skills in both speech and writing, which are valuable in the job market. You could consider sales, marketing, and HR or administration jobs. There may be some apprenticeships available and there are now some new Advanced Level Apprenticeships in journalism If you want to work with books and literature, look at library or bookshop work or you could work in admin for a publisher. For all these jobs you will be in competition with graduates, so you should look for opportunities for further training or take an office or business course to help you get in.

## ▷After a degree

### Working in English

English graduates have a wide range of careers open to them.

- *Teaching*–train to teach in schools, colleges or as a TEFL teacher (teaching English as a foreign language) English is taught at both primary and secondary levels. Postgraduate training is necessary for this.
- *Publishing*–be prepared to take any job in publishing and work your way up. Opportunities include copy-editing (checking a manuscript for accuracy, consistency and conformity with the publishers house style) or working as a researcher for non-fiction publications. Don't forget that there are now opportunities in digital publishing and e-books. Selling and marketing in publishing can provide good opportunities as can the legal site and publishing rights. There are opportunities in bookselling both in real and virtual shops.
- *Advertising, marketing and PR*–jobs such as copywriter, media planner or buyer, marketing assistant or PR officer. Entry could be via graduate training schemes or by working your way up from a junior job. There are postgraduate courses available in these areas, which could give you an advantage.
- *Journalism*–there are opportunities in printed, digital and broadcast journalism. Consider a postgraduate course to give you advantage. It is essential that you gain experience and can demonstrate your commitment by, for example, working for a student newspaper or radio station, or a hospital radio service.

You need to build up a good portfolio of experience and work to help you get in and progress.

- **_Other writing_**–the number of people who make their living from creative writing (novels, short stories and drama) is very small. Don't be put off, but remember that you will probably have to do your writing in your spare time to start off with. If you have some funds, there is always self-publishing but you will need to market your books to get sales. If you are happy to pursue other forms of writing, you might want to consider technical or non-fiction writing. There are now opportunities for writing on the web and in social media, blogs etc as many companies need full time staff to promote their web presence.

## Working outside English

Apart from those entering teaching, most English graduates do not use their knowledge of English literature professionally. However, you will have learned to propose ideas and theories and to think creatively. This can be useful in many careers including law and business (especially sales and marketing). For many of these careers, further qualifications or training either in or outside work will be necessary.

## Sources of information

National Council for the Training of Journalists (NCTJ)
www.nctj.com

Publishers Association
www.publishers.org.uk

www.whystudyenglish.ac.uk

'The sheer discipline of it, the amount of reading you do, I think it makes you quite confident. You can tackle anything, really.' Shona, taking a degree in English literature with philosophy

# English language and literature

In A level English language and literature, there is a strong emphasis on language and how it is used in different communicative situations. You learn to study systematically both written and spoken language by analysing different sorts of texts and transcripts, and by writing your own text and commentaries on the language with which you have created them. You will learn the skills of summarising, editing and recasting written material for practical purposes, and coursework will provide an opportunity for creative writing. In addition, you will study literature from various periods in the form of plays, short stories, novels or collections of poems. You will analyse the text and look at the representation of speech as well as exploring the stylistic and thematic issues. You will learn to write fluently and coherently.

*For details of higher education, careers and further information see the English language and English literature entries.*

# Environmental studies

*Studying environmental studies will give you the knowledge, understanding and skills to make informed judgements on current environmental issues. It is the study of the environment and the place of human beings within it. You learn the principles that are used to decide how to manage the environment and promote sustainability. You cover not only the scientific concepts that provide a basic understanding of the environment but also the social, economic and political aspects of environmental management.*

*You investigate how humans affect the world in which they live, and you will learn objective and critical approaches to environmental politics. Issues explored on the course include climate change, nuclear power, acid rain, air and water pollution, land use, ecosystem and habitat loss, endangered species, genetically modified (GM) foods, over-fishing, and organic versus chemical farming.*

## What do you study?

*AQA is the only exam board currently offering environmental studies.*

At AS you acquire a broad understanding of the environment and how it works and at A2 you expand your studies to gain a greater understanding of important environmental issues, develop your skills further and learn more about science and how it relates to the environment.

## The living environment:

- an introduction to the biodiversity of life on Earth
- reasons why the conservation of life on Earth is important
- methods that may be used to achieve effective conservation
- conservation in the UK, coral reefs, Antarctica and tropical rainforests
- 'Life processes in the biosphere' explores the ecological relationships between organisms and their abiotic and biotic environment (the six major abiotic factors are water, sunlight, oxygen, temperature, soil and climate; biotic means relating to, produced by, or caused by living organisms) in order to understand conservation problems further and how these may be managed.

## The physical environment:

- atmospheric gases, water and mineral nutrients and how they are essential for life on Earth
- human exploitation and management of physical resources to provide higher material living standards
- unsustainable natural resources.

## Energy resources and environmental pollution:

- future problems of energy supply and how these may be resolved; looking at alternative sources of energy
- properties of pollutants to explain why some materials or forms of energy cause environmental damage; the study of atmospheric, aquatic and terrestrial pollutants
- minimising releases, treating effluents and managing the damage caused by pollutants.

## Biological resources and sustainability:

- factors controlling human population growth in relation to the demands placed upon the planets resources and life-support systems
- food production and forestry systems and environmental problems caused by them, how these problems can be tackled
- study of the sustainability of human lifestyles.

In addition, you will develop skills in mathematical and statistical analysis.

Environmental studies involves classroom work, essay writing, discussions, research and class presentations. You spend time on laboratory experiments, fieldwork, surveys, role-play sessions, environmental impact assessments, cost-benefit analysis, computer modelling and energy audits. An example could be analysing the water in a local river using various tests to determine the pollution level. You visit relevant sites, which could be a nuclear reactor or nature reserve. You are encouraged to do as much reading around the subject as you can, especially about environmental issues in the news.

Although GCSE environmental science is available many people start the A level with GCSE biology, geography or combined science as it is not offered in some schools or colleges.

## Subject combinations

Environmental studies combines well with biology, geography, geology and chemistry.

If you want to take an environmental course at a higher level, biology and geography may be required or preferred, and, in some cases, chemistry. Maths or statistics could be useful as data analysis can be an important part of environmental degrees. Some environmental science or studies degrees are more issue-based, so you might consider A levels in economics, government and politics, or law.

# Higher education options

### Degree-level study

There are many degrees with the word 'environmental' in their title. The most widely offered are environmental science and environmental studies. These include the topics you will have already studied for A level environmental studies, although in much greater breadth and depth. They vary in the emphasis they give to basic scientific principles so you must check the course content carefully.

Examples of other environment-related degrees available include environmental geography and climate change, environmental geochemistry, environmental chemistry, environmental conservation, sustainable development, environmental planning, environmental forensics, environmental geography, environmental geoscience, environmental sustainability, environmental conservation, marine environmental science and global development and sustainability.

Degree titles are not always a reliable guide to content, so you should check carefully before you decide which courses to apply for.

Environmental engineering is another option (you will usually need A level mathematics and physics for entry). This is concerned with engineering techniques for solving environmental problems, such as water resource management, pollution, waste management and land reclamation. It is often combined with civil engineering. Another related degree is disaster management. Some environmental degrees offer a study year abroad or a sandwich placement.

### Degree subject combinations

Environmental science and environmental studies are available in combination with many subjects. Examples are environment and planning, environmental earth science with education, environmental studies and geographical information systems, and environment and business.

### Other higher education qualifications

You can study foundation degrees in related areas including conservation management, construction heritage and conservation management, countryside and wildlife management, countryside management, culture and environmental concerns, environmental conservation and countryside management, civil and environmental engineering, ecology and conservation management, environmental education, geography and the environment, landscape, heritage and conservation, marine ecology and conservation, regeneration and sustainability, sustainability and environmental management, sustainable construction, sustainable resource management, sustainable wastes and resource management, wastes management, wildlife conservation and habitat management, and woodland conservation management. There are also foundation degrees available in public and environmental health and in occupational health, safety and environmental management.

There are environmental science HNCs or HNDs, most of them designed as vocational training. Examples include environmental management and sustainability, conservation biology and green technology.

### Relevance to other subjects?
The environmental studies A level is concerned with the interaction between people and their environment, so it has a social science element that would be relevant to subjects such as sociology, history, politics, psychology, economics or law. It is also acceptable for courses such as countryside or land management or business administration.

### Important advice
If you are taking biology, geography, physics or science in society, there may be some slight overlap (depending on the options taken) so check the course content carefully if you are studying environmental studies with any of these subjects.

Try to get as much experience as you can if you are planning a career in the environment, such as voluntary work with a local environmental or conservation group.

## Future careers

### ▷ After A levels
Many companies now operate in a more sustainable and environmental way and there has been a rise in 'green collar jobs', which are jobs concerned with the environment.

You will usually need further training to make direct use of your environmental studies knowledge in a job. However, you may be able to work for one of the many groups and organisations concerned with environmental issues, especially if you have some experience of business or administration work. Your technical knowledge may be helpful in the preparation of publicity, or in local group activities and education programmes.

Experience as a volunteer may help you to obtain paid work later. The study of environmental studies will have given you the ability to take a logical approach to problems as well as developing good problem-solving skills, which could help you in careers in business administration, banking or finance.

## ▷After a degree

## Working in environmental studies

- *Environmental scientist*–working in a university or large commercial company in research or consultancy, a postgraduate qualification will be useful for this type or work.
- *Environmental health*–local government employs environmental health officers, whose responsibilities include noise control and food safety inspection (although here you would be in competition with graduates in food science).
- *Housing management, surveying and town planning*–you will need additional specialist qualifications.
- *Waste management*–organisations such as local authorities and private companies employ environmental scientists as recycling or waste management professionals.
- *Government agencies*–there could be opportunities with the Environment Agency or DEFRA as well as the Health and Safety Executive (HSE).
- *Nature conservation officer*–working for local authorities or national organisations.
- *Environmental organisations*–for example Natural England, the Royal Society for the Protection of Birds and the National Parks. These organisations recruit environmental scientists, as do environmental pressure groups such as Friends of the Earth. There is a lot of competition for jobs in these organisations and factors other than academic qualifications are important. You must be able to demonstrate enthusiasm for the work and a good portfolio of voluntary experience.

- ***Energy efficiency adviser or installer***–assessing how green houses are or installing green energy technologies in houses and businesses, for example solar panels or water reclamation systems; further training will be required.

## Working outside environmental studies

The general scientific education you will receive as part of an environmental science degree helps you to develop strong observation, data-recording, interpretation and IT skills, as well as the ability to write high-quality reports on your findings. These skills could help you in many careers such as business and finance, advertising and marketing.

## Sources of information

Chartered Institute of Environmental Health
www.cieh.org

Department for Environment, Food and Rural Affairs (DEFRA)
www.gov.uk/defra

Environment Agency
www.environment-agency.gov.uk

Lantra
www.lantra.co.uk

Natural Environment Research Council
www.nerc.ac.uk

www.environmentalcareers.org.uk

www.letsrecycle.com

'I did some local conservation work, helping tidy up the local park. It was something different to put on my personal statement.' June aged 19, on an environmental science degree

# Film studies

*The film studies A level has been developed to explore film as an art form, which although it was the major new art form of the 20th century is still developing today. You will learn to understand and appreciate how films communicate meaning and entertain us, their social context and the industry that produces them. The course covers the study of British and US films, and world cinema, and gives you the opportunity to make your own films and write storyboards and screenplays.*

## What do you study?

The topics covered are:

- *film form*–how the micro-features of a film work and produce meaning. Micro-features are elements of the film such as cinematography, editing, sound, performance and mise en scène (sets, props, costumes etc).

- *British and American film*–how the British and American film industries work. Who are the film audiences in the UK and how film is viewed, for example cinema, home cinema and on demand. Topics in British film include: What makes a film a British film and what genres exist? (e.g. horror and comedy). What are the characteristics of British film stars? (e.g. Ewan Macgregor or Julie Christie). British production companies like Ealing Studios or Working Title. How are films influenced by their cultural period? (e.g. the swinging sixties or Thatchers Britain). What about the social and political contents of film, such as those involving the crime culture? (e.g. *Bullet Boy* or *Get Carter*). How have other cultures arriving in Britain contributed to the British identity in film? (e.g. *Yasmin, Ghost,* and *Gypo*). You will also study aspects of finance, organisation, production, distribution and marketing within the film industry.

- *US film*–you will study and compare films from a specific genre or dealing with a specific theme. For example, two films dealing with specific theme such as *Double Indemnity* and *The Last Seduction, 42nd Street* and *Chicago, My Darling Clementine* and *Unforgiven.* You could also consider remakes such as *King Kong* (1933 and 2005) or *The Invasion of the Body Snatchers* (1956 and 1978).

At A2 you will develop your understanding of all the work youve been introduced to in AS with new topics. You might study world cinema such as Bollywood, Iranian, Japanese or Mexican cinema or international film styles such as German and/or Soviet cinema of the 1920s, surrealism and neo-realism and new waves. There are specialist studies in urban environments or the empowerment of women. There are topics covering early cinema, documentaries, experimental film and video, popular film and emotional response (e.g. what makes a weepie?). There is the opportunity to undertake a film project and make your own short film or write a screenplay.

There is a film studies GCSE available but you don't need this to take the A level.

Study includes film screenings and close analysis of sequences from different films, followed by essays, criticism and case studies. You will have the opportunity to produce work in the form of a screenplay, storyboard, film criticism, film or DVD either in a group or alone. You will be expected to take an active interest in film outside the classroom and be able to talk about it knowledgeably and critically.

An A level in moving image arts is offered by the CCEA examination board. It is an applied subject which examines the history, techniques and creative impact of film and equips students to make their own films, informed by that knowledge and those skills.

## Subject combinations

If you are considering a degree course in professional film production and direction you may need a portfolio or audition in addition to an interview. A level film studies can help with this. You could consider taking art and design or photography with film studies, as they will increase your understanding of how visual images are put together and how they can communicate different ideas.

Some art and design courses allow you to use film and video as part of the practical work. English literature helps you to express your ideas on paper and offer clear criticism of others work, using evidence from texts to back up your ideas. Communication and culture, media studies, history or modern languages also combine well.

Creative Skillset has created a network of Screen Academies that are recognised as centres of excellence in film education in the UK. Courses at these academies are at further education, degree and postgraduate level, as well as short technical courses. Go to the Creative Skillset website for more information.

# Higher education options

A level film studies is not necessary for film degrees. Note that for some of the more practical courses based at colleges of art and design, an Art Foundation course may be helpful to gain entry.

## Degree-level study

Film studies courses take a variety of forms: some focus more on the critical and historical study of film, others on the practical and technical skills involved in film making. However, many courses include elements of both. As film studies A level is not offered by every school or college, most degree courses start from scratch. You can then often decide on the direction that your own course will take through your choice of options, which cover specialised areas such as theoretical and analytical studies, camera techniques (using both film and video), scriptwriting and technical production.

Look out for titles such as film production, film and video studies, and moving image. You will also find more focused courses like digital film and visual effects production, film production technology, film production for the music industry, computer visualisation and animation, scriptwriting, special and visual effects for film and television.

## Degree subject combinations

Film studies can be combined with many subjects, for example, English or a language. Many film studies degrees are already combined degrees, as you study video, television, radio or digital media from a practical and/or theoretical viewpoint. If you are interested in the financial production side of film making you might combine film with business, entrepreneurship or management.

## Other higher education qualifications

Foundation degrees are available in creative film and moving image production, creative industries (film and video), film and media production, film and photography, film and television production technology, film and television production technology with sound, hair design and make-up for theatre, TV and film, post-production technology for film and television, and computer generated images. Courses can link into degrees or professional practice courses and some will require a portfolio of work for entry.

There are some HND and HNC courses specifically geared towards film and media. Course titles include applied multimedia, media moving image and digital film production. Postgraduate courses are available in film and all aspects of film making.

## Relevance to other subjects?

Film studies A level encourages you to develop observational, critical, written and practical skills. It helps you to look at creative products in detail in the context of the society or culture in which they were made. Film studies can lead to degrees in communication studies, English, American studies, sociology, psychology, and philosophy. It could also help you on drama or performing arts courses.

## Important advice

If you are considering a degree in film studies or a related area, start by investigating the exact contact and entry requirements of each course as they can vary a great deal. Try to find out what sort of jobs their graduates got after the course.

# Future careers

### ▷After A levels

The film industry is competitive but you might get in at a junior level with hard work and a bit of luck. Networking is very important in this industry. There may be administration jobs or you might get in as a runner for a film or television company. Runners help everything to run smoothly and provide a range of support in every area of film production. There may be apprenticeships available (see Creative Skillset website).

You could look at work in an area related to film, such as advertising, distribution (getting films to cinemas around the country) or marketing. Roles available are likely to be as an administrator or general assistant, and if you are good at networking and making useful contacts you may be able to get work from there.

### ▷After a degree

### Working in film or television

You should be prepared to get further training or to start in a junior position and work your way up. Postgraduate study could be an option to enhance your skills.

Most people earn a low wage, work extremely long and unsociable hours and are on short-term freelance contracts. If you are serious about a career in film you must be prepared to network and make contacts at every opportunity as you really have to build your career yourself. You must be prepared to work as a freelance and be self-employed.

Here are some examples of the types of jobs available to you:

- *Production runners or assistants*–help run the producers and directors offices, involved in films from planning to post-production. Tasks include booking crews, organising the shipping of equipment and arranging timetables. Could lead to production roles such as script supervisor.
- *Assistant directors*–work with the production manager to carry out many of the practical jobs needed during the production of the film. There are different levels of assistant director: first assistants have the most responsibility and help to maintain the shooting schedule; second, third and fourth assistants work with the first assistant and have decreasing levels of responsibility, carrying out tasks such as calling actors and delivering scripts and messages. This work can lead to the role of director, who takes full responsibility for the production.
- *Camera operators*–carry out the directors instructions regarding shot composition and development. Start as trainees.
- *Designers*–work in film, television or video and use technical and artistic skills. Work in this area can range from costume and set design to designing the continuity sequences used on screen between programmes. To enter this area, you need additional specialised training, which can often involve a postgraduate course or an apprenticeship.
- *Script writers*–work freelance and are commissioned by film or television companies. Writing for the screen is very different from writing a book and a good understanding of film terminology and techniques is needed.

For details of other jobs, visit the Creative Skillset website.

## Working outside film or television

Film studies graduates could enter advertising and marketing, journalism, publishing, research, and arts administration. They can also get into careers for graduates in any discipline such as business and finance or retail and management training.

## Sources of information

British Film Institute
www.bfi.org.uk/education

Film Education
www.filmnationuk.org

Creative Skillset
www.creativeskillset.org/careers

London Film School
www.lfs.org.uk

National Film and Television School
www.nftsfilm-tv.ac.uk

www.bbc.co.uk/careers

> 'It is really hard work, long hours—a big shock after college. You must learn to fit in with all sorts of people, if you don't, you don't work.'
> Damien, working as a runner after a film studies degree

# General studies

*General studies does what it says in the title. It is general but it means you study a wide range of subjects. Depending on the specification, you could study modules in culture, morality, arts and humanities, science, mathematics and technology (this does require some proficiency in maths), society, politics and the economy or thinking and analytical skills. There may also be the option to study a modern foreign language.*

As the subject is very broad so different types of teaching styles and approaches are used. These include discussions, debates, written and investigative work. As well as developing important thinking and communication skills, the course gives you the opportunity to broaden your general knowledge about a range of world issues and current affairs, e.g. human cloning, media censorship, the impact of globalisation, contemporary art, religious conflict and environmentalism. An interest in current affairs is vital for success in general studies.

General studies A level is a useful course for anyone wanting to show that they have studied a broad curriculum and can think critically and flexibly in examination conditions, rather than memorising information in a specialised area. It is sometimes not accepted as a third subject for university entrance. However, as a fourth subject it can be very useful to convince university admissions tutors of your general academic ability. Some students find that general studies helps their university applications as it teaches critical and thinking skills as well as giving you a broad outlook on a wide range of subjects. It can prove useful on a personal statement for university entry.

## Subject combinations

General studies is an excellent additional subject and will combine with a whole range of A level subjects. Some of the topics covered are similar to those in the science in society and citizenship A levels, so you should check to make sure these don't overlap.

It can be taken as a contrasting subject (for example, with specific science subjects) to give a varied and enhanced curriculum, or as a complementary subject (for example, with social science subjects) to give a thorough grounding in one field of knowledge.

## Important advice

Please note that general studies may not always count towards UCAS point offers. You will need to check with each individual institution.

> 'It sets you apart from students who have similar grades in other subjects but can't offer general studies. I always find that students who have taken general studies interview very well.' HE admissions tutor

# Geography

*Are you interested in the world around you? The world we live in is constantly changing. Think about natural and man-made catastrophes in the news such as flooding, earthquakes and war. Geography allows you to see why and how the world changes. It is multidisciplinary, offering the opportunity to develop a range of skills including investigative, IT, graphical, cartographical and statistical, numerical and research. You study a range of topics covering current major global concerns looking at issues like population growth and globalisation as well as tsunamis and volcanoes. The course will enhance your understanding of the environment and help you understand some of the pressing environmental, economic and social problems facing the world today.*

## What do you study?
*The topics listed give an idea of what could be covered. The exact content of AS and A2 specifications differs according to exam boards, so you will need to check with your school or college about the exact modules available to you.*

The study of geography is divided between two branches.
- **Physical geography**–is concerned with the Earth, its physical structure and the processes that take place on its surface, as well as physical hazards such as tornadoes, earthquakes and flooding.
- **Human geography**–looks at the activities of human beings in their physical settings; it addresses current issues, such as food shortages, war, immigration, population and sustainability.

A core theme at A level is the study of how the two branches of geography interact: the effect that the human and physical worlds have on each other. Contemporary concerns such as climate change and global warming are included in the specifications.

The topics covered include:

## Physical geography
**Biogeography**–ecosystems (communities of organisms and their environment), vegetation (why particular species of plant grow in particular parts of the world) and soils.

**Geomorphology**–the shaping of the Earths surface by the environment (wind, the oceans, glaciers, etc.) through the processes of glacier formation, weathering, erosion and desertification, and plate tectonics.

*Hydrology*–water on and just above the Earths surface: how it goes through a cycle by evaporation, rainfall and the return of water via rivers to the sea; how these processes can be managed by applied hydrology (dams, irrigation, hydroelectric power, flood prevention, etc) for our benefit.

*Atmospheric systems*–climate and weather, atmospheric pollution and global warming, the implications for human life.

*Coastal studies*–the processes that shape coastlines and their reaction to the impact of human culture.

## Human geography

*Economic geography*–the distribution of the worlds economic resources including agriculture, food, health, industry, economic development, tourism, energy and transportation.

*Population*–global population change, migration and resources.

*Settlement*–where and how people settle in different parts of the world: the location, character and structure of villages, towns and cities and how they grow, change and decline.

*Management*–of human geographical processes through planning systems.

GCSE geography is not always essential for A level study but most schools and colleges will assume some background knowledge. In the new specifications there will be more emphasis on mathematical skills so a good grade in maths GCSEs will help with your A level studies.

Apart from formal lessons, you will take part in classroom discussions and debates. You will learn how to obtain, record, represent, classify and interpret data of different types from both primary and secondary sources. This will include using software to manipulate geographical data. Fieldwork is an important part of the course and you may be examined on this. It involves measuring and collecting data, and conducting surveys using questionnaires and interviews. It might be in your local area or further afield, giving you the opportunity to observe and record in a variety of settings and landscapes.

## Subject combinations

Geography is a subject that falls neatly between the arts and the sciences and combines well with many subjects. The scientific nature of geography, especially physical geography, means that there is a useful overlap with biology, physics, environmental studies and geology. Some universities might not count geography as a whole A level if you also offer environmental studies. If you want to study environmental science at degree level you may need a science at A level. You should check this if you have a particular degree course in mind. The human, economic and social aspects of geography go well with A levels such as history, economics, politics, sociology and world development.

# Higher education options

Geography is a popular degree and a good grade in A level geography is needed for entry.

## Degree-level study

Geography can be studied for either a BA or BSc degree. The BA concentrates more on human geography and the BSc more on the physical aspects of the subject. A BA might include topics such as population studies, settlement, and distribution of wealth and resources. A BSc course is more likely to involve topics such as geoscience (the scientific study of the structure of the Earth and issues relating to natural resources) and hydrology (the study of the movement, distribution, and quality of water) and geomorphology (study of the origin and evolution of the earth's landforms, both on the continents and within the ocean basins). However, many universities allow for flexibility in choosing topics from both types of degree. Fieldwork is an essential part of geography degrees and may include overseas trips. You may wish to consider more specialised geography courses like applied, human or physical geography or degrees covering a specific area such as coastal geography, marine geography, environmental geography, global development and sustainability. Geography can be taken with education studies leading to qualified teacher status (QTS), qualifying you to teach the subject in state schools.

Your first year on a geography degree is likely to cover some of the topics you began at A level. However, its scope will extend to urban and rural studies, biogeography, and economic geography and development studies. There will then be specialised options such as medical geography (the characteristics of illness and disease in relation to where they occur), cartography and environmental monitoring, and impact assessment. There are specialised degrees in related subjects such as geographical information systems, human geography, natural hazards, disaster management and sustainable development.

## Degree subject combinations

Geography can be combined with one or more of many other subjects. Popular choices include economics, English, history, languages, mathematics and sociology. Biology, IT and environmental studies are also possibilities.

## Other higher education qualifications

There are foundation degrees available in geography and society, and geography and the environment as well as some related courses in ecology and conservation management and marine ecology and conservation.

HND and HNC courses are available in geography and also in environmental conservation management.

## Relevance to other subjects?

Geography A level can be used as a foundation for a wide range of other subjects, such as law, politics, economics, architecture, business studies and anthropology. It is useful for land-based industry courses. It would also be valuable preparation for degrees in environmental science, ecology, surveying, conservation, geology, travel and tourism, and any course that has an international dimension to it like European studies. Landscape architecture, meteorology, oceanography and planning are other possibilities.

## Important advice

You will need to examine course content carefully to find out which courses will be suitable for you. A geography degree can be useful for getting into environmental and conservation work. If considering this, it is important to build up a portfolio of voluntary and work experience in conservation before applying. This could be anything from helping to clean up a park at weekends through to a gap year spent in conservation work abroad or in the UK.

# Future careers

## ▷After A levels

The skills you will have learned on your course, like data handling, team working and IT plus an interest in the world around you, will be useful in all sorts of jobs such as business administration, insurance, retail, finance, media, and travel and tourism.

## ▷After a degree

## Working in geography

Your geography degree gives you many useful skills such as the ability to undertake research and analysis and to interpret data of all types. You will also be numerate with a good knowledge of global issues and the environment. There is a wide range of careers you could consider, although some will need extra study or training.

- **Environment and sustainability**–environmental campaigners, recycling officers, cycle route planners, environmental impact officers or disaster managers.
- **Planning**–surveying, town planning, landscape architecture, working for local or national government or in industry.
- **Mapping**–geographical information systems (GIS), cartography, aerial surveying and remote sensing.
- **Science and conservation**–hazard prediction and management, coastal engineer, flood protection officer, pollution analyst.
- **Travel and tourism**–travel agent, expedition leader, eco-tour guide.
- **Development**–aid worker, policy adviser.

## Working outside geography

Geography gives you many skills that could be applied to lots of different careers. There are opportunities in local government such as leisure, recreation and housing management. Having a numerate degree could get you into finance and banking, management training, marketing, advertising and the Civil Service; teaching is also a possibility.

## Sources of information

Ordnance Survey
www.ordnancesurvey.co.uk

Royal Geographical Society
www.rgs.org

www.geographyinthenews.rgs.org

www.geography-site.co.uk

---

'Geography is not only up-to-date and relevant; it is one of the most exciting, adventurous and valuable subjects to study today. So many of the worlds current problems boil down to geography, and need the geographers of the future to help us understand them.' Michael Palin, broadcaster

# Geology

*Geology is a branch of science concerned with the structure, evolution and dynamics of the Earth, and with the exploitation of the mineral and energy resources that it contains. If you have a science or geographical background, or just an interest in the planet Earth, geology offers a wide range of topical subjects.*

Earthquakes and volcanoes are always in the news and in late 2013 a new volcanic island was formed off the coast of Japan. Asteroid impact is now seen as a very real threat to the planet. These are all topics in geology A level, which offers exciting ways of understanding how the inner parts of the planet work.

There will be fieldwork at home or abroad, and the internet keeps you up-to-date with the latest geological events around the globe.

Geology combines well with science subjects like environmental studies, physics, chemistry or biology. If you are offering geography A level as well check to see if both are acceptable. Science GCSEs can be helpful and GCSE maths is sometimes required. If you are considering a degree in geology you will need to combine it with one or two science A levels. A level geology is not normally required for university entry as it is not offered in all schools and colleges.

Geology could lead to a career in the environment, prospecting for natural resources, climate studies, engineering, surveying, or monitoring volcanoes, earthquakes and other natural hazards.

British Geological Survey
www.bgs.ac.uk

The Geological Society
www.geolsoc.org.uk

# Government and politics

*Politics affects our lives every day. The results of national and local elections have far-reaching consequences in our lives as they influence education, health, defence and, on a local level, even how frequently our dustbins are emptied. We need to understand how politics works if we are to play a full role as a citizen in our democracy.*

*Government and politics is about much more than who is going to win the next general election. As a student of A level government and politics you will explore how political power is gained and used, and learn about how governments and other political institutions and systems work both in the UK and the USA. You look at political structures, such as the voting system and Parliament, and the case for and against changing those structures; the definitions and the functions of concepts such as democracy, justice and rights; and recent developments in the world of politics. You will also examine political ideas and concepts including other political ideologies.*

## What do you study?
*The topics listed give an idea of what could be covered. The exact content of AS and A2 specifications differs according to exam boards, so you will need to check with your school or college about the exact modules available to you.*

At AS you gain a broad understanding of the UK political system, including the role of elections, political parties and pressure groups and how policy is made.

You cover the central ideas of citizenship, democracy and participation and how the representative processes work in the UK. What is democracy and how does it differ from dictatorship? Voting and electoral behaviour; how the voting system works; what influences how people vote? Do elections guarantee democracy? What is the role of political parties? How important are pressure groups? The major institutions of contemporary UK government: their relationships with one another and their effectiveness. How adequate is the UK constitution? The UK does not have a written constitution but does have a constantly evolving collection of laws and principles, according to which the country is governed. What is the role and significance of Parliament? How powerful is the prime minister? Do judges deliver justice and defend freedom?

At A2 the specification includes a number of optional units and you might specialise in US politics or look at issues that are central to the study of modern politics, such as the environment, ideologies, globalisation, power, devolution and the European Union (EU).

Other topics include the representative processes of the US political system and their adequacy in terms of popular participation and full democracy, the institutional framework of the US government and the interrelationships between its legislature (Congress), executive (President) and judiciary (Supreme Court) and their role within the US Constitution the oldest constitution in the world.

Elections and voting, political parties, pressure groups, and racial and ethnic politics; political ideas and ideologies such as socialism, liberalism, conservatism, fascism, feminism and nationalism; power in modern society; Britain in Europe.

Issues such as: ethnicity and gender, the environment, education, the economy, perspectives on modern politics, participation and representation, globalisation, change and continuity, territorial politics, rights in practice and power in practice.

All these are studied in the context of current and recent issues, arguments and events. A GCSE in the subject is not required for study at A level but you must be enthusiastic about politics and have a good grasp of English.

You study through lessons, discussions, research tasks and may take part in mock elections or 'Question Time' sessions. You may listen to invited speakers, visit political organisations, the House of Commons or even Washington DC. You will be expected to keep up-to-date with current events.

## Subject combinations
Universities generally do not ask for any specific A levels for entry to degrees in government, politics or related subjects but some do have preferred subjects. Useful A levels include history, philosophy, geography, citizenship, English, economics, law and sociology.

# Higher education options

## Degree-level study
There is a wide range of politics degrees and many have their own specialisms. You will also find there are specialist degrees such as European politics and international politics, political economy, international relations, globalisation and political science.

The main areas of study are:

- **British politics**–constitutional reforms and the devolution/independence of Scotland, Wales and Northern Ireland. Britains membership of the EU, the euro and the sovereignty debate.
- **The EU and Europe**–comparing them with British and other political systems. Many universities offer courses focusing on the politics of other countries or regions such as the USA, the Middle East, Latin America, Asia, Africa or Australasia.
- **Political theory**–where you consider key questions about the nature of freedom and the strengths and limitations of democracy. Other topics include the relationship between government and society, the right of dissent and the limits of toleration, and questions of social justice and equality.
- **Elections**–and how they can change the course of a country. Studying elections can be about predicting results, trying to work out why people vote as they do, or even why they don't vote at all. Party campaigns, what policies are put forward and how parties select candidates.
- **International relations**–covers topics such as the role of international organisations (such as the United Nations), the strategies of various politicians on the international political stage, the role of international non-governmental organisations (for example large corporations) and vital international policy areas like the environment. It addresses questions such as why wars occur, how peace is negotiated and maintained, and international justice.

On many courses you can spend some time on fieldwork and this might involve working with a political party or pressure group, or you may even go abroad, observing the work of the European Parliament, European Commission or NATO.

## Degree subject combinations

Government and politics is available in combination with economics, history, philosophy, sociology, law and languages. There are also combinations with subjects like human rights and international relations, peace studies, conflict studies or social policy.

## Other higher education qualifications

There are no foundation degrees available in government and politics but there are some in related topics, such as community regeneration and community governance, community and public service and trade union studies.

There are no HNDs or HNCs available in government and politics but you might want to look at related courses in public services and legal studies. These are more vocational than degree courses and aim to prepare you for careers in public services or as a paralegal executive. (For more information on paralegals, see the entry for law.)

### Relevance to other subjects?

Government and politics A level gives you skills in how to develop ideas and arguments backed up with reliable evidence. This will be useful in many other subjects, especially economics, philosophy, law and history.

### Important advice

You must get into the habit of reading a quality newspaper regularly and keeping in touch with current events and issues. Applying what you learn to real-world events will make your studies far more interesting and give you a head start over other students, especially if you decide to apply for government and politics courses at degree level.

# Future careers

### ▷After A levels

It may be possible to get into jobs in national or local government. The study of government and politics increases your awareness of what is going on in the world and develops your skills of argument and discussion (both written and spoken), which can be used in many areas. Politics affects the work of the police and customs services, so an appreciation of issues such as immigration, civil liberties, and protest and pressure groups would be helpful in these careers. There may be apprenticeships in administration which will help you get in and the Civil Service has a Fast Track Apprenticeship scheme.

### ▷After a degree

### Working in government and politics

- *Elected politicians*–you usually start off by working unpaid for a political party, whether at a local or national level, and are then selected by the party to stand at an election for a council seat, European or parliamentary constituency.

- *Agents and researchers*—some people enter politics by becoming an agent for an MP (they are usually in the political party first) and there are opportunities to become researchers or assistants to MPs.
- *Political consultants and lobbyists*—employed by companies or other groups that want to see a particular issue raised and examined in Parliament.
- *Local government officers*—work at a local level in areas such as housing, roads and other public facilities.
- *Civil servants*—if you reach the senior grades in Whitehall, you will be advising government ministers on how policy should be put into practice. Recruitment to the senior Civil Service is through intensive selection tests, after which you are assigned to a particular department such as health, defence or education. Civil servants also work for the European Commission and a modern language up to A level standard is required for their fast-stream recruitment.
- *Other related jobs*—trade union work, political party organiser, academic teaching and research and political journalism.

## Working outside government and politics

A degree in politics is accepted for a wide range of careers. As a politics graduate you will be able to express yourself clearly in speech and writing. This makes you an ideal candidate for work in business, the media, journalism, management or the law.

## Sources of information

The Political Studies Association
www.psa.ac.uk

Civil Service careers
www.civilservice.gov.uk/recruitment/entry

Careers with the European Union
http://europa.eu/epso/index_en.htm

www.parliament.uk

www.w4mp.org

www.politicsresources.net

www.psa.ac.uk

---

'We learned about not just British politics but also political theory, e.g. communism, fascism etc. A level politics opens your eyes to how our country is run and governed, and is unique because there are no other subjects where you learn about how and why Britain is like it is today, from a political point of view.' Paula, with A levels in geography, history, government and politics and general studies, now taking a BA in government and politics

# Greek (classical)/Latin

### *Also known as classics: classical Greek and classics: Latin.*

*These subjects give you the opportunity to learn the ancient Greek and Latin languages (ancient Greek is known as classical Greek) and to study a selection of Greek and Roman literature. The cultures of ancient Greece and Rome are fascinating to study in themselves, and they are also the foundation of modern Western civilisations and cultures.*

*By studying Greek or Latin, you begin to appreciate the language and literature, history and society of the classical world and begin to understand how it has influenced our own. Studying classical languages also trains you in logical and analytical skills as well as providing a foundation for studying a modern language and English.*

## What do you study?

*OCR is the only board offering ancient Greek and Latin. This part of their classics suite, which offers four named pathways (Latin, classical Greek, classical civilisation and ancient history). There is a fifth pathway leading to a classics A/AS level, which offers combinations of units chosen from Greek, Latin and classical civilisation.*

- ***Knowledge and understanding of the language***–translating passages taken from the set texts as well as unseen passages of Greek or Latin into English. You carry out comprehension exercises similar to those you are used to in modern languages, and sometimes translate into Latin or Greek (this is known as prose composition). There is an option of translating English into Latin or Greek.
- ***Literary knowledge and understanding***–looking at how characters, thoughts, actions and situations are presented in Greek or Latin texts, how meanings are conveyed, whether directly or indirectly, and how the texts can be understood in their social, cultural and historical settings.
- ***Literary criticism and personal response***–considering the choice and arrangement of words, their rhythm and how the moods they convey are exploited in Greek and Latin literature, how to think about and explain your own response to the text. The texts studied could include those written by Homer, Lysias, Xenophon, Plato, Aristophanes, Euripides, Sophocles, Herodotus or Thucydides (for Greek) or Cicero, Ovid, Catullus, Propertius, Livy, Sallust, Virgil or Tacitus (for Latin).

Most people taking A level Latin will already have taken it at GCSE, but many take A level classical Greek as beginners.

Latin and ancient Greek stopped being everyday languages long ago. You cannot learn to speak them, or listen to the spoken language, as you do with a modern language. Instead, you work through reading and writing.

Classes concentrate on grammatical analysis, understanding, analysing and appreciating the literary qualities of the set texts and translation. However, the teaching of classical languages has gained from developments in modern language teaching, so it is not as different as you might expect. You may go on visits to museums or sites with links to the classics.

### Subject combinations

If you are looking at a degree in Latin or Greek and have the opportunity to take the language for A level, then you should. If you are thinking of studying both languages at university, you don't have to offer classical Greek A level, but a modern language alongside Latin would be helpful. Greek combines well with most A levels including history, modern languages or English. If you are considering a degree in archaeology then mathematics or a science, especially chemistry, would be useful as archaeology uses scientific techniques for the analysis of archaeological sites and remains. If you are considering medicine then plenty of anatomy and pathology terms are in Greek or Latin so it could be a useful subject along with your sciences.

# Higher education options

As the opportunity to study Latin or classical Greek is not always available in schools, some universities now teach them from scratch offering different routes to beginners and those with the A level. For classics degrees (Latin and Greek), you usually have to offer one or both of the languages (if only one, Latin is the usual requirement). There are a few classics courses where AS levels in Greek or Latin are accepted and some that will accept GCSEs in Greek or Latin.

## Degree-level study

The following options are open to you at degree level:
- a single-subject degree in either Latin or Greek (although often you can also study the other language as a minor or through options)
- a degree in classics (Latin and Greek) again, you can usually vary the proportions of the two languages, or concentrate more on one or the other as you progress through your degree.

In both these types of degree, you will spend much of your time reading Latin or Greek literature, developing your understanding and appreciation of the language. Naturally, the number and variety of writers that you study will expand greatly from your A level work. You may also have the opportunity to study the history of Latin or Greek. Some courses allow you to study the Latin used after the end of the Roman period (about AD 476) up to the Middle Ages (ending about AD 1500). In addition to language and literary work, you study Greek and Roman history, culture and society, mythology and religion and art and architecture. Most degree courses are very flexible and allow you to choose the proportion of the time that you wish to devote to each of these topics.

## Degree subject combinations

You can combine the study of Latin or Greek with many other subjects especially English, history, philosophy, archaeology and modern languages, although you will find combinations with computing and economics. Combining the study of a classical language with the modern languages that have developed from it can be very interesting. You can combine classics with modern Greek and with other modern languages like German, French, Italian and Arabic.

## Other higher education qualifications

There are no foundation degrees directly related to Greek and Latin but related subjects available include history, heritage and archaeology. There are no HNDs or HNCs in Latin or Greek.

## Relevance to other subjects?

The study of classical Greek and/or Latin can lead to many courses at university. It is a foundation for ancient history, classics, classical studies, languages, history, English, law, philosophy and theology.

Even if you don't think that you will want to take Greek or Latin beyond A level, don't rule it out at this stage. Your study of a language rather different from English, the alternative language-learning techniques demanded, and (for Greek) the mastery of a different writing system, provide good evidence of your intellectual abilities. Studying a more unusual subject provides a good talking point at interviews!

## Important advice

There is variation and flexibility in the exact texts and periods covered by different classics degree courses and a wide variety of courses in related areas, classical civilisation for example. You must think carefully about exactly which aspects of your studies of Latin or Greek you most enjoy and then find a degree course that fits your interests.

# Future careers

## ▷After A levels

Latin or Greek A levels are unlikely to lead directly to related work although if you work in law, you will find Latin useful. However, the different disciplines and techniques involved in studying a dead language in a more formal way suggest a clear, logical mind and a good memory. The study of classical languages will also help you in any language study you might do now or in the future. You could consider careers that are open to anyone with good A levels, such as banking, insurance, accountancy, retail or national or local government. Don't forget to look at Higher Apprenticeships in these areas which could lead to degree level study.

## ▷After a degree

## Working with Greek or Latin

There are only a few careers in which you can really use Latin or Greek and these, as you might expect, are concerned with passing on your knowledge to others.

- **Teaching Latin or Greek in schools**—this is the main possibility and the independent school sector offers most opportunities. If you are interested in teaching younger age groups (below A level), you would need to offer another subject such as history, religious studies, a modern language or English.
- **Teaching in higher education**—this is usually coupled with research and postgraduate study will be necessary.

- **Archaeology**—there may be some opportunities for graduates in Latin or Greek to work as archaeologists, discovering and studying the material evidence of early history. The work ranges from organising digs (excavations), through charting out farmland that may have once formed a Roman settlement, to the assembly and treatment of new pieces of evidence in museums. You would need to undertake further training, but work experience can be gained through taking part in digs during vacations or at weekends. Remember that you will be in competition with graduates who have specialist archaeology degrees.
- **Library and archive work**—there may be some opportunities in specialist classical libraries or archives. Further training would be required after your degree.
- **The heritage industry**—there may be opportunities to work in specialist museums or as tour guides or historic interpreters using your knowledge of Greek or Latin.

## Working outside Greek and Latin

Very few classics graduates end up working in a directly related area. However, most find that their skills are respected and valued by employers in other fields. Employers recognise that classics graduates can think clearly and logically and, because of this, careers in HM Revenue and Customs or as tax advisers are a popular destination for classics graduates.

Classics graduates go into a wide variety of jobs such as research, education, IT, librarianship or museum work, and many go into management and administration, the Civil Service, banking, insurance, advertising, publishing and journalism.

A degree in Latin or Greek would be a good background if you are thinking of a career in law (the study of Roman law is included in many law courses), or you could enter accountancy training at the graduate stage.

## Sources of information

www.classics.ac.uk

www.classicspage.com

www.onlinelatinschool.com

www.ancientgreekonline.com

'We cannot possibly understand our modern world unless we understand the ancient world that made us all.' June, studying history, Latin and French A levels

# Health and social care

*NB: This is based on the new A level specification available from 2014.*

**Health and social care is a huge and varied area of work, covering a wide range of professions. There are many opportunities in health and caring: this course gives you a broad understanding of health and social care principles, how the sector operates and the opportunity to develop skills in this area of work.**

**It is a broad-based qualification that encourages you to study in a practical way. The course helps you to develop a range of vocational skills that will be useful to you either for higher level study or in work and training.**

## What do you study?
*The topics listed give an idea of what could be covered. The exact content of AS and A2 specifications differs according to exam boards, so you will need to check with your school or college about the exact modules available to you.*

- **Effective care and communication**—it is essential to develop and maintain good relationships in this area of work. You are introduced to the communication skills used in health, social care, children and young people and community justice sectors. This could include hospitals, nursing homes, elderly residential homes, childrens homes, primary schools, nurseries, prisons, remand centres or detainee centres.
- **Understanding health conditions and patient care**—pathways develops your knowledge and understanding of a range of health conditions such as asthma, strokes and heart disease and the appropriate patient care pathways which are commonly followed, based on a patient-centred approach to care.
- **Life as a challenge**—explores a range of challenges faced by people due to physical disability, learning disability, mental health issues and social circumstances. These are physical challenge (such as cystic fibrosis and osteoarthritis), mental health challenge (such as Alzheimer's and bipolar disorder), social challenge (young carers and people in later life, adulthood) and learning challenge (such as autism and Down's syndrome).
- **Educating children and young people**—introduces you to the theory and practice of learning in education. It also gives you the opportunity to plan a learning situation yourself.

- **Learning and development**–factors affecting learning, development, health and well-being and theories of human development.
- **Practitioner roles**–aims to increase your understanding of the world of work in the health, social care, children and young people and community justice sectors. It also helps you to reflect on your own suitability for different job roles.
- **Food and fitness**–develops your knowledge and understanding of food components and balanced diets required to meet the dietary and nutritional needs of different client groups, and a range of different aspects of exercise that help maintain the fitness, health and well-being of individuals.
- **Using and understanding research**–gain an understanding of research and research methods within one of the following sectors: health, social care, children and young people or community justice, and analyse background literature related to your area of interest. You will carry out your own piece of research by choosing, designing and carrying out a simple study which will demonstrate your understanding of research methods.
- **Understanding mental disorders**–introduces you to different mental disorders, their causes, treatments and the impact of these on individuals and on their families, friends and carers. You will explore the role of services and professionals in supporting people with mental disorders and the impact of legislation on individuals and their treatment.
- **Diagnosis, treatment and preventative strategies**–a variety of diagnostic techniques and the principles and key points of practice of a range of common medical treatments. Also looks into ways in which common diseases and disorders can be prevented.

You will have the option to take other units, depending on your school or college.

There may be opportunities for work placements within caring or health establishments and you will use these experiences to support your studies.

## Subject combinations
Health and social care can be usefully combined with biology or human biology or other science A levels to support applications to nursing or

allied health professions careers. Combined with psychology or sociology, it could support social work or teaching applications. Note that if you are considering a career in medicine you will need to have two or three science A levels including chemistry.

# Higher education options

### Degree-level study
You could consider a wide range of courses, including health sciences, health, nutrition and exercise, health and well-being, nursing, midwifery, biology, health promotion, sports and exercise studies, teaching, social work, and paramedical degrees such as occupational therapy, paramedic science, speech and language therapy, audiology and radiography. Some competitive courses such as physiotherapy or paramedic science might ask for additional AS or A level study in biology, chemistry or physics and may specify certain subjects at GCSE.

### Degree subject combinations
There are lots of different options for combined study in areas such as health science or studies and biology. You can combine with subjects that are related, such as sport and exercise studies, but also with subjects such as marketing and business studies.

### Other higher education qualifications
There is a wide selection of foundation degrees covering many different areas related to health and social care. Examples of these are health and social care, health and social care of adults, complementary therapies, food, nutrition and health, health, exercise and fitness, sport fitness and personal training, healthcare science, dental hygiene and therapy, dental technology, paramedic science, spa management, animal science and management and veterinary nursing.

HND and HNC courses are available in various specialisms; examples include health and social care, sport, health fitness and exercise and sport and exercise science. There are also DipHEs in operating department practice.

### Relevance to other subjects?
The wide range of skills you will acquire from the health and social care course could be transferred to other areas such as hospitality and catering, leisure, recreation, tourism or business.

## Important advice

Make sure that you are taking the right selection of units for any careers you are considering and check that you choose the right additional A levels to support your applications. It is important to research carefully into the range of higher education courses available to you. Any work experience you can get in the health and social care field is advisable, as it will help your applications.

# Future Careers

### ▷After A levels

There are apprenticeships in health and social care at Advanced Level and Higher Apprenticeship level (see Skills for Care).

There will be opportunities in areas such as childcare (you will need further study to become a nursery nurse) but other jobs such as playgroup assistant or nanny may be available. There are opportunities to work as care workers in residential homes or healthcare assistants in hospitals. You could also consider becoming a classroom or teaching assistant, although you normally need to be aged 18 to start training. Your knowledge of health and social care could be applied to administrative jobs in the health service. There are also opportunities in the police, ambulance service and in jobs like airline cabin crew where your study could be put to good use with further training.

### ▷After a degree

## Working in health and social care

Health studies and science courses can vary in their content and may cover options such as health promotion, health information science or health service administration, which could lead into administration and management careers in the health service or the caring sector. Social care or social science courses can lead to management or administration (see the entry for sociology). If you have done a more vocational course specialising in, for example, nursing, podiatry, radiography or social work, then the routes into work are well-defined, although you might need further postgraduate study to qualify in some of these careers.

## Working outside health and social care

A good working knowledge of how social and caring services work could lead you to consider jobs in administration. This could involve dealing with the public, which would make good use of your communication skills. Your knowledge of the human body could lead to careers in leisure and fitness or medical sales. Other jobs you could consider would be the police, ambulance service or Armed Forces. You could enter careers for graduates of any discipline, which could cover a wide range of business and management areas.

## Sources of information

Health and care professions council
www.hpc-uk.org

NHS Careers
www.nhscareers.nhs.uk

www.skillsforcare.org.uk (for apprenticeships)

www.communitycare.co.uk

www.basw.co.uk/social-work-careers

*'I like the fact that everything you do is applied to real life. Going on a placement in a special needs unit has given me confidence and also helped me understand what we are learning.'* Zoe, studying health and social care, biology and psychology

# History

***Those who cannot remember the past are condemned to repeat it***
**George Santayana (1863-1952)**

*It is said that we can learn from the past to avoid the same mistakes in the future. The study of history is concerned with when and why things happened and attempts to analyse the significance of past events. The best reason for taking a history course is that the past fascinates you and you enjoy studying it. History combines the excitement of exploration and discovery with the sense of reward that comes from successfully confronting and making sense of complex and challenging problems.*

*The purpose of historical inquiry is not simply to present facts but to search for an interpretation of the past. Historians attempt to find patterns and establish meaning through the study of evidence. It provides skills and understanding that will always be valuable in any career.*

## What do you study?

*The topics listed give an idea of what could be covered. The exact content of AS and A2 specifications differs according to exam boards, so you will need to check with your school or college about the exact modules available to you.*

The revised history A level specifications still require that students study British history. Students will also be required to study topics from a chronological range of at least 200 years. The content also includes that students undertake a historical enquiry that is independently researched and that investigates specific historical questions, problems or issues. The A level will have a 20% non-exam assessment and the AS level will be 100% examination. There are a wide variety of history specifications for A level. Options on courses include world history, economic and social, modern and medieval history and there are wide choices available in each specification.

You could study the history of more than one country or state or the history of more than one period. You might cover aspects of the past through periods or themes, significant individuals, societies, events, developments and issues within a broad historical context or developments affecting different groups within the societies studied.

Examples of shorter or thematic papers:
- The reign of Peter the Great of Russia, 1682-1725
- Britain and appeasement, 1919-1940
- A new Roman Empire? Mussolini's Italy, 1922-1945
- The impact of Stalins leadership in the USSR, 1928-1941
- The impact of Chairman Mao, China, 1946-1976
- The campaign for African-American civil rights in the USA, 1950-1968
- The USA and Vietnam, 1961-1975
- British society, 1959-1975
- The Reformation in Europe, c1500-1564
- The triumph of Elizabeth: Britain, 1547-1603.

It is not essential to have studied history at GCSE in order to do the A level. Some degree courses in history require a modern language at GCSE.

History A level involves being able to read and absorb information quickly. There is never enough class time to cover every aspect of every topic, so the more reading you can do on your own the better. Class discussions form an important part of the course but they must be backed up by note-taking and reading. There will also be field study trips to places of historical interest.

## Subject combinations
If you want to study history at degree level then the A level is the obvious choice, although its not a strict requirement for many degree courses. You will need to develop skills in research analysis and interpretation to study A level history so you might want to choose other subjects that will provide supporting knowledge and skills.

Government and politics will add to your understanding of political ideology and the British political system, which will be useful if you are studying modern history. Sociology and economics also cover a number of topics relating to developments in the Western world, requiring the ability to research and interpret data critically. A level English will help the development of your assignment-writing skills. You might also want to consider combinations with modern foreign languages or classics.

# Higher education options

## Degree-level study

There are many history and history-related degree courses. The largest number of courses are in British and European history, although they do not all cover all periods. As at A level, course topics relate either to periods, geographical areas or themes. Some interesting options on courses include the social history of medicine, gender history, the crusades, intellectual and religious history, financial history, the history of technology and industrial relations. You do not have to opt for a degree covering the periods that you studied at A level so you have the opportunity to try something new.

If you are sure that you want to specialise from the start, there are specialised degrees like ancient history, economic and social history, American/Canadian history, medieval studies, Jewish history, peace/war studies and the history of Scotland, Wales or Ireland. Some modern history courses offer a year studying in Europe and some offer related work experience.

## Degree subject combinations

History can be combined with many other subjects. The most widely available are English, geography, languages, philosophy, politics and sociology. However, practically any combination is possible including combining with sciences.

## Other higher education qualifications

There are foundation degrees in history and heritage management studies; historic garden restoration and management; historic building conservation; libraries, museums and archives; history, heritage and archaeology.

There are no HNDs or HNCs in history although there are some courses for which an A level in history would be good preparation. HNDs or HNCs in information and office technology or business management, for example, would put to good use your experience of collecting and analysing information.

## Relevance to other subjects?

Even if you don't continue with your history studies, you will find that A level history is a well-respected qualification for many courses. In subjects like law, modern languages, English, politics, sociology, economics and business you will find opportunities to use your writing and analytical skills.

## Important advice

History is a popular degree. It would be an advantage to try to visit historical places that relate to your studies or interests. These include not only the great historic houses but sites such as Quarry Bank Cotton Mill in Cheshire, the Potteries Museum in Stoke-on- Trent and Ironbridge Gorge in Shropshire. Visit the various folk and local history museums around the country (especially larger ones like St Fagans National History Museum near Cardiff, where rural Welsh houses and workshops have been reconstructed). Do some research into them beforehand; so that you know what to look for once you get there. You should be prepared to do a lot of reading in your spare time. The monthly magazine, *History Today*, will give you a taste of different historical periods and topics before you study them in detail, as will the wide range of historical programmes on TV.

# Future careers

### ▷ After A levels

The wide range of skills and knowledge that you will develop as a history A level student will be helpful in finding employment. You will be able to think and argue logically, write well and be able to organise and analyse large quantities of information. These are the kinds of skills needed to work in areas such as administration, management, sales and marketing. With further training you might find work in libraries or archives and there are apprenticeships available in library and archive work.

### ▷ After a degree

### Working in history

There are only a few careers in which you can use your historical knowledge directly:

- **teaching**–teaching history is the most direct way to use and develop your subject knowledge. To teach in state schools you need to take a PGCE to give you qualified teacher status (QTS). University lecturing is a possibility after specialised postgraduate and research in history.
- **museum work**–work in museums (usually after postgraduate training).

- *archive work*–archivists are employed either by the Government (in record offices) by the media or industry. Again, further postgraduate training in information management would help your prospects.

## Working outside history

You will find history graduates working in many areas of management and administration because their eye for detail, research skills and ability to form logical arguments can make them ideal organisers of both people and resources. They also work for local and national government, in finance, marketing, sales and the media. History is often seen as a good preparation for a career in law (shown by the fact that some universities recommend A level history rather than A level law as an entry qualification to law courses).

## Sources of information

The Historical Association
www.history.org.uk

www.bl.uk/learning/histcitizen/index.html

www.spartacus.schoolnet.co.uk

www.historytoday.com

'When I graduated, I found employers were very aware of the competencies that we historians develop during our studies. My job is to analyse information and data relating to finance, and what impressed my employer was that I could easily adapt the skills I used at university.'
James, IT analyst with a BA in history

# History of art

*In history of art A level you study the work of artists, sculptors and architects, concentrating on the Western world. Works are studied in the light of the political, economic, social, religious and cultural context in which they were created. For example, did the artists work as servants of a religious or political leader, or did they see their art as personal expression? You learn about the artistic tradition in which the artists worked, and study the techniques that are used in painting, sculpture and architecture.*

## What do you study?

*AQA is the only exam board currently offering history of art (art of the Western world).*

For AS you will cover the following topics:

### Visual analysis and interpretation

You learn how to look at and interpret works of art such as painting, sculpture and architecture. How to interpret paintings taking into account such things as composition; colour, light and tone; materials and techniques. How sculpture can vary according to materials, techniques and processes, size and how architecture is influenced by site and location, materials and scale, and location. This will include appropriate architectural, art and art historical terminology.

### Themes in history of art

You acquire a knowledge and understanding of historical art themes in relation to examples of works of Western art and architecture, artists and architects drawn from classical Greece to the end of the 20th century (500 BC-2000 AD).

All works of art are studied in relation to the following themes and you look at each work in the light of these.

- **Materials, techniques and processes**–how works of art are produced.
- **Form and style**–how the formal features of art and architecture contribute to its style and meaning and how different styles have evolved.
- **Form and function**–the purpose and appearance of, for example, a building, and how to evaluate it taking into account its role as a functional building as well as an artistic work.
- **Historical and social contexts**–how to interpret works of art in the light of history and social history.

- **Patronage**—what influence artistic patronage has on works of art.
- **Social and cultural status**—how these influence art.
- **Gender, nationality and identity**—how styles evolve due to these factors.

At A2 you will continue your investigations and interpretations concentrating on one period in each of the two units. The periods are shown below and your teacher will choose the appropriate one.

In each topic you are required to have a detailed knowledge of formal features, materials, techniques and styles, and of the individual artists, sculptors and architects of the period. You will be examined on your understanding of the historical, social, economic and cultural contexts of the period as well the philosophy and art historical concepts of the time.

## Unit 3

### Art and architecture in 15th-century Europe
European painting, sculpture and architecture in the 15th century, for example the works of Botticelli, Da Vinci, Brunelleschi, Bosch and Raphael.

### Art and architecture in 17th-century Europe
European painting, sculpture and architecture in the 17th century, for example the works of Rembrandt, Vermeer, Wren, Van Dyck and Inigo Jones.

### Art and architecture in 19th-century Europe
European painting, sculpture and architecture in the 19th century, for example the works of Blake, Turner, Constable, Rodin, Rousseau, Barry, Pugin, Gilbert Scott.

### Art and architecture in Europe and the USA between 1946 and 2000
European and American art and architecture 1946-2000, for example the works of Hirst, Emin, Hockney, Warhol, Moore, Hepworth, Foster, Goldfinger and Gropius.

## Unit 4

### Art and architecture in 13th- and 14th-century Europe
European painting, sculpture and architecture in the 13th and 14th centuries, for example the works of Bellini, Van Eyck, Pisano and Giotto.

## Art and architecture in 16th-century Europe

European painting, sculpture and architecture in the 16th century, for example the works of Michelangelo, Palladio, Holbein and Bruegel.

## Art and architecture in 18th-century Europe

This topic deals with European painting, sculpture and architecture in the 18th century, for example the works of Hogarth, Adam, Vanbrugh, Gainsborough, Roubiliac and Reynolds.

## Art and architecture in Europe and the USA between 1900 and 1945

For example, the works of Lutyens, Epstein, Matisse, Picasso, Magritte, Klee and Miro.

There is no GCSE history of art and you are not expected to know a lot about art history before you start the A level although obviously it will help. You don't have to be good at painting or drawing but it may help you if have experience of art, photography, history, languages, politics or sociology at GCSE. The most important thing is a real interest and enthusiasm for art history.

History of art is based around the detailed study of works of art. You can expect a lot of group work, discussing images of the works, whether they are paintings, sculptures or buildings. There will be study visits to galleries in the UK and possibly in Europe, such as Florence, Paris, Amsterdam or Barcelona.

## Subject combinations

If you are thinking of studying history of art at degree level, it is a good idea to combine the A level with subjects that complement your work. Art and design, English, history, classical civilisation or religious studies would provide invaluable background knowledge. Languages (especially French, German or Italian) also combine well. Even if you don't consider yourself artistic, you may find history of art a useful accompaniment to other subjects. For example, combining history of art with a science-based subject may not seem an obvious choice but can be a help with careers such as archaeology and art restoration or conservation, which require scientific skills. The history of art A level provides a useful background for an Art Foundation course although you will also need a portfolio of art work for entry.

# Higher education options

It is not essential to have studied A level history of art in order to study it at a higher level.

## Degree-level study

A history of art degree will extend your studies much further than the Western world.

You may spend some of your time focusing on a single artist or artistic movement, but you will have the opportunity to study topics such as world cinema, photography and the art of other civilisations. Some courses include practical studio work in art or design. Many courses offer a study period abroad, ranging from a week, to a term or a year. Most of these visits are to Europe, although North America and Australia are possibilities.

## Degree subject combinations

History of art is available with related subjects such as fine art and also English, history and languages.

## Other higher education qualifications

There are no history of art foundation degrees although there are art and design courses, some with a module in art history. There are also plenty of practical courses including art and design in the creative industries (fine art), art of games design, art practice, computing (games design), contemporary applied art and design, contemporary fine art practice, design, fashion design, fine art, illustration, sustainable design and construction and visual merchandising and promotional design.

There are no HND or HNC subjects in history of art but plenty of practical art courses such as art and design, fine art, graphics and illustration.

There are also art history courses available at postgraduate level. If you are thinking about the practical study of art, you should consider taking an Art Foundation course, which will help you get into a practical design course.

## Relevance to other subjects?

The history of art A level will be useful for entry to humanities and social science degrees.

Alternatives to a history of art course include history of art and design, art history and visual culture, which look at all the visual aspects of society not just art, and so include the study of advertising, fashion design, television and film. Other courses you might consider include architecture, archaeology, furniture conservation, restoration and decorative arts, conservation and restoration, museum and gallery studies, and arts administration.

## Important advice

The best preparation for the study of art history at a higher level is to visit as many galleries, museums and churches as you can. Many art collections are now available on the web so you don't have to travel far. Most art galleries are free and you may find some near you.

# Future careers

## ▷ After A levels

If you intend to go into work straight after A level history of art you may find work as a junior assistant in a gallery, auction house, design company or antiques business. You could consider part-time study to further your knowledge in these areas. There may be apprenticeships in these areas of work.

## ▷ After a degree

## Working in history of art

Careers in or related to art history often require further postgraduate study.

Possible careers include:
- museum, gallery or the antiques business
- arts administration or management
- auctioneer or valuer
- picture researcher
- specialist art or architecture librarian/ archivist
- theatres, arts centres, arts sponsorship for large companies and the arts support schemes run by local authorities and central government
- heritage industries—many tourist attractions, historic houses or industrial archaeology sites have an 'art dimension'
- specialist travel and tourism (e.g. lecturing on art tours)

- art and design publishing, broadcasting and journalism
- conservation and restoration.

## Working outside history of art

You will find the skills and knowledge gained on a history of art degree useful for the many careers open to graduates in any subject, such as buying, marketing and selling, finance and administration. Teaching is another option.

## Sources of information

Association of Art Historians
www.aah.org.uk

The National Gallery
www.nationalgallery.org.uk

ICON (the Institute of Conservation)
www.icon.org.uk

www.getintoheritage.org

www.chart.ac.uk/vlib

---

'If you want to get into art conservation, make sure you get some sciences, especially chemistry, at either GCSE or A level.' Nomandi, taking a postgraduate qualification in fine art restoration after a degree in history of art

---

# ICT

*Here you get the opportunity to see how computer technology is affecting the world we live in. The practical use of software for problem solving and information by individuals, organisations and within society is the focus of the course. You will get an understanding of the ICT industry, the career opportunities available and the application of ICT principles. You will learn how to present and handle information, understand the function and forms of software and hardware, and how to plan and develop solutions to ICT problems. You will also learn to look at ICT from the user's perspective, including technical support and software development. The course helps you to develop a range of skills that will be useful to you either for higher level study or in work and training.*

*Note that it's not just about learning how to use spreadsheets and word processors but focusing more on using those applications to provide solutions for clients.*

## What do you study?

*Specifications vary and you may have the opportunity to choose different options depending on your school or college. There is also a computer science A level (see earlier entry) and an applied ICT A level available, the applied A level is more vocational and includes more coursework.*

The areas you could cover are as follows:

## Practical problem solving in the digital world

You learn about and make practical use of a range of applications software, hardware and communication technologies to address several different types of problem. The applications software used covers the processing of text, images, numbers and sound. You then use the software to solve practical problems and may be asked to use your knowledge of applications to work on different projects, for example:

- an electronic photo album
- a rolling multimedia presentation for a school open day
- a website for a local nursery
- blog for a local councillor
- invoices for a small business
- a set of podcasts for a teacher
- an interactive multimedia display for a tourist information centre.

You should show that you go through the various stages of using and implementing applications through analysing, designing, implementing, testing and, finally, evaluating your projects.

## Living in the digital world

We are living in a world where the use of ICT surrounds us and is taken for granted. It is increasingly important to be aware of the numerous issues arising from the use of ICT for individuals, society and organisations. The issues change rapidly and increasingly involve environmental and ethical issues.

You will gain a wider picture of the use of ICT so that you gain an understanding of basic terms and concepts involved in the study of the subject. You will learn to discuss and comment on issues from a position of knowledge by understanding how the whole subject works. You will consider the important issues involved in the use of ICT, the immediate effect on yourselves and the longer term effects on society and the world in general.

You will examine such questions as:
- why is ICT being used?
- is it appropriate to use ICT?
- what are the implications of its use for me, now and in the future?
- how does a particular use of ICT affect society?

## The use of ICT in the digital world

You learn about the fast changing nature of ICT, including developments in technology and ICT system capabilities, and how this might affect the world that makes use of ICT.

The content is designed to address issues associated with the management of ICT and its use within organisations. A range of organisations are studied, including charities, clubs and societies, small, medium and large businesses, both national and multi-national public and private organisations. The number of people involved could range from one or two to many thousands.

Each organisation will have the same ICT-related issues to consider on a scale appropriate to their own needs, for instance, the introduction and testing of ICT systems, the training and support needed for users of ICT systems and the outside organisations that affect the way the organisation runs its ICT.

## Coursework: practical issues involved in the use of ICT

You undertake a substantial project involving the production of an ICT-related system over an extended period of time. This will build your transferable practical skills.

An example of a project might be:
- a software solution, such as an e-commerce or multimedia system
- a training system, including training materials for a client; for example, a course for someone working from home
- a user support system, such as for a user help desk in a company or school/college, or a fault logging system
- a system for ensuring the security of an organisations ICT systems
- a system for communication within an organisation; for example, for how schools could use technology to communicate with students within the school or a communal diary system
- a system for evaluating new software to be purchased or for a new system to be installed, including hardware, software, communications, consumables and services
- a backup and recovery system and a disaster recovery plan for an organisation
- a system for managing customer feedback.

## Subject combinations

ICT goes well with subjects like business studies, media or languages. As ICT is such an important study area, you could combine it with health and social care, travel and tourism, or more traditional subjects like history, geography and sciences. Some pure computing degrees do require an additional specified A or AS level in maths or a science and if you are considering adding maths or physics, this could lead to engineering courses at degree level.

# Higher education options

### Degree-level study

ICT allows progression to many related degree courses such as computer networking, computer gaming technology, business information technology, computing for business, information and communication technology, e-commerce computing, internet computing and systems administration, business computing (e-business), and computing with digital media. The content of courses varies as some will be more computer science and maths-based, concentrating on artificial intelligence, robotics or software engineering, while others will be geared towards business computing systems. It is important to look at the course content closely to see what is offered. The course title may not tell you the exact content of the course.

## Degree subject combinations
ICT goes well with a wide range of subjects including humanities, social sciences and languages.

## Other higher education qualifications
Foundation degrees are available in computing, applied computing and ICT, and in related areas such as computer network management, computer network security, computer systems management, computing (networking and forensics), computing (networking), computing (business information systems), business and computing, computing technologies (media systems), computing and internet technologies, computing with database development, game and mobile app design, and web design and software development.

The HND courses available include: computing (business information systems), computer science, computer forensics and security, computing, computing (software development), computing and systems development, computing games development, computing and website development, computer-aided engineering, information technology (networking and security), computer systems support, computing (mobile computing) and computer networks and security.

## Relevance to other subjects?
ICT gives you a thorough knowledge of business and IT systems as well as problem-solving, analytical and project management skills. You could consider subjects like business studies or financial management, banking, insurance, travel and tourism, and leisure and recreation.

## Important advice
Make sure you find out about the facilities and equipment that will be available to you when you are researching higher level courses. It is also a good idea to investigate specific course requirements to find out whether additional A or AS subjects are advisable or certain GCSE subjects are required for entry to these courses. If you don't choose to

do an ICT degree, there are opportunities to take postgraduate qualifications in ICT after a non-related subject.

# Future careers

### ▷After A levels

You could enter employment as a trainee in jobs such as networking, technical support and systems design, helpdesk professional, PC support, database or network administrator. Your skills could open up opportunities in business administration or any area where knowledge of ICT is essential. There may are Higher Apprenticeships available in IT which can lead to degree level study (see www.e-skills.com).

### ▷After a degree

### Working in ICT

Depending on the content of your degree, these are the types of jobs that would be open to you:

- *help desk worker*—acts as the interface between ICT and the users or customer, advising and helping with any technical problems that arise
- *software engineer*—specifies, develops, documents and maintains computer software programs in order to meet client or employer need
- *database administrator*—responsible for the usage, accuracy, efficiency, security, maintenance and development of computerised databases
- *applications developer*—writes and modifies programs to enable a computer to carry out specific tasks, such as stock control or payroll, typically for technical, commercial and business users
- *systems operator (technical support)*—takes the specification for the requirements of a computer system and designs the system including hardware, software, communications, installation, testing and maintenance
- *systems developer*—sets up the computer operating systems and standard software services essential to the operation of any computer
- *information technology consultant*—gives independent and objective advice on how best to use information technology to solve business problems; the work includes analysing problems, making recommendations and implementing new systems

- *cyber security*–advises companies on the best way to secure their information and good working practices; a thorough knowledge of programming and applications is required for this, which is currently a shortage area
- *network engineer*–responsible for the management of a computer network. This will include software installation and configuration, upgrades, diagnostics and troubleshooting.

## Working outside ICT

You will have a good knowledge of ICT systems and applications, excellent communication skills, be able to think logically and have team-working skills. You could use these skills in many aspects of business including administration, sales and marketing. Teaching and training are other possibilities.

## Sources of information

www.bcs.org

www.e-skills.com

www.computing.co.uk

'You never stop learning; your degree is only the first step in a long journey.' Arthur, graduate software engineer with a BSc in computing

# Law

*In A level law you will study the English legal system. You learn how the rules with which we live are established, developed and administered. You explore many different areas of law and then assess the effects of these laws in everyday life. Both real and hypothetical cases are examined to highlight how the law works in practice. A level law provides you with a good general insight into the institutions and work of the English legal system and the people who work within it. It also gives you lots of transferable skills.*

## What do you study?

*The topics listed give an idea of what could be covered. The exact content of AS and A2 specifications differs according to exam boards, so you will need to check with your school or college about the exact modules available to you.*

Depending on the exam board, you study some or all of the following:

### The legal system

- *functions of law*—protection of rights/freedoms, balancing conflict of interests
- *how the law is made*—custom, precedent, EU law, legislation and its interpretation
- *legal disputes resolution*—the criminal and civil courts, tribunals, arbitration
- *the judiciary*—the role of judges and magistrates
- *the courts*—the criminal and civil courts and the role of the European Court of Justice, the jury system
- *the penal system*—sentencing and the treatment of offenders, and police powers
- *the legal profession*—the work of barristers, solicitors and legal executives, other sources of advice and funding

### Criminal law

- *the ingredients of an offence*—commission of the physical act, the mental element
- *homicide*—murder, manslaughter, corporate manslaughter
- *offences against the person*—assault, assault occasioning actual bodily harm, wounding and grievous bodily harm
- *offences against property*—theft, robbery, burglary, criminal damage, fraud offences
- *defences*—insanity, intoxication, self-defence, provocation, duress

- *other topics*–principles of criminal liability, law and morality, law and justice, being an accessory to a crime

## Civil law
- *civil law offences*–the law of tort (a wrong or harm caused to someone), negligence and liability, trespass, nuisance, defence

## Contract law
- *how a legally binding contract can be made and unmade*
- *contracts*–formation of contract, contractual terms, invalid contracts, discharge of contract
- *consumer protection*

You need to be able to write well, think logically and have a good memory. You must be prepared to study and understand a lot of written material. You will also get involved in debating. You will write essays that explore the relevant concepts and analyse them to reach a conclusion. In addition, you have to apply legal principles and cases to hypothetical problems and assess how appropriate they are to their solution. There will be visits to local and regional courts and you might get to visit places like the House of Commons, the Royal Courts of Justice and the Old Bailey.

### Subject combinations
The ability to express yourself clearly both orally and in writing is essential for the study and practice of law. You may wish to combine law with English or history to help develop these skills, and these are useful for entry to law degrees as many universities prefer essay-based subjects. Subjects such as business studies or economics can help you to understand the context in which legal work is carried out. Psychology, sociology, and government and politics can also provide a good foundation for further study in law-related subjects. Sciences can also be useful, especially if you want to specialise in something like intellectual property. A modern foreign language could open up the opportunity to study in another country and even gain a legal qualification there.

# Higher education options
An A level or GCSE in law is not essential for study of the subject at university. Some university law departments sometimes prefer students to start their degree course as a beginner in law so you must check this when researching courses. However, students who have studied law at A level can find that it gives them a head start at university.

Note that some universities use the National Admissions Test for Law (LNAT) to help them to select candidates you can find out more about this at www.lnat.ac.uk.

## Degree-level study

Law degrees consist of a core of essential topics, which are those you need to take and pass if you want to obtain the maximum exemption from professional examinations. They are:

- obligations (contract)
- obligations (tort)
- criminal law
- public law
- property law
- equity and the law of trusts
- European Union law.

In addition you might take options in family law, commercial law, tax law and environmental law. Some degrees include the legal practice (for solicitors) or Bar exempting courses (for barristers). As well as law degrees leading to a professional qualification, there are a number of other law-related courses such as criminology, human rights and criminal justice. The latter focuses on the people and institutions of the criminal justice system and how they respond to criminal behaviour. These subjects provide a good background for careers in the police, probation and prison services and within the criminal courts. You will also find courses in criminal law.

## Degree subject combinations

The core topics take up approximately half of your time, so it is sometimes possible to obtain full professional exemptions if you study law in combination with another subject. This is something to check carefully as you plan your UCAS applications. Perhaps the most popular subjects to combine with law are those that provide some complementary experience and therefore broaden your career prospects. Examples are politics, economics, sociology, psychology, languages and business studies. Many law degrees now offer a European or wider international perspective, in which you study the law of the European Union, or the law and language of one or more other countries. This is important as increasingly legal practice crosses national boundaries.

## Other higher education qualifications

There are many legal and related foundation degrees available, including law, criminology and criminal justice, policing law and investigation, police studies, legal studies, and paralegal studies and practice.

There are HNDs and HNCs in subjects such as law, business law, legal studies, business and law, and legal practice. Such courses are more vocational than degree courses, and can form a good preparation for a legal career outside the main legal professions as a court or police officer, for example.

Within the legal profession you could go into paralegal jobs, such as a legal executive or secretary, which could eventually lead to part-time study to qualify in law.

## Non-graduate route to law

There is a route to qualifying as a solicitor via the non-graduate Institute of Legal Executives (ILEX) route. This is the route for people who work in legal employment and study part time. It can be followed after A levels, foundation degrees or HNDs.

## Relevance to other subjects?

The law A level develops your ability to think logically, make balanced judgements based upon clear evidence, and understand the social effects and consequences of such judgements. It is a good basis for almost any social science course at a higher level, including sociology, psychology, politics, economics or business studies. Your practice in essay writing and mastering factual information would make you a good candidate for other subjects such as history, geography, English or classics.

## Important advice

Take this A level because you are fascinated by the subject not because you are thinking ahead to the career possibilities. Be aware that there is a range of approaches to law at universities, with a spectrum stretching from black letter law (the basic principles of law which are generally accepted and undisputed) degrees to welfare rights law, so you must research courses before applying.

Although law is an academic subject, it requires students to consider the practical effect of the theory by applying it to real-life situations. Go and sit in the public gallery at a local court to appreciate the impact that law has on everyday life. If you can, get some work experience with a law firm or lawyer.

# Future careers

## ▷After A levels

You won't come away from the law A level as a fully qualified lawyer. However, the course does provide valuable background knowledge if you want to work for a law firm in a support role and train part time. There are Higher Apprenticeships in legal practice that can lead to paralegal and legal qualifications.

## ▷After a degree

### Working in law

To specialise within the field of law it is necessary to gain additional qualifications after your degree:

- **barristers**–represent their clients in the courts. They must first take the one-year, full-time Bar Professional Training Course (BPTC), followed by a pupillage (apprenticeship) within a set of chambers for at least one more year.
- **solicitors**–draw up contracts, assess cases, provide advice and recommend courses of action to clients. First they must take the one-year Legal Practice Course (if they have a law degree) followed by a training contract with a law firm. Non-law graduates have to study for a Common Professional Examination (CPE) or a Graduate Diploma in Law (GDL) then follow the law graduate route.
- **paralegals**–legal support staff work under the direction of solicitors. There is currently no legal requirement for a paralegal to have legal qualifications, but most law firms want their paralegals to be law or LPC graduates.
- **conveyancers**–these are specialised property lawyers, drawing up and transferring leases or deeds for houses etc. You would need to do further study to become licensed.
- **the police**–the police force is a possibility and as a police officer you would apply your legal knowledge on a day-to-day basis. There are also administrative and specialist support jobs within the police.

### Working outside law

A law degree is well respected for many business or management careers. For example, all limited companies must have a company secretary, who has to take on a number of legal responsibilities. You might choose to enter another profession such as accountancy or human resources where knowledge of law could prove useful.

## Sources of information

www.barcouncil.org.uk

www.ilex.org.uk

www.theiop.org

The Law Society
www.lawsociety.org.uk

www.lawcareers.net

www.lnat.ac.uk

www.skillsforjustice.com

> 'Go to your local magistrates court and sit in the public gallery. It will give you an instant introduction to law. That's what hooked me.' Valerie, studying a BA in law

# Leisure studies

*The leisure industry is fast growing and ever changing, covering everything from theme parks, cinemas and museums to leisure centres, outward bound activities, fitness centres and spas. The course gives you an in-depth understanding of all aspects of leisure, both from the point of view of industry professionals and from the customers perspective. You will study the structure of the industry, leisure facilities, lifestyles and lifestyle management, and current issues in leisure. The course combines research, investigation and practical application to a wide range of leisure situations and prepares you for a career in the industry either through higher education or straight into employment. It also equips you with interpersonal and practical transferable skills that will be invaluable in any career.*

## What do you study?

*This A level is offered as a double award by AQA (12 units) and a single award (six units) by OCR and Edexcel. Check with schools and college to see what options are available to you.*

**The leisure industry today**–how the leisure industry works, what career paths are available, and how the industry might develop in the future.

**A people business**–investigating why customer service is so important and how interpersonal skills are used in dealing successfully with customers. You will learn about the leisure customer, how to handle complaints and how to measure, monitor and evaluate customer service procedures and practices.

**Leisure industry practice**–safe working practices in the leisure industry; marketing and budgeting; quality measures and key business systems used in leisure organisations.

**Working in leisure**–exploring the employment and training opportunities within the industry. You will cover human resources issues such as recruitment and selection and motivation of the workforce.

**Current issues**–investigating factors currently affecting the industry and analysing how they will affect the industry in the future.

Here are some examples of the other options that may be available to you:

- fitness training for sport
- leisure and the media
- leisure in the community
- lifestyles and lifestyle management
- outdoor leisure
- event management.

You might also have the chance to gain industry-related qualifications such as first aid, sports leaders, YMCA gym instructing or coaching awards, which will help you gain employment.

You will go on study visits to leisure and recreation sites. You may take part in activities such as coaching a group of young people, or outdoor adventure activities to give you an insight into how they are organised. In addition, there will be work experience, work shadowing, links with local employers, case studies and research, as well as practical projects.

## Subject combinations
Physical education, psychology, business studies, travel and tourism, modern languages or geography all combine well.

# Higher education options

## Degree-level study
There are sport and leisure management degrees and you also find them combined with related subjects like events management, or tourism and hospitality. There are specialised leisure degrees, for example entertainment management (where you might specialise in music or nightclub promotion, marketing, theatre or artist management), adventure sports and management, adventure and extreme sports management and spa management. Many courses offer a compulsory or optional sandwich placement and some have links with universities abroad, offering overseas placements.

## Degree subject combinations
It is possible to study a number of combinations of subjects, especially if you consider a combined or modular course. There are some directly related combinations like sports development but there are many other subjects such as geography, English, languages, media, history, business studies or computing.

## Other higher education qualifications
There is a wide choice of foundation degrees available including: health and leisure studies, leisure and hospitality, hospitality and tourism management, tourism management, sport and leisure management, leisure and events management, outdoor leisure management, health and personal training, spa management, outdoor adventure education, adventure tourism management, crowd safety management, cruise

industry management, event management, equine business and event management, golf management, sports development, and venues, events and hospitality management.

There are HND and HNC courses available providing a mix of practical experience and theory. Examples of courses are, sport and leisure management, hospitality management, and travel and tourism management.

### Relevance to other subjects?

There are many related areas to consider including hospitality and tourism or business and management. Psychology is another option and there are degrees combining sport and leisure with psychology and education, as well as degrees in sport psychology.

### Important advice

Try to get some work experience in the industry as this will give you a good insight into the work. Think about getting some industry-related qualifications in, for example, lifeguarding, sports coaching and leadership. It is also important to look carefully into higher education courses in leisure, sports studies and recreation as they vary a great deal. Some sports science courses, for example, may ask for a science A or AS level.

## Future careers

### ▷After A levels

An A level in leisure studies is a good foundation for a range of jobs in sports and leisure centres, local government, and leisure and recreation businesses. There are opportunities to go straight into the industry in jobs such as health and fitness instructor, personal trainer, pool lifeguard, leisure or sports centre assistant, sports retail, outdoor education tutor, coach, play leader, or jobs in administration within the industry. There would also be opportunities in the Armed Forces. For some of these jobs you will need further training, for example, an NVQ in exercise and fitness to become a fitness instructor. Apprenticeships will offer training towards these qualifications and career development training from professional bodies such as the Chartered Institute for the Management of Sport and Physical Activity (CIMSPA). Investigate Advanced Level and Higher Apprenticeships in leisure and hospitality. You might even be able to work your way up to degree level study via this route.

## ▷After a degree

## Working in leisure

The industry has expanded rapidly in recent years and this is likely to increase, especially with the growth in health spas, fitness centres and active lifestyles. Consumer expenditure on sports and leisure has doubled in the last decade and this has led to an increase in opportunities and jobs in health and fitness clubs, leisure centres and sports clubs.

Apart from trainee management jobs there are positions in the marketing, public relations, sales and sponsorship sides of the industry, which could involve working in a head office rather than a local centre. There will be opportunities both in the UK and abroad. Skills in this area will be transferable to jobs in the travel and tourism sector. You may find employment with hotel groups, or in jobs like an event organiser. You could also specialise in leisure retail or health and beauty management in places like spas. You will also find openings in the gambling industry, another form of leisure.

## Working outside leisure

You will have gained excellent customer service and communication skills as well as sales and marketing skills. These could be transferred to careers in business, administration and management.

## Sources of information

UK Active
www.ukactive.com

Chartered Institute for the Management of Sport and Physical Activity (CIMSPA)
www.cimspa.co.uk

SkillsActive
www.skillsactive.com

www.leisuremanagement.co.uk

---

*'I like the way you learn skills that you know will be useful in jobs. My work experience at the local pool has been really interesting. I'm getting things to put on my CV all the time.'* Helena, taking A levels in leisure and business studies

---

# Mathematics (including statistics and mechanics)

*Mathematics is a challenging subject and a vital tool that supports the study of other subjects. The A level shows you how mathematics is used to describe and predict a diverse range of things, for example, the way the economy works, the motion of the planets, the speed of a chemical reaction, the behaviour of large groups of people and the way decisions are made in business. Some A level topics follow on from GCSE. You study them in greater depth and then tackle harder and more complicated problems. You will also study new areas, with their own specialised techniques for solving whole new types of problems. Mathematics is a continuous discipline, which means that techniques introduced in one topic must be understood before moving onto the next.*

## What do you study?

*The topics listed give an idea of what could be covered. The exact content of AS and A2 specifications differs according to exam board, so you will need to check with your school or college about the exact modules available to you.*

Mathematics can be divided into two areas: pure and applied. Most courses consist of about half pure mathematics and half applied topics like mechanics, statistics or discrete mathematics. Exam boards allow choice between the areas by providing a range of optional modules. However, although the specification may allow choice, you might have to study what your school or college offers.

These are the main subjects covered:

- *pure mathematics*–algebra, functions and graphs, geometry, trigonometry and vectors, logarithms and powers, linear and quadratic equations, sequences and series, calculus and numerical methods. Pure mathematics is the foundation for much of the work you do in other areas as well as being the starting point for the study of mathematics at a higher level.
- *statistics and probability*–collecting and presenting data, combining probabilities, conditional probability, probability distributions, mean value and spread, frequency tables, cumulative frequency, hypothesis testing, correlation and regression. Statistics is used in all areas of science and the social sciences, including psychology, economics, business studies and management. This topic is good preparation for work or further study in any of these areas, especially as many degree courses include a compulsory module in statistics.

- **mechanics**–description of the way that objects move in terms of distance, speed, acceleration and time and how these are related, the action of forces on stationary and moving objects, momentum and energy, vectors and circular and oscillatory motion. Mechanics is important in physics and engineering and in subjects like architecture, physical geography and environmental science. It is the starting point for the study of more advanced topics at a higher level including relativity and elementary particles.
- **discrete/decision mathematics**–network diagrams, linear programming, route inspection problems, critical path analysis and algorithms. Discrete/decision mathematics is used in economics, management studies and computer science.

In addition there are other A/AS levels in mathematics:
- **further mathematics**–this course is for more able mathematics students who enjoy the subject and have a real flair for mathematics. In further mathematics courses, the ground covered is both broader and more difficult than the ordinary curriculum. In some cases, it consists of taking more of the optional modules in the ordinary curriculum but studying them in greater depth.
- **statistics**–provides a second subject for mathematics students but also an excellent option for anyone wanting to continue with a mathematical subject to at least AS level. A useful choice for degrees where statistics would be useful such as psychology, sociology or business studies.
- **use of mathematics**–involves the application of advanced mathematics in real contexts. It includes the use of computers and graphical calculators. Students are encouraged to apply mathematics in their other studies and interests. It is for students who don't want to undertake a detailed study of mathematics but would find a working knowledge useful in further training or study.
- **quantitative methods**–as maths is becoming so important in many other subjects, this AS level has been formulated to provide students using maths in biology, business studies, chemistry, computer science, geography, IT or psychology with the skills needed to solve the mathematical problems they may encounter in these subjects. It also reflects the growing needs for quantitative skills in employment and everyday life.

Learning mathematics means learning how to use it to solve problems and the only way you can do this is through practice. Classwork involves the teacher explaining new material and then working through examples. You follow this up by tackling new problems, which become more difficult. Some of this work will be done in class, but you should also expect to put in at least five or six hours per week outside lesson time. You do most of your work using pen and paper with the help of calculators (although some modules may be non-calculator) and you will use computers to model systems and try out ideas on a larger scale. Many people find that the change from GCSE to A level mathematics is a big one. As this subject builds continuously on previous work, it can become difficult if you get behind. You must have a very thorough grasp of the fundamentals, so that you can concentrate on the new material.

## Calculators

All the awarding bodies assume that you will use a scientific calculator in some examinations although there will be some non-calculator papers as well. Check with your teachers for advice on which calculators are acceptable.

## Subject combinations

Mathematics is used as a tool in many other subjects, from engineering and physics to social sciences and business. Depending on what you want to do, you can combine it with any other subject. If you are thinking of studying mathematics or a related subject at a higher level, you should think about combining it with a science. Physics is a useful preparation for degree courses that include applied mathematics. As well as overlapping with mathematics in some topic areas, physics also uses mathematics more than any other subject, so it can provide valuable practice and support.

Other sciences, and subjects like economics, also involve mathematics. You might consider further mathematics, as this covers more ground and gives extra depth to your understanding. Further mathematics is for very able mathematicians who want to undertake additional study. A level mathematics and physics are required or preferred for physics and most engineering degrees. If you are interested in these subjects, it is important that mechanics forms part of your A level course. If you intend to study A level biology, psychology, geography, sociology, computer studies, economics or business studies, you will find that the statistics in A level mathematics or statistics will be useful.

# Higher education options

A good pass at A level or equivalent is essential if you want to study mathematics successfully at a higher level. If you do not have mathematics at a high enough level you could consider a foundation year (see below).

There are different types of mathematics degrees apart from the BSc. There is a four or five year degree called MMath. Even though the first M stands for master, this is an undergraduate degree. The degree is intended for those who want a career in mathematics and/or to undertake postgraduate study in maths. The first two years are the same as the BSc, but the final two years are more demanding. If you enter university on one degree you can transfer to the other and as the MMath is tougher than the BSc, students who do not maintain a good average grade in their first two years usually transfer to the BSc in their third year. You will also find MSci degrees, which are comparable with masters level study.

## Degree-level study

Mathematics at degree level is a natural continuation of A level work in some ways. However, the rate at which you cover new material is much faster and degree-level study is more abstract than at A level and more difficult to relate to common experience.

The size of the subject means that most mathematics courses are flexible, particularly in the second and third years. There are also many specialist courses that allow you to concentrate on one area from the start. These include courses in the main areas of the subject, like pure mathematics, applied mathematics and discrete mathematics. Other courses concentrate on particular application areas like engineering mathematics or financial mathematics, mathematical physics and mathematics education (which leads to a teaching qualification in addition to a degree). Some courses offer a year abroad spent studying at another university and some offer industrial placements.

Note that some universities offer a foundation year for those not up to undergraduate level standard in mathematics. If you complete this successfully you can transfer to a mathematics or mathematics-related degree.

## Degree subject combinations

You may want to combine mathematics with a completely different subject to provide variety, but there are also plenty of opportunities to take combined courses in which mathematics and the other subject support and complement each other. Such subjects include physics (there are also specialist mathematical physics courses) or statistics.

## Other higher education qualifications

There are foundation degrees in education and training for maths and numeracy specialist learning assistants in secondary schools (mathematics and education) and in related subjects like accounting, business, engineering and IT. There is an HND in mathematics and computing, again consider related areas such as business, accountancy, engineering and IT.

## Relevance to other subjects?

Mathematics A level is accepted as a good entry qualification for almost any other subject at degree level. It is needed for most physics and engineering courses and is strongly recommended or compulsory for many chemistry courses. Although not always a requirement for courses in biological sciences, it can be very useful, especially if courses contain statistics. Statistics is useful for social science courses such as psychology, geography, sociology, business studies and economics, and is required for some of the more mathematically orientated economics courses. Mathematics is useful for computer science and is compulsory for some of the more theoretical courses.

Mathematics can provide useful support for courses in economics and business studies. A level mathematics can be used as an alternative to A level physics for entry to some courses. For example, the A level requirements for medicine, dentistry and veterinary science are usually for mathematics or physics in addition to chemistry (usually compulsory) and biology (usually recommended).

## Important advice

In order to succeed in mathematics you must work consistently over a long period. You get into a regular routine of work that will allow you to build up your skills and knowledge. If you are considering a gap year before a mathematics degree it is important to check with universities to see how they view it. Some universities feel that you lose continuity in your studies. If you decide to take a gap year, it would be wise to keep up your mathematics during your time out and revise it just before starting your course.

# Future careers

## ▷After A levels

An A level in mathematics is in great demand by employers. Even when a job does not require specific mathematical knowledge, employers find that the discipline learned through studying mathematics helps you think clearly and logically. You will find people with A level mathematics working in areas that make obvious use of mathematical skills, such as accountancy, banks and financial services, but you are equally likely to find them working as a retail manager in a shop or department store, or as a website or computer games designer. Look at Higher Apprenticeships that may be available to you after A levels.

## ▷After a degree

### Working in mathematics

There are many areas where you can use the expertise developed during your degree. These include the following:

- **business, finance and accountancy**–this is the single largest career area for graduates in mathematics and statistics. Accountancy will require further training and there are opportunities in private practice, local and central government and business. Banks and other financial services companies like to recruit mathematics and statistics graduates to their management training schemes
- **IT**–some graduates go into mathematical computing, but the majority go into more general areas such as programming, systems analysis or consultancy
- **actuarial work**–graduates start as trainees and take professional exams
- **management**–mathematical techniques are used as management tools for solving a variety of complex problems in production, distribution, marketing and financial investment
- **technology**–industries such as aerospace, renewable energy and telecommunications employ mathematics graduates for analysing data and working on the design of products or industrial control systems

- **education**–there is a demand for qualified mathematics teachers so you may qualify for financial help with your training
- **research**–nearly 23% of mathematics graduates go on to further study or research in mathematics. However, the number finally making a career in research is very much smaller. Some large companies and government organisations also employ research mathematicians, but again the numbers are small compared to the number of graduates.

## Working outside mathematics

As most jobs involve some use of numerical or financial data, mathematics graduates are well placed in the job market, provided that they can bring other skills like communication, team working and management potential. Many employers are more interested in a mathematicians ability to analyse and solve problems than any specific mathematical training. Employers include local government, the Civil Service and all areas of industry and business.

## Sources of information

PSI (Statisticians in the Pharmaceutical Industry)
www.psiweb.org

www.ima.org.uk

www.rss.org.uk

www.mathscareers.org.uk

www.theorsociety.com

---

'The maths department offers lots of extra help, which I wasn't aware of before I got here; there are weekly maths surgeries where postgrads are available to help you, a scheme where first years can buddy up with a mentor and tutors who are very supportive.' Justin, first year BSc maths

# Media studies

*Media and communications are one of the UK's biggest industries. Media reflects and influences all aspects of our society. In media studies you will gain an understanding of all types of media including film, music, newspapers, radio, magazines, games and social media such as Facebook, blogs and Twitter. You will develop an understanding of media products and how they are researched, produced, distributed and consumed. You will learn theory and critical analysis as well as some of the practical and technical skills involved in producing media products.*

## What do you study?

*The topics listed give an idea of what could be covered. The exact content of AS andA2 specifications differs according to exam boards, so you will need to check with your school or college about the exact modules available to you.*

*Note that there is also a media: communications and production A level offered by Edexcel.*

***Media products and their audiences***–films, TV, radio, newspapers, magazines, games software and web-based media; their target audiences, how they are produced, distributed and consumed by their audiences. The forms and conventions of different media genres, such as broadcast fiction, film fiction, documentary, lifestyle, music, news and sport.

***Media issues***–media regulation, the relationship between the media and society, censorship and violence, advertising, global media, media and collective identity, and media in the online age.

***Key media concepts***–you carry out a textual analysis of a piece of media such as a radio play or TV drama. You will analyse how the piece is put together and different techniques used in the production. For a film this could be camera angles, lighting, and sound and editing techniques.

***Practical techniques***–learning the technical skills to create media products and creating your own. You might create a video, DVD, music jingle or a website.

A GCSE in media studies is not required for this course but you would be expected to be familiar with a wide range of media products.

Practical classes involve learning how to research and create a piece of media. You might make a trailer for a TV soap, documentary or thriller, an advertisement, a short interview or news round-up for a radio broadcast, a design for a new womens magazine or create a website. When you are presenting results of any research or project you will use appropriate technologies such as a PowerPoint presentation, a blog, a podcast or a DVD or memory stick with extras.

## Subject combinations

Media studies complements many other A levels because it covers such a wide range of subjects. If you are thinking of studying media at a higher level, then English, communication and culture, sociology and psychology could prove useful. For practical courses in media production, it may be an advantage to have an art and design A level, or even maths and sciences for the more technical courses.

# Higher education options

An A level in media studies is not required in order to study the subject at a higher level.

## Degree-level study

Courses in media studies vary greatly. You will find some are more general humanities type courses and others are more practical. Many institutions offer practical courses in subjects such as digital media and media production (some media production courses have specialisms such as scriptwriting and radio). Note that some courses might ask for either an Art Foundation course and/or a portfolio for entry. There are also sandwich courses available with a placement in industry which could prove very helpful for your CV/portfolio.

You will also find more specialist courses such as journalism, broadcast journalism or social media. If you don't want to specialise at first degree level there are opportunities for postgraduate study in media specialisms such as journalism.

## Degree subject combinations

The subjects most widely available in combination with media studies are English, history and politics. If you want to get a job in the media, which can be difficult, it would be a good idea to combine media studies with a subject that might help you to get a start in your career, such as business studies, politics, modern languages, the digital industries or sciences. You can take media studies as part of a modular course, allowing you to study a wide range of other subjects.

## Other higher education qualifications

There are foundation degrees available in media, media practice and media production. You will also find lots of related courses such as business and media production, broadcast media, commercial video with multimedia, computer games and interactive media, creative film and moving image production, editorial and news media design, digital media and marketing, film and media production, interactive media and web analytics, journalism and practical media, live television production, media advertising, media writing with production, radio production, social media, sound and music for new media, television production, and visual media production.

Media studies can be taken at HND or HNC level and courses include creative media production, interactive media, media technology, film-making, practical journalism and interactive media games art and animation.

## Relevance to other subjects?

Media studies A level helps you to develop useful skills relevant to a number of other subjects. Your ability to analyse and criticise visual, written and audio information in relation to cultural and social factors would help with subjects such as English, history of art, drama and theatre studies, design courses, archaeology, anthropology, philosophy and modern languages. Your understanding of the political and social influences at work in the media would also help you in the study of most social science courses, such as sociology, psychology, politics or history.

## Important advice

There are many media courses on offer. If you are even remotely considering a career in the media, you should make sure that the course you choose offers the balance that you want between practical and theoretical work. It is a good idea to check out the range of practical facilities offered, such as recording equipment and editing facilities. Make sure you research the destinations of graduates from your chosen courses and check what links they have with employers.

If you are interested in studying a non-media related subject at a higher level, you should make sure that the universities or colleges you are considering will accept media studies. Don't forget that if you are planning a career in the media you should be building up experience now, even if it is on the school website or hospital radio. Also networking is key to a media career so start building up your networks now.

# Future careers

## ▷After A levels

Media studies is useful in many areas of work, particularly if they involve communication and up-to-date media knowledge. The media industries are difficult to get into, so your A level won't guarantee you entry. Unless you are prepared to start at the bottom as, for example, an office assistant or runner and work your way up, you will need further qualifications and experience. In media you will need to be good at networking and making the right contacts to progress in your career. There are apprenticeships in creative and digital media offered through Creative Skillset.

## ▷After a degree

### Working in the media

It is hard for media studies graduates to get started in media. Any contacts made during your degree may eventually become useful to you so it is important to keep networking and get as much relevant work experience as you can, to build up your CV/portfolio. Organisations such as the BBC offer work experience placements and you may be able to arrange your own work placement or internship. If you are hoping to enter TV or film production, you should be prepared to get further training, or to start in a junior position. You may have to arrange and finance extra training yourself to get you the right skills and knowledge.

Don't forget that the media industry is a very broad one and covers not only the obvious jobs in journalism, interactive media, film and TV. There are also opportunities in animation, computer games, advertising, facilities (specialist technical services to film and TV), photo imaging and publishing.

Here are some examples of popular jobs in the media:
- **talented creatives in advertising**–they are always in demand, as they provide an essential source of imaginative ideas in the creation and selling of products
- **journalism**–in radio, TV, newspapers, magazines or digital/social media
- **production/broadcasting assistants**–in film and television they help to run the producers and directors offices, involved in programmes from planning to post- production

- **technicians**–technical jobs arranging lighting or sound in studios or on location for outside broadcasts
- **researchers**–these work mainly on factual research for programmes, including films and documentaries.

## Working outside the media

There are many career areas where you could make use of your knowledge and skills. Your understanding of how images are created and the effect that they have on consumers would be useful in public relations. Marketing may also be a good choice, as it involves identifying the kind of product that the public would like to buy, and managing the packaging, advertising and selling of that product. You will have developed good communication and teamwork skills, which could be applied to many areas of business.

## Sources of information

www.bbc.co.uk/jobs

www.bfi.org.uk/education

www.bima.co.uk

www.creativeskillset.org/careers

www.digital-apprentice.co.uk

www.filmnationuk.org

www.itvjobs.com

www.ukfilmcouncil.org.uk

'Make sure you do your research thoroughly before you finally decide on a course. Go to as many open days as you can and look at the facilities. Don't forget there are virtual open days if you can't get there. Don't be afraid of just emailing or ringing up universities for information and advice.' Josie, aged 25, working in PR after a broadcast journalism degree

# Modern foreign languages

*It has been predicted that the top five languages spoken by 2050 will be Chinese, Spanish, English, Hindi-Urdu and Arabic, and that out of these, the most widely used in business will be Chinese, Spanish and English.*

*Whatever you might make of these predictions, neglecting languages in business means ignoring significant potential markets. Apart from the business aspect, language study not only gives you language and communication skills, but also a way of understanding a society and its culture. It is also interesting to note that the internet is not all in English, with the top five languages being English, Chinese, Spanish, Japanese and Portuguese.*

A range of modern foreign languages is available at A level, including French, German, Spanish, Russian, Italian, Greek, Japanese, Chinese, Polish, Turkish, Arabic and Urdu.

You are expected to develop a much deeper understanding of how the language works than at GCSE. You are encouraged to learn languages within the context of the culture, society and way of life of the countries where they are spoken, including current issues affecting the country. You might also focus on how the language is used in business; the top business languages required by UK employers are currently Mandarin Chinese, French, German, Spanish, Polish, Russian, Arabic, Portuguese, Japanese and Korean.

**Mandarin** is one of the fastest growing languages in the world. With over a billion speakers, in China and other nations, it is quickly becoming one of the most popular second languages particularly amongst professionals. More businesses are now expanding into China or using suppliers and manufacturers within the country, which means that there are more opportunities for multi-lingual employees.

While many people focus on the up and coming economies around the world, you shouldnt ignore the benefit of learning core European languages, including French, German, and Spanish. As well as being the important languages within the Eurozone, all have a global reach, covering the Americas and Africa.

**French** is the most popular choice. France is one of our nearest neighbours and for a country so close, French culture, philosophy, literature and view on life are quite different from our own. Studying French brings you into close contact with the country's traditions and gives you direct access to its rich literary and artistic traditions.

Becoming fluent in French you won't just be able to converse with professionals in France, but also in parts of Canada, North and West African nations like Cameroon or Senegal and Switzerland.

**Germany** is a centre for finance and manufacturing in Europe, so many businesses in the UK and throughout the world have established trade links in the country. So, just as with any language, it can be hugely advantageous to develop proficient German skills, particularly if you are looking to develop within your career. German has many similarities to English, and some English learners find it easier to pronounce than French. One major difference between German and either English or French is that German grammar makes more use of inflection changes of word ending to indicate a change in meaning (as in English singular and plural, for example). This means that getting started can seem more difficult than with a language like French, but once you are over this hurdle, you can progress at a similar rate. Once you have the basics, German can provide you with an understanding of a culture with a complex political history and a rich literary, musical and dramatic tradition. It is also spoken by some eastern Europeans.

**Spanish** is a language that you may find quite easy, especially if you have already studied French (although it gets more difficult later). It is the world's fourth most widely spoken language (after Chinese, Hindi and English) and has the advantage of opening up the language and literature of most of Latin America as well as Spain. Spanish is an important language in the USA as well. Equally, the Spanish language has travelled throughout the world, most notably in South and Central America where it is still the predominant language.

**Italian**, like Spanish, will be easier for you to learn if you have already started French. It is perhaps less likely than French, Spanish or German to be useful to you in your career (it has fewer speakers than the big three) but is still an important business and cultural language.

**Russian** is another language that has experienced huge growth in recent years, closely mirroring the increased trade with businesses in Russia, Kazakhstan and other surrounding nations. As demand for Russian speaking experts increases, so too does the value placed on developing fluent language skills. Like China, Russia has grown to become a centre for many burgeoning industries, particularly gas and oil production. Companies from around the world are flocking to former Soviet states to establish business links and broker deals, adding further value to mastering the Russian language. Russian is more difficult than the other frequently taught languages, not least because it has a different alphabet. However, most learners soon master this and find it to be a rewarding language to learn.

**Polish** has become popular since Poland joined the EU. Many Poles work in the UK, and UK citizens are setting up businesses and buying property in Poland.

You might want to consider one of the non-European languages now available at A level. As well as providing the opportunity to study cultures outside Europe, they open up many employment opportunities. This is particularly the case for languages connected with areas of economic importance like India and the Far East.

## What do you study?

*The topics listed give an idea of what could be covered. The exact content of AS and A2 specifications differs according to exam boards, so you will need to check with your school or college about the exact modules available to you.*

Command of a second language is usually broken down into four skills writing, reading, speaking and listening (understanding the spoken language).

**Writing** the ability to communicate in the written language using the appropriate style and form for the communication required. This may involve tasks such as writing a reply to a formal or informal letter, job applications or writing a promotional leaflet. You may be expected to express your ideas in the form of essays and short-answer questions on a wide range of topics including social issues, the arts, education or literature, written in your chosen language.

**Speaking** the ability to express yourself clearly and correctly through spoken language. You will be encouraged to develop a wide vocabulary and practise speaking in the language as often as possible in order to develop a comfortable and grammatically accurate style. All specifications require an oral exam, and you will be given plenty of practice at taking part in general conversation as well as speaking on specific topics.

**Reading** you will be encouraged to read texts regularly in your chosen language. Some of these may be literary texts in the form of plays, poetry or prose. You will read newspapers and magazines in the chosen language to develop your vocabulary and comprehension. You will be tested, mainly in the chosen language, with comprehension questions of various types.

Some demand short answers or are multiple-choice questions, but others require more extensive writing. One purpose of this is to demonstrate your understanding of what you read; in the case of literary work, your appreciation is assessed as well as your understanding.

*Listening* gaining skills in listening and understanding the language, including its informal use by native speakers. This is usually done using material taken from the media such as radio, satellite TV, cinema, DVDs or the internet. While working on all these skills you learn about the society, culture, education, institutions and economy of the country or countries where the language is spoken. The exams will effectively test your knowledge of these issues as well as your command of the language. Study of literature is a smaller item in the specifications than it used to be, having largely been replaced by the study of present-day society and issues. However, literature including that of the past is itself a part of society and most students will study some texts.

Unless you are a native speaker of the language in question, a good pass (GCSE at grade A or B) in the language is usually required in order to take the A level. Some schools offer languages for beginners at A level.

There are many ways that you can spend your time in class when learning a language: this is partly because different ways of learning reinforce each other, and variety helps to cater for your learning style. You will work individually and in groups with written texts from newspapers and magazines and multimedia recordings. You will watch recorded pro-grammes and films and then discuss them, working on the vocabulary that you learn and the grammatical points that they illustrate. Outside class, there is a good deal of time spent committing things to memory especially vocabulary. There may be the opportunity to go on a trip to the relevant country or you may be able to go on an exchange programme and live in the country for a while.

## Subject combinations

If you are thinking of specialising in modern foreign languages at degree level, you may prefer to make an early start by studying two languages for A level (although you can nearly always start a second language as a beginner at degree level). If you take two languages, you should find that the skills and knowledge relating to the workings of one language will help you with the other. This is also the case if you combine a modern foreign language with an A level in classical/ ancient Greek or Latin. You could combine a language with many other subjects including business, ICT and sciences.

# Higher education options

There are opportunities to study language degrees without having an A level in the language and you will learn the subject from scratch (also known as *ab initio*). However, for French degrees virtually all institutions require A level French (a few will accept an A level in another language). The same applies to a lesser extent to German and Spanish. For other languages universities will expect students to be beginners. However, a language A level, even in a different language, will help as it proves you have language learning skills and experience.

## Degree-level study

Language study at degree level varies considerably from one place to another. At some, you would find a big difference from your A level studies as you would spend a large proportion of your time studying literature. At others, the focus remains on practical language use and the study of contemporary society.

A popular option is to build on your existing skills and knowledge by continuing with your A level language and starting a new one alongside it. At some institutions you can choose from a wide range of languages that may not have been available to you at A level, such as Scandinavian languages, Portuguese, Arabic, Chinese, Japanese or African languages.

Another option is a regional studies course, which allows you to study one or two modern foreign languages alongside the economic, political, social, legal and cultural climates of that country or region. European studies is the most widely offered but there are also emerging degrees in Asia Pacific studies and Latin American studies. It is assumed that you already have a strong grasp of your major chosen language, unless it wasn't available to you at A level.

On nearly all language degrees you will spend some time abroad. This is usually the third of your four years. The way that you spend this year depends in part on your own preference, but also on the arrangements that have been developed over the years. For example, students going to France are most likely to work as an English language assistant in a secondary school or college, while those going to Russia usually spend their time on special courses of study at a university. However, opportunities to work as an employee in a business or similar organisation are also possible.

## Degree subject combinations

Modern foreign languages can be usefully combined with a wide range of other subjects. With increasing economic, political and cultural contacts throughout the world, a carefully chosen combination can increase your employment options. Economics, business studies, engineering, marketing, politics, a science subject or law could be particularly appropriate. Combined subject degrees are available almost everywhere. Some institutions have created specialised European or international degrees in subjects such as engineering, sciences and law (where you may study French or German law and language, or European Union law, as well as English law). In these, your language study is more likely to be integrated with your study of the other subject than it is in a standard two-subject degree course. You will find specialised combined degrees to cater for emerging markets: Chinese, for example, can be combined with business management and marketing.

## Other higher education qualifications

There are no foundation degrees in modern foreign languages but some HNDs and HNCs in tourism management offer options in modern foreign languages.

## Chartered Institute of Linguists qualifications

The Chartered Institute of Linguists runs qualifications in translating and interpreting. These can be studied full or part time.

## Relevance to other subjects?

Even if you decide not to study modern foreign languages by themselves at a higher level, you will find your study valuable. A knowledge of a modern foreign language at A level would help in the study of English, especially English language, history, politics and philosophy. If you are interested not just in one or two languages but language in general, you might consider a degree in linguistics, in which you study the development of human language: its structures, history and use. Since linguistics study must be backed up with examples from particular languages, knowledge of a modern foreign language will be very useful to you; you can also combine language study with linguistics.

## Important advice

No matter how much classroom work you do, there is no substitute for experiencing a language first hand. Try to visit a country where your chosen language is spoken and spend time listening to it and speaking it, as well as absorbing the country's culture. It's easy to listen to the radio on the internet and this can only help you with your studies. Nearly all universities have language centres, so even if you decide not to study your languages as part of a degree, you are likely to have the opportunity to continue your studies part time at a university language centre.

# Future careers

### ▷After A levels

You will find the level of language that you achieve with A level study is an advantage when you apply for practically any sort of job, especially with companies trading internationally. There are some opportunities to go straight from A levels into a job where your language skills will be used every day, such as working for an airline as cabin crew or ground staff, or within the travel industry, perhaps as a rep for tour companies at home or abroad. You must try to maintain and improve your language skills as they can get rusty. Also languages are constantly evolving so you need to learn new words as they arise.

### ▷After a degree

### Working in modern foreign languages

Language-based careers are a popular choice for language graduates. You normally have to undertake further specialist training if you wish to become a professional linguist. There are three traditional language-based career roles interpreters, translators or teachers. These can be combined in a number of careers:

- *interpreters*–these translate the spoken language, normally into their own mother tongue. Interpreters provide an essential link between businesses or governments during negotiations or they may work translating for foreign nationals abroad. The work may be face-to-face or over the telephone. This kind of work requires further training and fluency in two foreign languages, preferably including a degree in an unusual language. There is a shortage of interpreters with English as their first language and two other languages, especially in the UN and European Parliament.
- *translators*–these work with the written language and the normal practice is to translate into the native language from the second language, not vice versa. They are often self-employed and work

mainly for businesses. Some translators group together to form agencies offering translation in a wide range of languages.

- **teachers**–language teachers are always in demand so the more subjects or languages you are able to teach, the more valuable you are likely to be.

- **linguists**–within the Diplomatic Service, linguists can be both translators and interpreters. They may find themselves working in the UK or within an embassy abroad, where they play an important part in daily communication between countries and the trading, cultural and political decisions that are made.

- **travel and tourism**–there are many opportunities here, whether you are working in the UK or abroad, ranging from tour guide to management positions. You could be using your languages on a daily basis and your knowledge of the country and culture to help you communicate effectively

Apart from these jobs, in a recently survey it emerged that 74% of employers want language skills. Here are some examples of jobs where languages will be useful:

- **computer games translator**–translating computer games into other languages

- **website translators**–more and more websites are multi-lingual or need to have a version for different language speakers

- **football analyst**–watching and analysing the latest European football matches and producing reports on the failures and successes of the team. These are passed on to traders to aid investors in betting more successfully

- **international relocation manager**–working for large international companies to help staff relocate to new countries. You organise housing, schools for their children and removals

- **group tour organiser**–organising tours for musical groups like orchestras or theatre companies; organising and booking venues, hotels and transport

- **journalist**–using your language skills to research and write articles for magazines

- **press conference assistant**–interpreting for foreign language speakers at press conferences. Think of all the football players and managers who may need this service

- **recruitment consultant**–recruiting globally in a wide range of employment sectors.

You will find languages skills in demand in most areas of work. Examples of areas using languages skills include: IT, creative and media, national and local government, hospitably and tourism, manufacturing, construction, property management, engineering, finance and business.

## Working outside modern foreign languages

Graduate linguists are good candidates for most jobs open to graduates in any subject as they are flexible thinkers, imaginative and creative. They also have an understanding and appreciation of other cultures. Many find that they do not use their languages at the start of their career for example, they may be engaged in general management training. If they maintain their language skills there could be opportunities to use them later on.

## Sources of information

www.iol.org.uk

www.whystudylanguages.ac.uk

www.ilovelanguages.com

www.thirdyearabroad.com

---

'In an increasingly competitive job market, proficiency in a foreign language can give you added value when applying for jobs.' Mike, graduate recruitment consultant

---

# Music

*If you are a keen musician, this course gives you the chance to develop your musical abilities and knowledge in a wide variety of ways. You will be able to demonstrate your skills in musical performance and study musical theory, composition and the history of music. Some specifications allow you to study world music, folk music, jazz, and music for film and TV as well as the classical music of Western European cultures. Students learn to work together well in addition to developing performing, composing and critical or analytical skills. The course is valued by employers and universities because it develops versatility, creative ability and good communication skills.*

## What do you study?

*Music A level specifications are broadly alike, but have different emphases within them. Most allow you to choose where you want to place the emphasis of your own studies. You study a number of the following, depending on the course options you choose. Some offer different pathways for composers and performers.*

- **Listening**–developing your ability to listen to and analyse music through a variety of exercises such as dictation, analysis of performance errors and stylistic description of samples of music.

- **Performing**–preparing a recital lasting between 5 and 16 minutes (depending on the exam board), there may also be ensemble playing and technology-based performances.

- **Analysis and appreciation of the elements of music**–learning about musical structures and techniques such as sonata form, rhythm, harmony and counterpoint (the combination of two or more simultaneous melodies, as in a fugue).

- **History of music**–studying topics relating to the music of a particular period or type. Examples of topics set include music for film and television, popular music and jazz, and the Western classical tradition. Other topics include 18th/early 19th century orchestra, jazz 1920 to 1960, solo instrumental chamber or orchestral repertoire from the period 1700 to 1830 and popular instrumental music from 1900 to the present day. The scope of a topic is often quite wide, since it includes the influences of music from other periods or countries on the music in your study.

- **Composing**–learning the techniques of musical composition, partly through the imitation of styles, in which you have a degree of choice. Examples of styles might include choral harmonisations in the style of J.S. Bach, keyboard accompaniment in the

211

early Romantic style, minimalism or more recent developments such as the popular song, folk, club dance, hip-hop, musical theatre and world music. As well as composing, you will carry out exercises in arrangement the preparation of a given piece of music for a particular instrument or group of instruments. Your work will be submitted for the exam in the form of a folio and/or a recorded version, and you may be required to write a commentary on your work. Some exam boards require composition as part of a formal examination.

A good grade (B or above) in GCSE music may be required before you can study the A level. You will be expected to play a musical instrument to a certain standard, which can vary between Associated Board of the Royal Schools of Music grade 4 and 6, depending on your school or college.

In some ways, music is like a language. You have to learn how it is put together (techniques such as harmony and types of musical form) and how it conveys feelings, mental images and moods. As with learning a language, improvement comes largely from exposure and lots of practice. Much of your time will be spent listening to music, discussing and analysing what you have heard and developing your ability to listen actively. Your ability to analyse different pieces of music depends on your experience of a wide variety of different types of music, so as well as your set work you should go to as many live music events as possible. If your course involves performance, you will have to spend quite a lot of time practising your instrument or instruments.

### Subject combinations

Music can be combined with any other A level. If you are thinking of studying music in higher education, especially if you are thinking of a singing career, languages are very useful. If you are considering a course in music technology or electronic music, mathematics, physics or computing will be useful.

## Higher education options

A good pass in A level music is usually required in order to be able to study it at a higher level. For many courses you have to pass a performance test and/or offer a pass at a high level (usually grade 8) in the Associated Board of the Royal Schools of Music graded examinations.

## Degree-level study

Depending on your interests you can take a music degree course at university, where you will be studying alongside students in other disciplines, or at a music college (conservatoire), which is geared more towards performance.

Music courses usually lead to either a BA (Bachelor of Arts) or BMus (Bachelor of Music) degree. The BMus is much the same as a BA but when an institution offers both a BA and a BMus, the BA is typically broader in scope while the BMus concentrates more on composition, history or performance. You should check the course details carefully. You would probably spend the first two years of a music degree course developing the skills and knowledge that you gained at A level, your understanding of music theory and history, and your performance skills. In the final year, you have the chance to concentrate on the aspects of music that you find most interesting.

Your specialised options might include the study of a particular period of musical history, works written for choirs, the piano, stringed instruments or another family of instruments; non-classical music, such as jazz or rock; or the use of computers in music composition. Some institutions also offer the chance to spend part of your time studying abroad in a conservatoire or university.

There are also degrees concentrating on specialist areas like popular music, song writing, music production and musical theatre.

**Conservatoires:** as mentioned earlier, these offer more performance-based degrees and have a separate application and selection process.
- Birmingham Conservatoire
- Leeds College of Music
- Royal Academy of Music
- Royal College of Music
- Royal Conservatoire of Scotland
- Royal Northern College of Music
- Royal Welsh College of Music and Drama
- Trinity Laban Conservatoire of Music and Dance

The Guildhall School of Music and Drama does not recruit through CUKAS. Applicants should apply direct.

You can research courses on the Conservatoires UK Admissions Service (CUKAS) website, www.cukas.ac.uk.

## Degree subject combinations

University-based courses give you the opportunity to study music as part of a combined degree scheme or modular course, with a wide range of other subjects. You might consider a performing arts or creative arts course, in which you can usually study a combination of drama, music and visual art. Alternatively, you can combine music with any other subject including business, maths, English, history or modern languages. You could also study music education if you wish to teach.

## Other higher education qualifications

There are foundation degrees in music, commercial music, community music, creating music performance, applied music practice, music (performance and production), music performance (heavy metal), music performance (popular music), music composition for film and media, music technology, song writing and DJ and electronic music.

HNDs and HNCs are available in music performance, music business, music production, music technology, sound engineering and urban and electronic music.

## Relevance to other subjects?

An A level in music doesn't have to lead to a music course at a conservatoire or university. Many people find that their musical knowledge and understanding of the language of music is extremely useful in subjects such as drama, modern foreign languages, philosophy, linguistics and communication studies. There are also specialised music technology courses and music industry business courses.

## Important advice

The selection procedure for a higher level course in music can be very tough. You may be required to reach a performance level equivalent to the Grade 8 practical music examination. If you do not have this, you might be asked to submit a certified audio or video recording of your performance for review, as evidence of equivalence. In addition to a general interview, you may be asked to perform a piece of music and to take a listening test and a sight-reading test, or something similar. Find out whether you are likely to have to attend a practical audition.

# Future careers

## ▷After A levels

An A level in music may not lead directly to a music career but it can give you an advantage in careers where musical knowledge would be useful. Provided you don't mind starting at the bottom and doing junior jobs like running errands and making the tea, you might find work in the recording industry, for a music magazine or website, or at a radio station. There may also be apprenticeships in the music business. A level music can be used as a general qualification for entry to careers in many businesses or organisations.

## ▷After a degree

### Working in music

Many careers relating to music involve additional training and experience before they can really take off properly. These include the following:

- **performing**—as a soloist, part of a small ensemble or larger orchestra, or as a piano accompanist for other performers. This sort of work requires a very high standard, continual practice and often unsocial working hours. There is also a good deal of competition and you will have to take whatever work you can get. If you have the relevant experience and ability, you may be able to supplement your performing income with private or school teaching.
- **media**—there is an increasing demand for music of all types for broadcasting on radio, TV and the internet, and therefore a number of career opportunities in the areas of presenting, writing (for computer games, for example) and in music technology generally.
- **teaching**—including private tuition to individual students, as well as class teaching in schools. For teaching in state schools, you will need a recognised teaching qualification. You may also gain work as a peripatetic teacher, moving round to different schools to give lessons.
- **music technician**—as a technician rather than a performer, you might be responsible for sound quality or technical equipment either in the recording studio or as part of a team at a performance.

- **music business management**—organising performances, contracts, rehearsals and publicity on behalf of musicians. You might work for a large symphony orchestra, jazz band or pop band.
- **composing**—not many people earn a living as composers and usually build up their careers gradually. They might work on commissions awarded by advertisers or television and radio producers, often spending weeks working painstakingly on pieces lasting only 15 seconds.
- **music therapy**—working with adults and children with injuries or disabilities, making use of both the physical skills and emotional dimension of music to develop or restore peoples abilities. You would need a further qualification for this.

## Working outside music

Because of the option to teach, quite a high proportion of music graduates do work professionally in music after they graduate. Some use their practical skills and knowledge in other careers. Some of these will have a connection with music, including arts administration, libraries and publishing. Others take further training and enter completely different careers.

## Sources of information

British Association for Music Therapy
www.bamt.org

Incorporated Society of Musicians
www.ism.org

www.creative-choices.co.uk

http://getintomusic.org/

---

'It was great to have the opportunity to explore and learn about music from around the world as well as different historical periods and styles. The fact that you are being taught by staff who are leaders in their areas of study is inspiring, because they pass their enthusiasm on to you.'
Judith, BMus graduate

---

# Music technology

*Technology in music is now part of our everyday lives. It is used in all areas of music from classical through to hip hop, grime and grindie. Music technology teaches you how to use this technology to arrange and compose music. The A level gives you the opportunity to develop your musical abilities, study composition and arrangement, and acquire skills in sequencing and multi-track recording.*

*Music technology A level is part of the A level music curriculum. In order to get onto the course, you must be able to play an instrument to a reasonable standard. Schools and colleges have varying requirements but, in general, it ranges from Associated Board of the Royal Schools of Music grades 4 to 6 with a reasonable knowledge of music theory, usually at grade 3 or higher. GCSE music may be a requirement unless students have previous experience. No experience in music technology is required.*

## What do you study?

*The topics listed give an idea of what could be covered. The exact content of AS and A2 specifications differs according to exam boards, so you will need to check with your school or college about the exact modules available to you.*

*Sequencing, recording and producing*—learning the skills required to produce accomplished musical performances in a range of styles using sequencing software, and using the processes of multi-track recording to produce finished mixes in a range of musical styles. You will also learn how to record live instruments.

*Arranging and improvisation*—this involves taking a motif or melody and developing it into a full arrangement to be presented as a score or finished recording on CD.

*Composing using technology*—developing the ability to use computer software and multi-track recording techniques to create compositions to a brief.

*Listening and analysing*—the study of the styles most common in popular music through listening. You study the development of popular music styles from 1910 through to the present day. These styles and trends range historically from ragtime and Dixieland jazz through to recent developments in club music and electronica. You develop the ability to analyse the musical, technical and stylistic features of music and consider the impact of technology on music.

Other topics you might study include popular music covering areas such as rock and roll, rap and hip hop, reggae, heavy rock, soul, indie rock, punk and new wave and club dance. You might also study music for the moving image, which includes music for films and television, and words and music (the relationship between words and music).

Much of your time is spent in practical study, creating recordings and sequencing using a range of technology. You will have the opportunity to record original compositions and develop arrangements from lead lines and short motifs. Outside class, you should spend as much time as possible listening to a broad selection of music, learning to recognise the musical structure and the technology used.

## Subject combinations

If you wish to study music technology at a higher level, you should select other A levels from mathematics, physics, ICT, electronics or music depending on the content and requirements of the course. Some courses will require music A level in addition to music technology, or require you to reach a certain standard of performance (which could include an audition).

# Higher education options

## Degree-level study

Music technology is a popular area of study and attracts students from both musical and technical backgrounds who want to learn about both cutting-edge technical and creative developments in the field. There is a variety of degrees available with varying titles including music technology, creative music technology, creative sound production and music and sound. Degrees may be based in music colleges or music or engineering departments at universities, depending on the content. Some are technical and concentrate on the practical skills of sound engineering, whereas others are a mixture of music and music technology; many require some competence in performing music at certain levels. They may be entitled BMus, BSc, BEng or BA degrees depending on the content. As you might imagine, the BEng courses are for those wishing to become audio engineers and designers of electronic instruments, studio equipment and music systems. There are related courses in sound technology and sound engineering and production, smart systems and music technology.

There is a list of courses accredited by the Association of Professional Recording Services (APRS) available on their education website, JAMES (Joint Audio Media Education Services); see *Sources of information*. The courses are accredited if they meet industry needs, so could help you get employment after you graduate.

## Degree subject combinations

Music technology combines well with music, performing arts and media courses. There are specialist combinations available with electronic engineering, pop music performance, radio broadcasting and film production. You could consider combinations with management or ICT and you will also find music technology combined with science subjects.

## Other higher education qualifications

Foundation degrees are available in music technology, creative sound technology, audio and music production, commercial music performance and production, DJ and electronic music, live sound, music production, music production and artist development, music production and creative recording, music production and performance, music production and sound design, popular music production and sound and music technology.

There are HNDs and HNCs in music technology, sound engineering and multimedia integration, music production, media technology (music and sound engineering) and urban and electronic music.

## Relevance to other subjects?

Depending on your interests you could consider popular, commercial music or media studies. There are also sound engineering and electronics courses. If you are interested inthe music business, there are courses in music industry management and music journalism.

## Important advice

Music technology degrees vary in their content and specialism, so you must research the different courses to find out which is the best for you. Course requirements also vary, as well as the standard of musical performance required, so be sure to contact universities and colleges directly to find out what would be suitable for you. It is also important to ask them what sorts of jobs their graduates go into.

# Future careers

## ▷After A levels

You might start as a junior in a recording studio, or as a runner or messenger in the music or TV industries. You might find work in a radio station, the film industry, assisting with live sound at concerts and the theatre, or possibly administration work with music and other media publications. There would also be opportunities in music, computer or electronics shops. (See also the information under this heading in the music entry.) Sound and music technology apprenticeships were launched in September 2013.

## ▷After a degree

## Working in music technology

Depending on the content of your degree, here are some of the careers you could consider:

- audio production
- audio sales
- audio systems maintenance
- broadcast (radio, television, internet)
- equipment design
- events management
- independent musical composition and performance
- live sound production/engineering (gigs, theatre, events)
- media production
- multimedia authoring
- music education: teaching, lecturing, research, technical support
- music for new media (interactive games, the web)
- music for time-based media (film, video)
- music production
- music technology journalism
- recording artist
- research and development
- software design
- sound capture (sound engineering)
- sound design
- sound design and post-production for film, television and radio
- studio engineering/ studio management
- television and radio engineering and production.

Some of these areas cross over into the more creative aspects of music. The work could be freelance and/or on short-term contracts, so you are likely to be self-employed.

## Working outside music technology

You would have knowledge of IT and engineering so you could consider working in the IT or engineering industries, which might require further training. If you have a strong interest in the music industry, there could be opportunities in music management and administration, arts administration, journalism and marketing.

## Sources of information

www2.aprs.co.uk

www.bpi.co.uk

http://ccskills.org.uk/

www.creative-choices.co.uk

www.jamesonline.org.uk
(for list of accredited higher and further education courses)

www.soundonsound.com (online magazine)

> *'I was able to use the recording studio facilities to record local bands in my spare time. This will help my CV and I will have a portfolio of professional demos ready for when I graduate.'* Mitch, on a BSc in music technology

# Performing arts

*The course is all about the performing arts industry and the different careers and progression routes through it. You will be able to specialise in one or two areas. You don't necessarily have to be able to dance, sing, act and play an instrument to a high standard for this course, although if you can do more than one it will be helpful. It would be helpful to have already achieved a GCSE in dance, drama, music or expressive arts for this course.*

*This A level is a broad qualification that encourages you to study in a practical way. It is designed to help you develop a range of vocational skills that will be useful to you either for higher level study or in work and training.*

*N.B. There is also a course entitled performance studies (OCR).*

## What do you study?

*Specifications vary, but in all you will investigate the industry and jobs within it, develop your own performing arts skills, and get involved in all aspects of organising and producing productions.*

**Investigating the performing arts industry**—looking at how the business part of the industry works, how decisions are made and how it is financed and marketed. Knowledge and understanding of the past and the important developments that have taken place in the performing arts this will be useful to you in developing your skills, creating your own performance pieces and discovering what has influenced your own work.

**Exploring skills for performance**—assessing and building up your own skills in one or more of the specialisms offered: dance, drama, music, music technology or the technical and production aspects of performance. This will depend on your own interests and what is available in your school or college.

**Exploring repertoire**—researching stylistic conventions, interpretation of repertoire.

**Creating work for performance**—creating your own performance or showcase; this could be something totally original or adapted from another source. You work with others in a project management team through the whole creative process, culminating in the event itself, which improves your skills in all the different areas.

**Performance practice**—learning what is involved in performing work as a performer, including safe working practices.

*Professional practice: production demonstration*–learning about carrying out a production role in response to a brief or commission, developing your production skills and demonstrating them in practical work, producing a final product or providing a practical application in performance. You might work as a member of a production team (for example, front of house, stage management, or as a lighting and sound technician) or design something for the production such as a costume, mask, prop, puppet or set.

*Employment opportunities in the performing arts and how to get work*– looking at the different jobs and opportunities available, how people and companies promote themselves, and also topics such as terms and conditions of employment. You need to learn about effective self-promotion, attitudes, survival skills and self-employment.

You will study through a programme of assignments, which will include practical performing, and there will be tests, set assignments, projects and case studies, some of which will be assessed externally. You may keep a working log detailing all aspects of the development process of an assignment or project including research, exploration, practical application and ongoing evaluation. In group work you may have to prepare supporting documents explaining how the performance was prepared and how you were involved in the creative process. You will go on visits to performing arts venues and see productions. There may be speakers from the industry.

## Subject combinations
A levels in media studies, music and English language would combine well, and also subjects such as history and psychology.

# Higher education options

## Degree-level study
Courses are divided into practical performance or technical courses, and more academic studies. There are courses in performing arts where you can study one or two types of performing arts, and specialised drama, dance and music colleges where you would concentrate on one. Technical courses include stage management and costume design. Apart from courses entitled performing arts, other course titles to look out for include: contemporary and performance practice, performance design and practice, acting for stage and screen, media performance, musical theatre, and acting, stage combat and contemporary circus and physical performance.

## Degree subject combinations

Performing arts is available with related subjects such as music, choreography and dance, drama, choral studies and events planning.

## Other higher education qualifications

You will find a wide variety of foundation degrees, which provide employment-related courses in many specialisms within the sector. Apart from performing arts foundation degrees there are degrees in: acting and contemporary theatre making, acting performance, circus arts, costume construction for stage and screen, creating performance, dance theatre performance, drama, performance and arts management, event management, music, musical theatre, performance (physical theatre), performance and events production, performance practice, performance production, performing arts (acting, dance and creative technologies), performing arts (contemporary theatre performance) ,performing arts (dance), performing arts (drama and theatre), performing arts and the community, performing arts music, performing arts technologies, professional acting, sound, lighting and live event technology, and stage management and technical theatre.

There are also HNDs and HNCs in performing arts and examples are: performing arts, performing arts (acting), performing arts (dance), performing arts (music performance), performing arts (performance), musical theatre and popular music.

## Relevance to other subjects?

Look at degrees in arts administration, leisure and recreation, hospitality management, and events and exhibition management.

## Important advice

You need to get as much experience of performing arts as you can, either in or outside education. If you do not intend to become a performer, there are opportunities to learn about technical support. Join a local drama group and get experience of stage management, costume and make-up. Get involved with school and college productions.

# Future careers

## ▷After A levels

Most students who want to perform or learn technical skills will go on to higher education. You will need to get more experience and training and make useful contacts. Jobs available after A levels could include administration and support in performing arts organisations, box-office work and other front-of-house work in theatres. There may be some practical junior jobs available in costume, scene construction or props. Apprenticeships might also be available at this level although likely to be on the technical/admin side.

## ▷After a degree

### Working in performing arts

If you start work as a performer you will need to attend auditions and build up your experience. You may need to find yourself an agent to help you get work. If you have studied technical skills, this is a similar route: you will start at a junior level and build up experience and contacts. With a performing arts background you could go into teaching, which would require further training. There are opportunities in arts administration and community arts work (promoting performing arts in the community). You could also consider retailing (music shops, costume hire companies) and general administration or management in performing arts.

### Working outside performing arts

As you will have learned valuable transferable skills on the course, such as communication, you would be able to go into many areas of work including business and retail. Sales and teaching would give you a good opportunity to use your communication skills. (See also the music, dance, drama and theatre studies entries.)

## Sources of information

Association of British Theatre Technicians
www.abtt.org.uk

Council for Dance Education and Training
www.cdet.org.uk

Incorporated Society of Musicians
www.ism.org

http://ccskills.org.uk

www.dramauk.co.uk

www.stagemanagementassociation.co.uk

http://getintotheatre.org

---

'The show must go on, even if you aren't feeling up to it. You need self-discipline and real determination to succeed.' Letitia, student on a performing arts degree

# Philosophy

*If you have ever seen The Matrix film trilogy and wondered about some of the issues in the films you will already have had an introduction to some of the key questions studied in philosophy. Why are we here? What is the truth? Do we just fit in with the way things are or question them? If you have watched the Walking Dead series this may well have thrown up similar questions.*

*The word philosophy comes from the ancient Greek word meaning love of wisdom. The Greeks founded philosophy and the issues they considered are still pursued by philosophers today. As an A level philosophy student you will be asking questions like: Is there anything that we can really know with certainty? What is justice? How is the human mind related to the body? Are there any absolute moral values?*

*The point of philosophy is not so much to answer such questions (although you may find more satisfying answers than you had before) but to learn how to analyse and approach them. Developing such skills will be worthwhile for your further studies and in your daily life. The skills that you will develop through your study of philosophy, such as arguing logically and lateral thinking, are extremely relevant to our information-based economy and are transferable to many other academic subjects.*

## What do you study?

*The topics listed give an idea of what could be covered. AQA is the only board offering this specification.*

You will gain an understanding of some important philosophical ideas, their historical presentation and their contribution to modern thought.

You will strengthen your capacity for analysis, reasoning and judgement; spot flaws in logic; learn how to argue logically and confidently; understand views different from your own; and be able to oppose others arguments.

The AS specification will give you a broad introduction to the study of philosophy and its key themes.

You will cover the following themes:
- reason and experience
- why should I be governed?
- why should I be moral?
- the idea of god
- knowledge of the external world
- tolerance
- the value of art
- god and the world
- the debate over free will and determinism.

At A2 you will develop your understanding of key philosophical concepts, themes, texts and techniques and specialise further, choosing two themes to study in depth and focusing on philosophical problems through the study of a key text.

- **Philosophy of mind**–what is the mind? What is its place in nature? What is the relationship between mentality and physicality? How are mental states identified, experienced and known?
- **Political philosophy**–this theme covers philosophical questions concerning how human well-being can be helped or hindered by the organisation of society and political structures.
- **Epistemology and metaphysics**–epistemology: do we know anything for certain? Is there any difference between knowledge and belief? Metaphysics: the branch of philosophy responsible for the study of existence. It answers the question What is? It encompasses everything that exists, as well as the nature of existence itself. It says whether the world is real, or merely an illusion. It is a fundamental view of the world around us.
- **Moral philosophy**–are there moral truths and if so what is their nature?
- **Philosophy of religion**–how should we understand religious belief? Are the claims made by religious believers a distinctive kind of theory or hypothesis? If so, are the arguments used and conclusions reached reliable? How do these aspects of religion weave into the fabric of religious belief and inform our understanding and evaluation of it? To what extent do different religions compete with or even undermine each other?
- **Philosophical problems**–you will study classical philosophy texts and look at the problems raised by these philosophers. You will need to be familiar with the text and will be required to develop and explore the problem areas identified within it. You will be expected to use this knowledge as a springboard for wider discussion and engagement of issues, and apply your acquired knowledge to philosophical problems raised in the text. The texts are works by Hume, Plato, Mill, Descartes and Nietzsche.

There is no GCSE in philosophy although OCR offers religious studies GCSE with an emphasis on philosophy and ethics. However, for the study of this subject at A level you will need an enquiring and open mind, as well as the ability to write in good, clear English.

Class discussion based on your reading is an important aspect of studying philosophy, as it has been for hundreds of years. Be prepared for the reading to be difficult at first, until you get used to the way that philosophical arguments are presented. There may also be the preparation and delivery of student presentations and group topics. As you might expect, your written work will be in the form of essays and you will be expected to undertake a lot of independent study. You must be able to work hard to grasp some difficult concepts and then be able to cope with class discussions that will test your understanding and your viewpoint.

## Subject combinations

You are unlikely to be asked for particular A level subjects if you apply for a university course in philosophy, although mathematics may be a preference for courses involving formal logic. Otherwise, your ability to form logical arguments would be helped, and in turn reinforced, by studying subjects such as English, history, politics, psychology, religious studies and critical thinking.

# Higher education options

It is not necessary to have an A level in philosophy in order to study it at a higher level.

## Degree-level study

Philosophy degree courses vary a great deal in content. Some place a great deal of emphasis on the traditional study of the great philosophers of the past, such as Aristotle, Plato and Descartes. Others focus on modern issues relating to politics, psychology, education and religion. All of them encourage you to form and defend your own ideas. Most courses begin with a year spent introducing you to the main strands in philosophical argument and other courses are even broader to begin with, starting with a general foundation course covering other humanities subjects as well as philosophy.

As you progress through the course you will find yourself with an increasing number of options, with some third years having no compulsory topics. Options could include history and the philosophy of science, feminist philosophy (theories about the position of women in society), aesthetics (how we judge beauty and art), or the works of particular philosophers such as Hegel, Nietzsche or Wittgenstein. You can specialise in European, natural or mental philosophy.

## Degree subject combinations

On many courses you have the option of continuing to study philosophy alongside another subject, and there is a wide range of subjects in the arts, humanities and sciences. There are also several degrees combining three subjects from philosophy, politics, economics, psychology and history. These degree programmes are designed so that the subjects throw light on each other, although you can usually select options in order to weight your own course in the direction of just one of the subjects. Other popular combinations are politics, economics, religious studies, history and modern languages.

## Other higher education qualifications

As foundation degrees are vocational, there are none in philosophy. You might want to consider those available in law, politics or community studies.

There are no HNDs or HNCs in philosophy although an HND in legal studies or business law is one possibility, as it gives you plenty of opportunity to use your experience of logical argument and can provide the foundation for a career in law.

## Relevance to other subjects?

Philosophy helps you to think about and understand important and complex ideas and issues, and encourages you to look at them critically and sensibly. You will be able to use ideas from present-day thought as well as evidence taken from the works of thinkers throughout history. This experience would provide a good basis for many subjects, including politics, law, theology/religious studies, economics, history, sociology, linguistics, drama and classics. Also look at subjects like human rights or international relations.

## Important advice

You cannot be a lazy thinker in philosophy and your commitment to the subject will be clear from the amount of reading that you do. Interviews for higher level philosophy courses often involve discussion of what you have read, not just the books on the set texts for your A level subject. The more you read in philosophy, the better you will become at forming intelligent arguments of your own.

# Future careers

## ▷After A levels

Philosophy is not a vocational subject so won't lead straight into a particular career. It does help you to become a clear and critical thinker who can put together a reasoned, intelligent argument. These skills are valuable to employers in many areas, including administration or any job requiring organisational skills. You would be an effective member of any team where the powers of persuasive argument are important such as in marketing or sales.

## ▷After a degree

### Working in philosophy

Careers linked directly to philosophy are limited as there are very few full-time philosophers. The nearest you might get to working as a philosopher is by teaching or lecturing in schools, colleges or universities. If you want to teach in a state school you will need to offer an additional National Curriculum subject such as history, or government and politics, as well as studying for a postgraduate teaching qualification (PGCE). Only if you become a philosophy lecturer or writer will you get the chance actually to do some philosophy of your own. This could involve further study at postgraduate level.

### Working outside philosophy

Most philosophy graduates go on to work in areas that enable them to use their ability to ask intelligent questions, analyse a problem and come up with a reasoned decision. Many philosophy graduates find employment in management or administration, where the ability to make informed decisions (often on other peoples behalf) is extremely important. Others use their powers of argument in sales, advertising and marketing, targeting potential buyers for a product and finding the most effective way of selling it. Financial jobs are also a possibility as are jobs in law or politics. Some graduates go on to work in journalism, the media, publishing or social work.

## Sources of information

Royal Institute of Philosophy
www.royalinstitutephilosophy.org

www.bpa.ac.uk

www.alevelphilosophy.co.uk

www.philosophynow.org

> 'A philosophy degree has trained the individual's brain and given them the ability to provide the skills we require and clients demand. These skills include the ability to be analytical, provide clear and innovative thinking, and question assumptions.' Russell, director of a management consultancy

# Photography

*In photography A level you study different aspects of photography allowing you to display your creative abilities and understanding of different areas of the subject. This will give you opportunities to specialise in areas other than lens-based imagery, such as digital imaging and the moving image. The specifications are both theoretical and practical. On the theoretical side, you study cultural, historical and contemporary practice and its use as a means of visual expression and communication. On the practical side, you learn how to choose and treat subjects for photographs as well as how to take, develop and print images of your own.*

## What do you study?

*The topics listed give an idea of what could be covered. The exact content of AS and A2 specifications differs according to exam boards, so you will need to check with your school or college about the exact modules available to you.*

You will cover a broad range of topics, which could include:
- portraiture
- documentary photography/ photojournalism
- landscape photography urban, rural and coastal
- working from objects for example, still life and the natural world
- digital imagery how photographic images can be edited and manipulated
- photographic installation, video, television and film.

In addition, you could also cover some of these topics as you work through the course.

***Exploring visual characteristics***—how to represent people and human situations, inanimate objects and the living world through the medium of photography.

***Interpretation of the subject***—the different ways of representing the subject of a photograph and the effects they create.

***Light sources***—how to manipulate light for effective photography.

***Cameras and related equipment***—understanding and assessing the photographic equipment available.

***Sensitive materials and processing***—the detailed techniques and knowledge required for developing photographs.

***Colour photography***—how it is created and how its technology differs from that used for black-and-white photography.

***Photography in the mass media***—the role played by photography in communicating information to the public, and the creation of images as a means of entertainment.

***The moving image***—similarities and differences between photography and film, video and television, as a means of communication.

***How to interpret and work to a brief***—an important skill to develop.

It is not essential to have GCSE photography to take the A level.

Practical work is an extremely important part in this subject. The work involves selecting and preparing subjects, whether in a studio or natural setting, in landscapes or cityscapes, then checking and adjusting lighting before taking the final photograph. You then develop, edit and print the photographs. The pictures that you create during this time will contribute to your exam portfolio, which should show a variety of techniques and subjects. Theory work involves classroom discussion of photographs and other visual media, together with note-taking and essay writing. You will visit photography galleries, exhibitions and trade shows.

Research and development of ideas form an important part of the course. You will need to be self-motivated and work outside lecture time. You might be asked to provide your own equipment, such as an SLR camera, filters, tripod and memory stick, although sometimes these can be borrowed from your school or college.

The assessment will include producing a portfolio of work, controlled assignments (where you will be given preparation time and then controlled time to finalise your work) and you may have to prepare a personal investigation with a related written personal study.

## Subject combinations

If you want to study photography beyond A level, you will be expected to have a good portfolio. It would be useful to choose other A levels that will help you with this. An obvious choice is art and design, although you must ensure that the subjects do not overlap too much, as the two A levels might not be accepted for entry to higher education.

Media studies includes the investigation of visual images as a means of communication, so could be a good choice. If you want to broaden your studies and increase your job opportunities, consider languages or business studies as these are useful in most careers. Finally, if you think that you might aim for a career in technical photography (medical or forensic photography, for example), physics, chemistry or mathematics would be good choices.

# Higher education options

A good portfolio of photographic work is often a major entry requirement for higher level photography courses. Most people produce this as part of a one-year Foundation course in art and design, which is available at many colleges and schools of art, as this is the usual entry route. However, some exceptional students can get in with just A levels or equivalent.

## Degree-level study

Photography can be studied as a single subject. Apart from degrees entitled photography, you will also find course titles such as contemporary lens media, photographic art, photographic practice and contemporary photography.

Courses vary in the amount of practice and theory involved, but most provide the option of specialising in particular areas of photography during the second or third year. This could include medical, landscape, nature, portrait, industrial, still life and cinema photography. There are also courses specialising in documentary, marine and natural history photography, fine art, fashion photography, press and editorial photography and photojournalism.

## Degree subject combinations

There are options to combine photography with related subjects such as video, fashion and brand promotion, public relations or digital imaging as well as with many other subjects. Studying for a combined degree may increase the options open to you after your degree. Look at subjects such as business studies or languages, which would benefit your future career whatever you decide to do.

## Other higher education qualifications

Not to be confused with the preparatory Art Foundation courses, foundation degrees are available in photography, applied photography, action photography, photography and digital imaging, commercial photography, contemporary photography practice, creative and editorial photography, digital photography, professional photography, photo imaging and location photography. There are HNDs and HNCs available in photography and digital photography. Again, as with degrees, for some courses you may first need to take a one-year Foundation course in art and design.

## Relevance to other subjects?

Other subjects where photography A level would be an advantage are media studies, film studies or cultural studies, history of art, or any art and design specialism, such as graphic design, fine art (painting and drawing) or sculpture.

## Important advice

It is never too soon to start gathering work together for your portfolio. Get into the habit of carrying a camera around with you to take advantage of photo opportunities. The work that you do outside your lessons is just as important as what you do in class.

# Future careers

### ▷After A levels

You could go on to train as an assistant to a professional photographer, gaining experience as you go along. Starting salaries are often low, but you get the opportunity to learn on the job and, if you're lucky, to make use of the facilities or equipment. There could be opportunities in camera and photographic equipment shops and you might also want to consider a job on the reproduction and development side of photography. This could be a high-street laboratory or professional development laboratory, responsible for anything from holiday snaps to wedding pictures or commercial photos. Provided that you have a good enough portfolio and your own equipment, you might consider approaching local newspapers for work, photographing newsworthy events. This would be on a freelance basis, but again it is good for building up your experience and portfolio. There could also be opportunities to work for the police or the Armed Forces. There are photography and digital imaging apprenticeships available.

### ▷After a degree

### Working in photography

Professional photographers work in studios or on location. Some are employed by newspapers, industrial or architectural companies or by businesses compiling professional portfolios for models or actors. Many photographers are self-employed (at least 50%), and are responsible for finding their own work, running their business and the creative photographic work itself. Photographers specialise in many different areas and the direction that you eventually take could be by careful planning or by chance. Specialist areas include product or food photography (for cookery books and magazines, or any product that must be made to look as attractive as possible), fashion styling, police work (creating photographic records of criminals, scenes of crime and evidence) or travel photography. Digital imaging is an expanding area, using photographic materials as the basis for the kind of computer-enhanced images that we see around us in advertising, on DVDs and in films. Finding work in photography can be difficult as it is very competitive, so a creative, imaginative and committed approach to the job search is the key to success. You will need to have a good quality portfolio in order to approach employers, develop a creative CV, set up your own website and use the networking opportunities provided by social media.

## Working outside photography

As competition in professional photography is intense and careers insecure many photography graduates use their skills in a slightly different context. For example, an understanding of the power of the visual image is important for anyone working within advertising. They can work as photographic archivists, responsible for the organisation and storage of photographic history or documentary evidence, which must be easily accessed when needed by publishers, newspapers or even the police. There are also jobs within areas of film and television, including direction, production, editing, computer graphics, set design/dressing and lighting. Here the work is far more concerned with the moving image rather than the static one, but a sense of form, colour, light and framing are all just as essential.

## Sources of information

Association of Photographers
www.the-aop.org

British Institute of Professional Photography
www.bipp.com

British Journal of Photography
www.bjp-online.com

Royal Photographic Society
www.rps.org

www.creativeskillset.org

> *'Make sure you learn dark-room skills as this forms the basis of everything you do.'* Yolanda, studying A level photography with French and art

# Physical education

*Studying physical education gives you the opportunity to develop a theoretical understanding of the physiological, psychological and sociological factors that underpin sporting performance as well as gaining practical experience. It is a well-respected academic subject, offering you the opportunity to explore sport on a national and international level. It has never been so much in the spotlight with the current focus on healthy lifestyles, and the 2012 Olympics which encouraged more people to participate in sports of all kinds. The specifications focus on participation and performance in physical activity as part of a balanced, active and healthy lifestyle.*

## What do you study?
*The topics listed give an idea of what could be covered. The exact content of AS and A2 specifications differs according to exam boards, so you will need to check with your school or college about the exact modules available to you.*

- *Opportunities for and the effects of leading a healthy and active lifestyle*–applied exercise physiology, how the human body works: the anatomy and physiology of the human body and how the body responds to physical activity and assessing fitness; nutrition and physiological, biomechanical and psychological factors in sport.
- *The critical sports performer*–analysis and critical evaluation of the factors that improve or optimise performance; factors affecting the nature and development of elite performance. You will also look at the roles of umpires, referees and coaches as well as other sports leaders.
- *Sociocultural and historical effects of participation in physical activity*–the current state of sport both in the UK and globally. The legacy of the 2012 Olympic games. Participation in sports and recreation, including healthy lifestyles and contemporary health concerns.
- *Optimising performance*–applied physiology, energy sources and systems, aerobics and anaerobics, muscles, preparation and training, sports supplements, specialised training, sports injuries, mechanics of movement, sport psychology.
- *Acquiring, developing and evaluating practical skills in physical education*–in some specifications the practical demonstration of skills is from a choice of activities such as team games, gymnastics, dance, athletics, skiing, snowboarding, canoeing/

kayaking, climbing, horse riding, mountain activities, orienteering, rowing and sculling, sailing, windsurfing, kitesurfing, track/road cycling and swimming.

It is not necessary to have taken GCSE physical education in order to study this A level. However, if you have taken this GCSE course and/or biology, you may find it useful in the transition to A level work.

The course involves a mixture of practical and theory work, with the opportunity to work on your own sporting performance. You will learn theory, observe sporting performances and may analyse your own performance on video or by keeping your own personal diary.

## Subject combinations

If you are considering a degree in physical education (or sports science) then at least one science from biology, human biology, chemistry or applied science is recommended. Physical education also goes well with subjects such as history, sociology and psychology. If you are considering sports or leisure management, business studies or leisure studies A levels would be good choices.

# Higher education options

## Degree-level study

There are three main areas involved in studying physical education (or sports science) at degree level:

- sports psychology
- exercise physiology–nutrition, diet etc
- sport biomechanics–the analysis of physiology during sporting activities.

Within these you will find a variety of modules, examples are: foundations of sport and exercise psychology, bioenergetics of human movement, foundations of exercise physiology, anatomy , professional and academic skills for sport, data analysis in sport and exercise, foundations of biomechanics, applied exercise physiology, sports nutrition, exercise prescription and instruction, cognition and emotion in sport and exercise psychology, biomechanics and kinesiology, research in sport and exercise, performance analysis, applied sport and performance psychology, applied strength and conditioning, working with a client, professional issues in sport and exercise psychology, applied performance analysis, contemporary coaching issues, exercise referral, professional development and employability. Some courses will include a work placement.

You will find specialised sports science or sports studies courses available, such as sports and exercise science, physical education and coaching, sports coaching, sports psychology, sport rehabilitation, sports conditioning, rehabilitation and massage, sport technology and sport development. There are also courses in sport management and sport business. Degree titles vary and can include physical education and health and fitness in their titles. There are also physical education degrees incorporating teacher training.

## Degree subject combinations

You can combine sports science or sports studies with related subjects, like human biology, or with management courses, such as tourism, leisure or outdoor recreation. You could also consider combinations with business, ICT or languages.

## Other higher education qualifications

Foundation degrees include areas such as sport studies, sport science, sport coaching and performance, sports coaching and physical education, sport coaching and fitness therapy, sport development (physical education), community sports development, health and personal training, sport injury and treatment and sports rehabilitation.

Specialist courses are available in cricket coaching, football coaching, football development, rugby coaching and performance, equine sports coaching, sports coaching (European judo), golf management and golf performance.

You could consider related courses in sport and leisure management, sports club management, sports journalism, management of sport, sport and adventure management, sports surface management or surf science and technology. HND courses available include sports studies, sports coaching, sport science (outdoor recreation) and sports development and coaching.

## Relevance to other subjects?

Look at courses in leisure and recreation management and hotel and hospitality management. You could also consider courses in psychology or sociology, youth work or teaching.

## Important advice

In order to keep up with the practical component of the course you should follow a training regime (or continue with any existing programme that you may have).This should include general cardiovascular work together with some resistance training. A general pattern of healthy living, such as a healthy diet excluding cigarettes and alcohol, is regarded as essential. As there are so many related higher level courses in the sports, fitness and leisure sector it is advisable to start researching courses as early as possible to find the ones most suitable for you. Remember to ask about the destinations of the graduates from any courses you are considering.

# Future careers

### ▷ After A levels

A knowledge of physical education could help you work within the sports and leisure industry in a job such as a leisure centre assistant. You might also consider sports coaching, lifeguard or personal fitness instruction work (depending on any extra qualifications you may have gained). Retail sports shops or jobs in IT and administration connected to the sports industry could also be options. The National School Apprenticeship scheme offers apprentices in schools, some specialising in sport. There are also apprenticeships in sports coaching, and leisure and recreation management.

### ▷ After a degree

### Working in physical education

About one in five sports science graduates go into professional jobs in sports straight after graduating.

*Health and fitness industry*–this is a major career option for graduates in sports studies so you might consider a career in the management of fitness, leisure centres, health clubs or spas. You might start as a personal trainer, which can offer a good route into the industry. You may also find jobs in local or national government such as an active lifestyles officer who promotes healthy living and lifestyles in the community.

*Coaching*–this ranges from high-level activities (such as the Olympics) to providing for the needs of young people in the community. It also connects with the popular world of personal development training, especially in large corporate companies. Local councils are increasingly recognising the need for young people to be able to access sporting facilities, and the need for professional coaching in this area is now widely acknowledged. With the legacy of the 2012 Olympics, this has become an expanding area.

**Sports development officer**–promotes sports locally within the community, often targeted at a particular group, for example young people. You would work for local or national government.

**Teaching**–you would need to study for a Postgraduate Certificate in Education (PGCE) after your degree unless you choose a course which includes education and qualified teacher status (QTS).

**Outdoor activities manager or leader**–managing an outdoor activities centre, offering instruction to a wide range of people, or becoming a leader where you offer people instruction and encouragement.

**Sports marketing and media**–this ranges from being an events manager and being involved with the general business of putting on events, to gaining sponsorship or becoming an agent for sportspeople. This often involves establishing links with the corporate and business world and is a rapidly developing area.

**Postgraduate study**–just over 13% of sports science graduates go on to further study, which could be in sports science, health and nutrition, management and physiotherapy. Sports science graduates wanting to qualify as a physiotherapist will need to take a pre-registration postgraduate course.

## Working outside physical education
Your degree could equip you for careers in management, banking and insurance, the social services, the police, the fire service and the Armed Forces.

## Sources of information

British Association of Sport and Exercise Sciences
www.bases.org.uk

Sport England
www.sportengland.org

Sportscotland
www.sportscotland.org.uk

Sport Wales
www.sportwales.org.uk

UK Sport
www.uksport.gov.uk

Careers in sport
www.careers-in-sport.co.uk

National School Apprenticeship Scheme
http://schoolapprenticeships.co.uk

SkillsActive
www.skillsactive.com

---

*'It's such a satisfying job. I organised some 'Walking for health' walks locally. It got people out of their cars and provided a chance to experience the health benefits of a short stroll.'* Doug, active lifestyles officer, with a degree in sport studies.

---

# Physics

*Physics is unique. No other subject allows you to gain such a deep understanding of the way the world works. It can stretch to study of the space and universe but is also down to earth and includes items that we take for granted in the modern world like mobile phones, the internet, PCs and the power that runs them. It is an exciting and creative science, which is constantly evolving as new discoveries are made.*

*Studying physics is all about observing natural phenomena, trying to understand them and predicting what might happen in new and unknown situations. You learn about a wide range of theories explaining and predicting the way in which the physical world behaves. It's a broad subject involving experience and observations, theory and maths, ICT, materials and information theory. As a physics student, you must be able not only to follow and construct logical arguments but also to use your imagination and intuition to see how what you have learned can be applied to new situations. Physics is continually developing with new theories and practical techniques so offers a unique base from which to meet the demands of new technologies in our ever-changing world. This also means that the range of careers and opportunities is ever-growing.*

## What do you study?

*The topics listed give an idea of what could be covered. The exact content of AS and A2 specifications differs according to exam boards, so you will need to check with your school or college about the exact modules available to you. N.B. There is also an A level in electronics.*

All physics specifications include the following:

- **the properties of matter**–solids, liquids and gases; mechanical, thermal and electrical properties explained in molecular terms
- **the properties of materials**–including density and Young's modulus
- **mechanics**–including motion along a straight line, projectile motion, Newtons laws of motion, energy and power
- **oscillations and waves**–mechanical and electromagnetic waves, sound and optics
- **quantum phenomena**–photo electricity, energy levels and photon emission, wave-particle duality
- **atomic, nuclear and thermal physics**
- **fields**–force fields, gravitational fields, electric fields, capacitors, magnetic fields, electromagnetic induction, particle accelerators, fundamental particles
- **electricity**–electrical quantities, resistance and resistivity, circuits and components, alternating current, direct current circuits

- **further mechanics**–including momentum, circular motion and simple harmonic motion.

You may also study a range of other topics, which will include more advanced theoretical work and some specific applications of physics. You may also learn practical techniques such as planning, implementation, analysis, evaluation and communication.

Examples of other topics are:
- **medical physics**–imaging, ultrasound and other techniques for the diagnosis and treatment of illness
- **astrophysics and cosmology**–the study of stars, galaxies and other heavenly bodies
- **telecommunications**–commercial and industrial applications of radio waves and digital techniques
- **energy**–the production and conservation of energy
- **applied physics**–rotational dynamics, thermodynamics, engines.

There are physics A level specifications driven by real-life applications, focusing on the practical activities and applications of physics. Examples are physics in context and advancing physics (which was developed with the Institute of Physics).

These courses cover topics such as the study of digital imaging in medicine, human perception, digital communications, designer materials, wave and quantum behaviour, photons, space and time, gravitational fields, the expanding universe, liquid nitrogen, plasmas, electromagnetic machines, electric and magnetic fields, fundamental particles, ionising radiation and radioactive tracers.

A good grade (C or above) in physics or science and additional science at GCSE is usually required to study A level physics. You will also need to be able to use mathematical formulae confidently.

You learn through a combination of theory and practical work. Theory is taught through lectures explaining conceptual physical models. You develop your understanding of much of the theory by applying it to increasingly complex problems, and you will be expected to read textbooks and scientific journals to increase your understanding. Practical work is used to learn experimental techniques, to place the theory in context and to help develop a deeper understanding of physical phenomena. You will learn the selection and use of different types of equipment, processing of data, making observations and measurements, and the analysis and evaluation of results.

## Subject combinations

Physics combines well with other science subjects, but maths will be particularly helpful and relevant as there is so much maths involved in the study of physics. You should take A or AS level mathematics if you are thinking of a degree in a physics subject or engineering. Further maths is useful for some engineering courses, such as aeronautical engineering. Physics A level combines well with chemistry, leading to medical courses and many technology and science-based courses like chemical engineering, materials engineering and textile science and technology.

Physics could also be combined with A level electronics or design and technology for engineering design or product design courses.

If you are not quite up to standard for entry to an undergraduate physics degree, there are foundation years available for some courses, which are designed to fill gaps in maths and physics and prepare you for entry onto the first year of a degree.

# Higher education options

## Degree-level study

Traditional physics courses give you a solid grounding in modern and classical physics along with the associated mathematics and experimental techniques. Important areas covered include mechanics, relativity, quantum physics, electromagnetism, waves and optics, atomic and nuclear physics, particle physics, oscillations, thermodynamics, lasers and solid-state physics. Teaching is through lectures and lab work, backed up by tutorials and/or problem-solving classes. The three-year courses are broad in scope, while the four-year courses lead to the qualification of MPhys or MSci and aim for the greater subject depth you need if you want to practise as a physicist in research or in industry.

There could be specialised options, such as astrophysics, cosmology, biophysics, applied physics, atmospheric physics and environmental physics. Maths features in all physics courses, both as a language through which physics is expressed and as a method for the development of the subject and for problem solving. If the maths side of physics particularly appeals to you then you could consider a degree in theoretical physics.

Some applied physics degrees are sandwich courses, which involve placements in industry. There are some sandwich courses available in pure physics, where the placement could be with a wide variety of employers or research establishments, for example British Aerospace, the National Physical Laboratory or National Oceanography Centre. Or your placement could be abroad, for example at the high-energy research centre (CERN) in Geneva, the WSL Institute for Snow and Avalanche Research in Davos, or the Max Planck Institute for Solid State Physics in Stuttgart.

## Degree subject combinations

You can combine physics with virtually any subject, although some subjects are closely related, like electronics, astronomy or mathematics. If you think you might not want a purely technical career, combining physics with management, business studies, ICT or a modern language would be a good preparation for careers in management, business or industry.

## Other higher education qualifications

There are foundation degrees available in physics, applied science and clinical technology which could lead into linked degree courses or employment. There are no HNDs or HNCs in pure physics.

## Relevance to other subjects?

Physics A level is useful for many related degrees, such as engineering, materials science or geophysics. There are also courses in engineering physics, which are designed to combine education and training in the branches of physics that have been identified as important for the development of a professional engineer. Many medicine, dentistry and veterinary science courses specify A level physics or mathematics as a requirement. The mathematical basis of physics makes it a good preparation for many other subjects. For example, there is increasing emphasis upon scientific research methods and statistical analysis in courses such as psychology, sociology, economics and business studies, so there are many options.

## Important advice

Have a look at the content of courses to see which ones inspire you. There could be sponsorship for physics or engineering degrees. This is competitive, and sometimes the closing dates are before the UCAS closing dates.

# Future careers

## ▷After A levels

There are related jobs such as a laboratory technician, and there are apprenticeships available. Having studied physics you will have good problem-solving, research and report-writing skills, so you could consider opportunities in many other career areas including business and finance.

## ▷After a degree

## Working in physics

Physics graduates can use their particular skills and knowledge in working for a wide range of employers including:

- **engineering and electronic companies**–researching and developing new products
- **utilities providers**–particularly telecommunications, power and transport
- **energy**–this could be in traditional fields, such as gas, oil and electricity, improving fuel efficiency and output, or research into new or renewable sources like wind and wave power
- **medical physics**–magnetic resonance imaging (MRI) scanners, lasers used in surgery, ultrasound, therapeutic radiography for treating cancer
- **materials industries**–including steel, plastics and ceramics producers and companies using these materials
- **radiation protection**–monitoring emissions and ensuring the safe disposal of radioactive waste. This could be within Public Health England
- **defence**–employed by agencies and contractors of the Ministry of Defence, you might design and implement new weapons systems and technology, and intelligence systems (e.g. through communication satellites)
- **space science**–researching other planets, building satellites and space probes, collecting information about the universe and its origins
- **schools and colleges**–physics teachers are in demand, and there is extra financial help available for teacher training in science subjects
- **research**–in research scientist jobs for government departments and commercial companies.

Many physics graduates move on to further study after their first degree (roughly a third), taking courses such as PhDs and MScs in subjects such as accelerator physics, applied mathematics, astrophysics, nuclear engineering, audio acoustics, radio imaging, computer software technology with network management, information technology, plasma physics and radiation detection.

## Working outside physics

Physics is a subject providing strong academic and technical training. The IT industry employs many physics graduates as software engineers, programmers, systems analysts and IT consultants. As a physics graduate you could enter a wide variety of careers including accountancy, technical sales and marketing, banking, finance, or local and national government.

## Sources of information

Institute of Physics
www.iop.org

Careers in physics
www.physics.org/careers

Science Museum
www.sciencemuseum.org.uk

Search for physics courses
www.myphysicscourse.org

www.physlink.com

> 'A physics degree opens the doors to many careers. Employers love problem solving and analytical skills and people who are good with numbers and computers.' Luke, taking BSc physics

# Psychology

*Psychology is the study of human experience and behaviour. It tries to help you understand both your own and other's behaviour. If you have ever wondered why you feel stressed out, forget important information or laugh at jokes you don't understand, then psychology can provide you with answers. As a student of A level psychology, you are introduced to the main branches of the subject and the issues that they address. Ultimately, these are all concerned with understanding what people think and do, and why.*

## What do you study?

*The topics listed give an idea of what could be covered. The exact content of AS and A2 specifications differs according to exam boards, so you will need to check with your school or college about the exact modules available to you.*

- **Method**–how psychologists collect, analyse and interpret data about thought and behaviour
- **Perspectives**–different approaches to the study of the mind and behaviour
- **Social psychology**–how the individual and social forces interact
- **Cognitive psychology**–how we obtain, process and remember information; language and its relation to thought, including memory and eyewitness testimony
- **Individual differences**–personality, intelligence, normal and abnormal behaviour, mental illness and its treatments (including anxiety disorders and autism)
- **Culture and identity**–whether human abilities are related in any systematic way to human groupings by culture, race or gender
- **Biological psychology**–how our biological and physiological make-up relate to thought and behaviour; issues include motivation, emotion, awareness, sleep and stress, factors affecting stress, coping with stress and managing stress
- **Developmental psychology**–how we change during the course of our lives, including social and cognitive development, language acquisition, childhood, adolescence and old age
- **Comparative psychology**–the similarities and differences between human and animal thought and behaviour; the extent to which what we learn about animals can be applied to humans; ways in which evolutionary ideas can be used to explain human and animal behaviour

- *Health psychology*–how our physical and psychological well-being may be interrelated; addictions and eating disorders
- *Educational psychology*–how we learn and how this might be influenced by how we are taught.

A GCSE in psychology is not needed to study A level psychology but you will need GCSEs at grade C or above in English, mathematics and possibly a science. Maths is especially useful, because of the statistics involved in psychology.

A lot of work in psychology involves discussion of different theories of why people think and behave in the way that they do. You are encouraged to form your own ideas and opinions and to back these up with evidence from your own experience as well as research carried out by others. You should be prepared to do a lot of reading and research in your own time. You spend some time learning how to carry out research and methodology in psychology, including how to design an experiment or other research project and how to draw conclusions from your results.

## Subject combinations
Most degree courses do not specify particular A levels for psychology degrees, although for some biology is quoted as being desirable. Some courses involve quite a lot of experimental design and analysis, however, and mathematics and sciences are often mentioned as being preferred. Other courses don't involve much quantitative work, and for these any A levels of a suitable grade are acceptable. GCSE maths and English and, sometimes, a science are often essential requirements for entry to degree-level study in psychology. The main thing is to get high grades in your A levels as psychology is a very popular and competitive degree.

# Higher education options
An A level in psychology is not essential for study of the subject at a higher level, but it is definitely preferred now that the A level is more widely available in schools and colleges.

## Degree-level study
A psychology degree can be orientated towards science (when it will usually be a BSc degree) or arts (usually a BA), the main difference being the amount of emphasis on experiment and quantitative analysis. A BA course will include some quantitative work but will focus more on theories and topics within psychology that rely less on statistical data or

quantitative investigation. Such topics include the ethics of psychology (the potential power that a psychologist has in terms of knowledge about peoples behaviour and emotions, and how this power can be abused), or theories of how we may develop particular personalities.

Instead of a straight psychology degree, you might consider a course that is more focused, such as health, forensic or sport psychology. There are some broader courses available such as behavioural science (usually combining psychology and sociology, sometimes with animal behaviour, biology or anthropology) or cognitive science (combining psychology with computer science especially artificial intelligence, the modelling of thought processes using computers).

If you are considering becoming a psychologist, you must make sure that your course is recognised by the British Psychological Society (BPS) (see *Sources of information*).

## Degree subject combinations

Psychology is available in many combined degree schemes, so it can be studied in combination with practically any other subject. You could consider subjects that are connected or complementary such as sociology, criminology, social anthropology, child development or exercise psychology. There are also more mainstream combinations available such as computing, mathematics, business studies, English, geography and management.

## Other higher education qualifications

There are foundation degrees available in psychology, psychology with sociology, psychology and crime, psychology and counselling, counselling and psychotherapy, psychology and health studies and animal behaviour and psychology. There is an HND in applied psychology.

## Relevance to other subjects?

You will find your A level in psychology useful in other subjects at degree level. It provides grounding in research methods, analytical skills, essay technique and logical problem solving, all of which will be useful for subjects such as sociology, economics and geography. If you are more interested in people, then counselling could be another option.

## Important advice

If you are considering a career in psychology, you should check that your chosen degree programme has been validated by the BPS as giving the Graduate Basis for Chartered Membership (GBC), especially if you want to work in the National Health Service. If the course that you take doesn't provide this, you may have to sit more exams after leaving university to meet the entry requirements for professional psychology training. Be aware that psychology is a very competitive subject so you will need high A level grades for entry to degree courses.

# Future careers

## ▷After A levels

If you intend to go into work straight after A levels, you are likely to find that many employers value the knowledge and skills you have gained from the psychology A level. Your communication and research skills will be valuable in business, sales and marketing, the media and the health sector.

## ▷After a degree

## Working in psychology

There are many options if you want to become a professional psychologist but you will need to undertake postgraduate study for nearly all of them. You are likely to have to get some practical work experience before you start your specialist postgraduate training.

- *Clinical psychologists* work directly with patients in a hospital or as part of a community healthcare team. They may also undertake research.
- *Counselling psychologists* help individuals, couples, families and groups who are having problems with normal life. They help people to understand their problems and make their own decisions. They may work in GPs surgeries, counselling organisations, academic and business settings, or privately.
- *Educational psychologists* work with children and young people who may have learning difficulties or behavioural problems.
- *Forensic (criminological and legal) psychologists* work with other professionals in the courts and prisons. Their work ranges from assessing the mental competence of offenders to participating in the day-to-day running of prisons.
- *Health psychologists* assess peoples attitudes, behaviour and thinking about health and illness. They work with other health professionals to help in communication with patients, and investigate how peoples beliefs may affect their treatment.

- **Neurophysiologists** try to understand the relationship between the brain and psychological processes. They work towards the rehabilitation of patients who have suffered brain injuries, or perhaps have had their brain function affected by conditions such as strokes. They may be employed in the NHS or in the private sector.
- **Occupational or industrial psychologists** advise firms on the recruitment and training of staff in organisations and on improving the working environment.
- **Sport psychologists** work in competitive sport and recreation, increasing awareness of the relationship between the mind and physical performance.

## Working outside psychology

Even if you don't want to become a psychologist, you might use some of your psychology skills in your chosen career. Your understanding of individual and group behaviour will be especially valued in social work, human resources, sales, marketing, careers guidance, and general administration and management.

## Sources of information

British Psychological Society (BPS)
www.bps.org.uk

Careers in Psychology
www.careersinpsychology.co.uk

---

*'It relates so well to real life and you start to understand why people behave as they do.'* Adam, A levels in psychology, biology, physical education and sociology

# Religious studies

*Religious studies provides you with a better understanding of world religions, philosophy and ethics. You certainly don't need to be religious to study it and students of any or no faith at all will find it an extremely challenging subject. You may study different religions in depth or concentrate on issues such as war, terrorism, morality and aspects of politics. You will gain an understanding of other people's views and how to look at things from another person's viewpoint. You will gain useful debating, discussion and research skills.*

## What do you study?

*The topics listed give an idea of what could be covered. The exact content of AS and A2 specifications differs according to exam boards, so you will need to check with your school or college about the exact modules available to you.*

Specifications have a wide variety of options; some let you focus on one or two religions, some cover the philosophy of religion and ethics while others are more theology based and centre on the Bible. The following gives you some idea of possible options.

- ***Philosophy of religion***—this covers the philosophical arguments about the existence of God and the problems with these arguments. It includes studying about the nature of God and the need to prove God's existence, arguments for the existence of God based on apparent order and purpose in the world, the problem of evil, scientific explanations, life after death, religious experiences, miracles and atheism.

- ***Religious ethics***—this covers the relationship between morality and religion and the various ethical dilemmas people may face. It includes studying ethical theories, ethical language, objectivity, subjectivism and relativism, utilitarianism, situation ethics, justice, law and punishment, war and peace, medical ethics and sexual ethics. Throughout these topics examples are drawn on from world religions, the media and contemporary society. You will consider scholarly contributions to these topics, such as those from Aquinas, Paley, Swinburne, Hume, Kant, Plato and Aristotle.

- ***The history of Christianity***—the early Christian church starting with the church as portrayed in the New Testament through its development and expansion to the fifth century AD. The medieval and modern Christian Church monasticism, the Reformation, non-conformity, Christian theology in developing countries.

- *Religion, art and the media*
- *Studies of the Old and New Testaments*—or scriptures from other religions
- *Religion and contemporary society*
- *Specialism in a world religion*—including Buddhism, Christianity, Hinduism, Islam, Judaism and Sikhism.

It is not essential to have studied GCSE religious studies in order to take the A level the examination boards clearly state that the course is intended to be accessible to students of any background. A good grade in GCSE English or history would indicate that you could cope well with the researching and writing involved.

## Subject combinations

Religious studies can be combined with almost any other subject. If you are considering religious studies at a higher level, you might consider studying an ancient language, classical civilisation or philosophy. More common combinations are history, sociology, drama, English literature, media studies, psychology and business studies.

# Higher education options

It is not essential to have an A level in religious studies in order to study it at a higher level, but normally at least one essay-based subject is required.

## Degree-level study

Religious studies generally examines religion as a worldwide phenomenon. It includes the study of the major world religions. You study the history of the religions, the moral issues that they address, and their place in the world today. Theology or divinity degrees concentrate on Christianity. You might learn Biblical Hebrew and/or New Testament Greek, and the emphasis is on the study of Christianity from its inception to the present day. This includes an examination of its cultural, ethical, philosophical and historical developments. Biblical studies deals specifically with the Bible, its content and the changing approaches to it over the centuries.

Specialised courses are available in Islamic studies, Jewish studies, Jewish history and a course entitled religion in the contemporary world, which combines humanities and social sciences to explore the complex relationships between religion and society.

## Degree subject combinations

There are many joint degree courses available and you can combine theology or religious studies with most subjects. The most popular options are history, English, philosophy, sociology or languages. You could also combine with related subjects like church history. Specialist degrees such as Islamic studies can be combined with Arabic and Jewish studies can be combined with Hebrew.

## Other higher education qualifications

There are some foundation degrees available in Christian theology and ministry and these are geared towards those wishing to work in the church.

There are no HNDs or HNCs available but many universities and colleges, including theological colleges, run diploma and certificate courses of various kinds, some of them part time or as evening classes. Some offer courses for the University of Cambridge Certificate in Religious Studies and many run their own courses, most of which are intended for those planning a career in the Christian ministry.

## Relevance to other subjects?

There are many other degree courses you could consider with a religious studies A level, such as American studies, combined studies, English, history, law, philosophy, politics, psychology, social science and teaching. It is acceptable as an entry qualification for any humanities or social science course. Anthropology, which involves looking at human culture in all its forms, including the role of religion and ritual in developed as well as primitive societies, would be particularly enhanced by a knowledge of religion and religious behaviour.

## Important advice

Make sure you research degree programmes carefully as some degrees just focus on one or two religions, whereas others cover many different faiths or broader issues. Some courses offer the opportunity to study abroad at another university or to study a particular religion during the summer vacation, for example in India. You should make sure the course matches your interests. If you are not sure whether you want to do your whole degree in religious studies, you might want to look at courses where you can combine subjects or have the option to add to or change your subjects after the first year.

# Future careers

## ▷After A levels

Religious studies A level is regarded by many employers as a reliable academic qualification. It suggests that you can communicate your ideas clearly and effectively and have strong written and verbal skills. It is a useful additional A level for many careers and would be acceptable for many jobs including business and administration, retail, the Armed Forces and social care.

## ▷After a degree

### Working in religious studies

There are a number of careers related to religious studies, most requiring some further training:

- **teaching religious studies in schools**–there are some openings for religious studies teachers in primary and secondary schools; to teach in state schools you must have followed a degree leading to QTS (qualified teacher status), or have taken a one-year Postgraduate Certificate in Education (PGCE) after your first degree. Opportunities may be available to teach in colleges and universities.
- **ordained ministry or other full-time careers in the church**–this requires additional training over a number of years. You must have total commitment and dedication.
- **museum work**–you might be able to use your knowledge of different religious traditions and their historical development by becoming a specialist in the field of religious artefacts. A postgraduate qualification would help in this type of work.
- **research and teaching in universities**–staff in universities usually carry out research as well as teaching, and there may be opportunities as research assistants. You could be involved in researching anything from ancient Hindu traditions to the modern evangelical movement in the USA.

### Working outside religious studies

Only a few graduates in religious studies go on to a career with a religious organisation. Most use their skills in other areas, ranging from caring professions and charity work to business. Remember that a large proportion of graduate jobs are open to graduates in any subject, so if you are interested in a religious studies degree, don't worry about it being a disadvantage to you in the future. The critical thinking skills and the understanding of people developed in a religious studies degree will help you at many levels in the world of work.

## Sources of information

www.reonline.org.uk

www.rsrevision.com

'I enjoyed my degree; it taught me how to think logically, research effectively and also how to understand people. It certainly helped me get my first job.' Nigel, investment banker, with a degree in theology

# Science (Applied)

*For this course you study how science is used in industry, commerce, research and for the benefit (or otherwise) of the environment. It concentrates on how to approach scientific problems and aims to develop the practical skills that you need to solve these problems. It gives you the opportunity to study science without specialising at this level. Your studies will be balanced between biology, chemistry and physics and you may have the opportunity to choose units that lead to a particular pathway.*

*You will develop a range of skills that will be useful to you either for higher level study or in work and training. This A level is available as a double and a single award.*

*GCSE science and maths are recommended to help you get the most from this course.*

## What do you study?

*The topics listed give an idea of what could be covered. The exact content of AS and A2 specifications differs according to exam boards, so you will need to check with your school or college about the exact modules available to you.*

Possible topics for the different awarding bodies are: analysis at work; cells and molecules; chemicals for a purpose; choosing and using materials; energy transfer systems; finding out about substances; food science and technology; forensic science; investigating science at work; monitoring the activity of the human body; synthesising organic compounds; the physics of sport.

You also learn how to plan and carry out scientific investigations.

## A2

Possible topics include: applications of biotechnology; colour chemistry; controlling chemical processes; ecology, conservation and recycling; ecology and managing the environment; electrons in action; investigating the scientists work; materials for a purpose; physics of performance effects; sampling, testing and processing; the actions and development of medicines; synthesising organic chemicals; the healthy body; the mind and the brain; the role of the pathology service; working waves (looks at a range of applications of electromagnetic waves, such as communications fibre optics, mobile phone networks and satellites).

You study in a practical way and concentrate on the knowledge, skills and techniques found in real-life situations. You study with a combination of practical portfolio building and tests, combined with lectures and workshops, experiments and investigations, fieldwork and visits, case studies, research assignments and detailed reports on science topics and issues. There will be industrial visits, and speakers from industry will come in to give you up-to-date information on the current labour market and issues that affect them. For the A2, you have the opportunity to carry out a practical investigation of your choice, which will give you practical experience and the chance to learn new skills.

## Subject combinations

Think carefully about how applied science will fit in with your other subjects. There may be some overlap with other sciences such as biology, human biology and chemistry A level courses, and your teachers may recommend studying applied science instead of these subjects, rather than alongside them. A level applied science is a good choice for students considering higher education in any science-based course, including: nursing, midwifery, physiotherapy, paramedic work and sports science.

In addition, applied science can be used to support subjects such as physical education, psychology, sociology or other applied A levels such as health and social care or business. If you are aiming for a particular career path or degree course, you will need to check with the relevant university or college to find out whether your combination of subjects is acceptable.

# Higher education options

## Degree-level study

The double and single awards in applied science are acceptable for entry to higher education and you could consider a whole range of science-based degrees depending on the units that you have chosen. Some courses may ask for additional AS or A2 levels in certain subjects.

Courses you could consider include biological science, biomedical science, environmental science, forensic science, health sciences and food or sports science. Engineering subjects are another possibility. It is worth investigating integrated science courses. These are designed for industry and they require graduates with a broad mix of skills. The courses develop skills in science, technology, engineering, IT and maths, alongside high-level skills in interpretation of knowledge and analytical thinking. You could also consider degrees in nursing and teaching or other health-related careers such as radiography, occupational therapy or paramedic science. There are also foundation years available on some courses if you do not reach the standard for degree level entry. The foundation year is designed to get you up to standard for degree level entry.

## Degree subject combinations

A scientific degree could be combined with a whole range of other subjects, such as business studies, languages, arts and humanities. If you are considering this, you must check that the content of the course will allow you to progress, especially if you are considering a pure science career.

## Other higher education qualifications

There are foundation degrees in science and you could consider a wide range of applied foundation degrees covering different scientific specialisms, such as:

- animal science and welfare
- applied science
- biological sciences
- biomedical science
- chemical science
- equine science
- food science and technology
- forensic science
- healthcare science
- marine science
- marine sports science
- oral health sciences
- paramedic science
- pharmaceutical science
- sports science
- veterinary nursing science.

HND and HNC courses are available in applied science and applied areas such as agricultural science, applied chemistry, beauty therapy sciences, biomedical sciences, biological and chemical sciences, environmental science, forensic science, horticulture, conservation management and sports science.

## Relevance to other subjects?

You will have gained analytical skills and the ability to think and present information in a logical way, so many other subjects could be open to you such as business, management and accountancy.

## Important advice

There is such a wide range of science-based courses available you need to do a lot of research to find out which ones are suitable for you. Don't forget to check out the facilities available at universities. If you are not sure where a course might lead in the future, then ask what happened to previous graduates.

# Future careers

### ▷After A levels

You could go straight into employment as a laboratory worker in an analytical or quality control laboratory, hospital testing laboratory, educational science department, or a similar area of practical science. Other options could include dental technology or animal nursing. There are apprenticeships available in areas like life sciences, chemical science and healthcare science as well as engineering. Higher Apprenticeships can lead to degree level study.

### ▷After a degree

### Working in science

Science graduates are in demand and highly valued. You will find scientists right across industry, in the health service, government establishments, and research and educational institutions. Obvious jobs are in research and development, but science knowledge can be useful in marketing and sales in science-based companies. The government employs scientists in administrative and consultancy capacities and there could be opportunities in related areas such as legal work (licensing drugs, for example) and information science. There is also a severe shortage of science graduates entering teaching and there are financial incentives to encourage them to train.

## Working outside science

A science degree will provide you with good problem-solving skills as well as a good scientific and maths grounding, so you could consider trainee schemes in many areas including accountancy, banking, ICT and retail.

## Sources of information

Biochemical Society
www.biochemistry.org

Institute of Biomedical Science
www.ibms.org

British Science Association
www.britishscienceassociation.org

Cogent (apprenticeships)
www.cogent-ssc.com

Institute of Physics
www.iop.org

NHS Careers
www.nhscareers.nhs.uk

Royal Society of Chemistry
www.rsc.org

Future Morph
www.futuremorph.org

Society of Biology
www.societyofbiology.org

Women in Science
www.wisecampaign.org.uk

'The organisation we studied was a zoo, which was really good fun. We looked at the conservation they do and the captive breeding programmes. We met people doing real jobs. You don't realise what goes on behind the scenes.' Anna, taking A levels in applied science and biology

# Science in society

*Everybody is affected by the big issues in science. Think about global warming, hurricanes, sustainability, food additives, genetic engineering and swine flu, TB and HIV.*

*The course aims to develop the knowledge and skills for you to understand how science works, analyse current issues involving science and technology, and be able to communicate this understanding to others. It enables you to become scientifically literate. This is something that will be needed more and more by students, whether or not you are studying science.*

*Science in society is relevant whatever subjects you are studying. If you are not specialising in science it gives you the opportunity to keep up to date with a fast-moving subject.*

The course will enable you to:
- take an informed interest in media reports about issues and events involving science
- develop and be able to express an informed, personal point of view on these issues
- make use of your understanding of science in everyday contexts and in making decisions about your own lifestyle and choices in your life.

You will need to have studied science to GCSE level to take this course.

## What do you study?
*Science in society is available from AQA. There is also a science AS, only available through OCR. The specification for this AS is similar to that of the science in society AS.*

Throughout the A level you study these common themes:
- The methods of science, data and their limitations
- establishing causal links
- developing and testing scientific explanations
- modelling of complex situations (A2)
- science as a human activity
- the scientific community, science and society
- relationships between science and society
- assessing impacts of science and technology: risk and risk assessment and making decisions about science and technology

In the AS there are two units. The first is about exploring key scientific issues and covers:

- the germ theory of disease
- impact of infectious diseases now
- transport issues
- medicines
- ethical issues in medicine
- reproductive choices
- radiation: risks and uses
- lifestyle and health
- evolution and the universe.

You then examine scientific explanations of:

- the germ theory of disease
- cells as the basic units of living things
- the gene model of inheritance
- radiation and radioactivity
- chemical substances and chemical reactions
- energy: its transfer, conservation and dissipation
- The theory of evolution by natural selection
- The interdependence of species
- The scale, origin and future of the universe.

You will explore reading and writing about science through coursework, covering critical accounts of scientific reading and the study of a topical scientific issue.

Unit 2, called reading and research, gives you the opportunity to research and report on a topical issue, and to review some popular scientific literature and then write about it.

In A2 you study further key scientific issues

- cells, chemicals and the mind
- nature and nurture
- watching the brain working
- responding to global climate change
- energy futures
- sustaining the variety of life on earth.

You then investigate science explanations:
- neurons and their interactions
- the functioning brain
- gene expression
- chemical cycles
- the radiation model
- energy: sources and uses
- biodiversity.

The final unit is a case study of a current scientific issue.

## Subject combinations
Science in society can be combined with any subject whether science, arts or humanities.

# Higher education options

## Degree-level study
If you have specialised in other subjects for a specific degree area, science in society will complement these A levels in your degree area of choice. It is especially useful for medical degrees, environmental sciences, human and biological sciences. It gives breadth to arts and humanities degrees and an added dimension to courses such as journalism or law.

There is a degree in science and society at University College London which looks at science and technology in its varied and complex modern forms. It covers how social, political and cultural forces and values shape scientific practice and technological innovation as well as the effects of science and technology on society.

## Other higher education qualifications
There are no foundation degrees, HNDs or HNCs in science and society although plenty available in science and applied science.

## Relevance to other subjects?
Science in society contains elements of science and humanities so a wide range of related courses is available, depending on the other subjects studied.

## Important advice

Look at science and technology related stories in the media and think about how the science is expressed and explained and how the story is written. Start analysing this and being critical of popular science items and articles.

# Future careers

### ▷After A levels

The mixture of problem-based learning and consideration of current issues in science and technology makes the course a good additional qualification for many careers in business, science and technology.

### ▷After a degree

The study science in society degree is designed to allow you to gain understanding of the discipline and to develop intellectual, practical and transferable skills, such as critical thinking, retrieving, researching and analysing material, time and project management and working effectively both alone and as part of a team. It will prepare you for many careers, especially those at the interface of professional science and the wider culture. Graduates from this course typically go into careers in the areas of science policy, think tanks, charities, science communication, journalism, education, museums, finance and law.

### Sources of information

Science in Society (Nuffield Foundation)
www.nuffieldfoundation.org/science-society

Institute of Science in Society
www.i-sis.org.uk

# Sociology

*Sociology is concerned with why society works in the way that it does, and the extent to which our behaviour and even our opportunities can be shaped by our social class, age, gender, disability and race. It questions the society in which we live in order to understand the relationship between individuals and institutions such as the education system, religion and the mass media. Each of us is a member of a variety of social groups. In A level sociology you are required to take a step back from your personal interpretation of the world and look at how you too may have been influenced or shaped by these groups.*

## What do you study?
*The topics listed give an idea of what could be covered. The exact content of AS and A2 specifications differs according to exam boards, so you will need to check with your school or college about the exact modules available to you.*

**Methods**–how sociologists obtain information about society; the advantages and disadvantages of different methods of research.

**Social differentiation and stratification**–social inequality and difference, social class, ethnicity, gender and age; how these affect an individuals access to work, wealth, education and other social resources.

**The family**–types of family structure and how families differ across social groups; marriage, divorce and gender roles; the position of children in the family and wider society.

**Education**–the relationship between social class, social mobility and education; how culture is passed on through education; educational institutions; the curriculum; educational achievement between genders and different ethnic groups.

You are also likely to study topics from the following:
**Deviance and control**–how to define antisocial behaviour; the possible causes and outcomes of crime; how social order and control are achieved through laws and social norms (generally agreed codes of behaviour); who has ultimate responsibility for social order, and what are its benefits or negative side effects? Suicide as a social issue; the role of the mass media in defining social deviance.

**Health, welfare and poverty**–definitions of poverty and the reasons for its continuation; distribution of wealth and income; poverty and exclusion; the role of the welfare state.

*Sociology of youth*–key concepts and the social construction of youth, the role of youth culture/subcultures in society, the relationship between youth and subculture and the experience of young people in education. Mass media and popular culture how the media reflects or influences culture and ideas; ownership and control of the media; selection and presentation of news and information. How the mass media presents age, social class and ethnicity.

*Communities and nations*–the formation and maintenance of communities; urbanisation and its effect on communities; nationhood and relations between nations.

*Power and politics*–how political systems work; authority (positions of power and control) and ideology (political ideas and theories); states and governments; political parties and pressure groups; feminism, environmentalism and other social movements.

*Global sociology*–development and underdevelopment of different countries; cultural, political and economic relationships between societies; industrialisation and the environment.

*Religion*–the role of religion in society (as a conservative influence or agent of change); religious institutions and how they are changing; religions in a multicultural society.

You don't need GCSE sociology to take the A level, but it will obviously help you with your further studies. You will need good English skills, as the exams involve essay answers, and also maths, as there are lots of statistics to analyse.

The course contains a lot of reading, essay writing and class discussion. DVDs, newspaper articles and the web are also used to show how sociology relates to the world around us. You may go on visits, for example to the public gallery of a court to see a variety of different cases. You may hear speakers such as the police or someone from a different religion talking about how it affects their life and how they live.

## Subject combinations
Sociology could combine with and complement subjects such as government and politics, psychology or economics and would also combine well with health and social care or arts subjects. If you are considering a BSc in sociology or social sciences, it would be a good idea to combine sociology A level with a more numerate/quantitative subject such as maths, statistics or computing. For these courses you will need

at least GCSE maths to cope with the research and statistics involved in the courses.

# Higher education options

It is not necessary to have studied A level sociology in order to study it at university, although the background knowledge provided by your A level would certainly help with the first year of your degree.

## Degree-level study

A degree in sociology may be a BA or BSc. In some cases this indicates whether the approach is more on the arts or the science (specifically quantitative) side. This means you should check the content of each course carefully before applying.

The first year of a sociology degree course covers some of the topics you will already have looked at during your A level studies, but in much more depth. Many first-year courses are quite broad, offering you a general introduction to the social sciences. They may include options in the study of social policy, psychology, economics, politics and languages.

In your second and third years, you will be able to specialise in areas that particularly interest you, for example, gender and sexuality, social justice, culture, race, religion or social policy. You can combine sociology with many subjects, but the most widely available are history, politics, psychology, economics and English. There are combinations in related areas such as criminology and social policy. You will also find social work courses combined with sociology or applied sociology. These courses include the necessary assessed practice towards qualification as a social worker.

## Other higher education qualifications

There are foundation degrees in social sciences and in combination with psychology. There are related degrees in public and community services, children, parenting and communities, community development, community health and wellbeing, community leadership, community learning, community policing and justice management, community studies (development and youth work), housing, communities and regeneration, professional studies in youth, community and families, social policy, health and housing, and youth and community development.

HND and HNC courses are available in social sciences or social studies, with some specialist courses in criminological social sciences and health and social care management.

### Relevance to other subjects?
One of the most popular alternatives is to take a degree in social work, and to qualify as a social worker. (N.B. It is possible to take a postgraduate qualification after other degrees for social work training.) Other popular options are public services management, community studies and counselling degrees. You could also look at criminology or criminal justice, cultural studies, politics, housing studies, development studies, economics, geography and history.

### Important advice
For entry to teaching, there are a few social science PGCE courses, which are specific to the 14 to 19 teaching age groups. The courses include sociology but may ask for another subject specialism such as history, religious education, economics or psychology. You might consider a joint degree in sociology and another subject, if you want to study sociology without jeopardising your chances of going into teaching later on. It is important to check the acceptability of your intended degree carefully with postgraduate teacher training providers before you start your degree course.

# Future careers

### ▷After A levels
Employers will value your understanding of human social behaviour as well as your research skills. Career opportunities include working for the government, market research, human resources, the police or prison service. If you want to go into social work later on, you could build up experience by working in a social services support job, e.g. as a care assistant. There are apprenticeships in health and social care and Higher Apprenticeships in care leadership and management.

## ▷After a degree

## Working in sociology

*Social researcher*–working for market research organisations, charities, educational organisations, local or national government; may require getting further qualifications in information management or social research methods.

*Social worker*– supporting and advising people who experience health or social problems within the community; you would need to do postgraduate study for this unless qualification was included in your first degree.

*Teacher*–in a school or college, for which you would need a PGCE. See the *Important advice* section for more information.

*Administrator*–for local government in departments such as education, housing or social services, central government or charities.

*Counsellor, welfare worker or community advice worker*–working in a variety of settings, providing support and advice to a range of clients. You would need further training.

## Working outside sociology

You will have developed valuable research skills as well as your knowledge of society, which would be useful in a range of careers from advertising, marketing and human resources through to the emergency services.

## Sources of information

The Social Research Association
www.the-sra.org.uk

British Sociological Association
www.britsoc.co.uk

Skills for Care
www.skillsforcare.org.uk

www.sociology.org.uk

---

*'I enjoy sociology because it is relevant to everyday life. You can see the concepts involved in sociology every day, which makes it interesting.'*
Charlie, 16, studying sociology, English, psychology and law

# Travel and tourism

*Travel and tourism is very broad and includes not only package tours, special interest holidays, travel by train, boat, coach, car and plane, but also theme parks, zoos, historical sites, and houses and museums. If you think about your local area you are sure to identify some places of interest worth visiting. This course is aimed to give you an understanding and overview of the travel and tourism industry today. You learn to appreciate how it is always evolving as customers needs and trends change. A good example of this is the trend towards staycations people holidaying in the UK rather than abroad. It is also a highly competitive industry. You also look at issues such as customer service, quality and responsible tourism.*

*This A level is available as a double or as a single award.*

## What do you study?
*The topics listed give an idea of what could be covered. The exact content of AS and A2 specifications differ according to exam boards, so you will need to check with your school or college about the exact modules available to you.*

- **The travel and tourism industry**—looking at the industry and at how and why it grows and develops. You will learn what mix of organisations make up the UK travel industry and the significance of the industry to the UK economy. You will investigate the wide range of careers available in the industry and identify those jobs that will suit you. This might include looking at employment overseas and the types of skills and personal qualities required.
- **Customer service**—very important in a highly competitive business. You will find out how important it is that all staff in the industry receive comprehensive induction and training packages. You learn about different types of customers, how to deal with complaints and how to measure, monitor and evaluate customer service procedures and practices.
- **Travel destinations**—learning about the major continental European and long- haul destinations for UK tourists, studying their location and finding out what makes them attractive to different types of tourism. You will look at the different types of transport available, especially as customers are becoming more environmentally aware. You will study attractions in the UK for overseas visitors.
- **Range of holidays**—looking at the range of different types of holidays available; you may have the opportunity to undertake a

specialised study of a particular type of holiday, which could include special interest and activity holidays, guided tours, sports tourism, ecotourism, adventure tourism or cultural tourism.

- **The impact of tourism and current issues in the industry**–this covers the ecological impact of tourism development and responsible tourism, as well as other issues such as the use of technology and how global tourism is developing. It also covers the economic impact of tourism, and the trend of people having staycation holidays in the UK rather than going abroad.

In addition, there are other units offered (according to the specification), which include the following topics:

- international travel
- event management
- organising travel
- ecotourism
- working overseas
- tourism development
- the guided tour
- adventure tourism
- hospitality, including corporate hospitality
- marketing in travel and tourism.

You will undertake work experience, day and residential visits both in the UK and possibly abroad; you may learn practical skills (such as ticketing) and foreign languages. You will put on a real travel and tourism event for fellow students or the general public, and visit trade shows and exhibitions. You are likely to undertake a project for A2. You may have to pay towards any residential courses.

## Subject combinations

Possible useful combinations include foreign languages, physical education, psychology, geography, media studies and business.

# Higher education options

## Degree-level study

There are degrees in travel and tourism and travel and tourism management. You will also find many related and specialist degrees, for example, adventure tourism management, adventure and extreme sports management, airline and airport management, cruise management, ecotourism, hospitality management, sports tourism, travel journalism, hotel and resort management, tourism management and marketing, leisure and recreation management. All these degrees would give you the opportunity to develop your skills further and are likely to include placements in the UK and/or abroad.

## Degree subject combinations
It is popular to combine travel courses with a language, geography or business studies and there are related combinations on offer such as hospitality, tourism and events management.

## Other higher education qualifications
Travel and tourism foundation degrees are widely available and you will also find a variety of foundation degrees in specialist areas of the industry such as events and tourism management, international tourism management, tourism business management, tourism management (aviation management and operations) and tourism park management.

HND and HNC travel and tourism courses are available and again there are specialist courses such as international tourism and event management, and tourism and hospitality management. You could also consider related HNDs such as hospitality or leisure and recreation management.

## Relevance to other subjects?
Look at business studies or retail management, marketing or public relations courses.

## Important advice
Keep up-to-date with innovations in travel and tourism as it is a fast-changing industry. Consider how volcanoes, economic downturns or civil unrest have affected tourism. Look at trends such as sustainable tourism, adult gap years and the impact of the London Olympics. Attend travel shows and talk to travel companies. Work experience or work shadowing would be useful to help you decide if this type of work is for you. Also think about learning a foreign language.

# Future careers

## ▷After A levels
Your skills from this course could lead to a wide range of employment opportunities, especially if you have taken some extra vocational

qualifications and/or a language. You could consider jobs in travel agents, airline cabin crew, car rental, cruise ships, airport ground staff, hotel administration/reception, travel call centre work, conference planning and resort representative work. There are apprenticeships available in travel and tourism.

## ▷ After a degree
### Working in travel and tourism
Travel and tourism graduates often join large travel companies in head-office functions such as financial control, personnel or marketing. They may also work in travel agents, tourist attractions, tourist information or in specialist travel areas such as adventure, sports tourism or health and fitness holidays. If you are willing to travel and broaden your experience this can really help your career.

### Working outside travel and tourism
Your customer service, business and organisational skills will be transferable to a lot of other careers such as hospitality and catering management and the leisure industry. You will also have options for working in general business, administration and management.

### Sources of information
ABTA
www.abta.com

Association of Independent Tour Operators
www.aito.co.uk

Institute of Travel and Tourism
www.itt.co.uk

World Tourism Organization
www.unwto.org

VisitBritain
www.visitbritain.org

---

'Get a part-time job in the industry while you are studying. I worked part time as a hotel receptionist and that helped me get my first full-time job in the same hotel.' Natta, hotel reception manager with a BA in hospitality and tourism management

# World/global development

*Are you concerned about poverty and discrimination here and around the world?*

*How can we help people to get out of poverty? Should the government provide more overseas aid, and what happens to it when it is given? How can we make trade fair? What about healthcare in other parts of the world? How would local health provision affect someone who is HIV positive?*

*World development A level will help you to gain an understanding of global issues and their impact on people and societies. It explores the need to develop a more just and fair society and considers the issues of poverty, inequality, fair and unfair trade, globalisation, debt, conflict, the arms trade and environmental sustainability. These are issues that shape our and everyones lives.*

## What do you study?

*World development is offered by WJEC and Edexcel offers global development.*

In world development there are two main areas that are studied:
- development, resources and global citizenship
- poverty and inequality.

And at A2:
- theories and concepts of development
- one of the following themes: economic development, political development or social development.

You will study global issues, economic growth and the development of a sustainable, one world vision. You will examine the forces at work in the processes of globalisation and interdependence. You will consider how development takes place and how a more just and equal society might be achieved; for some people, basic needs such as water supplies are important, for others it is their working conditions in a factory making fashion clothing. You will look at local, national as well as international issues, evaluating approaches such as fair trade, community action and government support. You will be challenged by issues of poverty and discrimination locally and globally. The course contains aspects of other subjects such as economics, geography, sociology, politics, economics, citizenship, history and business studies.

## Subject combinations

The course combines well with many subjects, especially geography but also with business, sociology, economics, modern languages and politics.

Languages could be particularly useful if you plan eventually to work abroad. There is no reason why world development cannot be combined with science and maths, especially if you are interested in sustainable technology or global challenges.

# Higher education options

## Degree-level study
Relevant courses are available in international relations, international development, third world development and charity development. Some courses include work placements in the UK or abroad, sometimes included as an assessed module within the degree.

## Degree subject combinations
Economics, peace studies, politics, history, modern languages, English as a foreign language, law, geography, sociology, business studies and economics are possible combinations.

## Other higher education qualifications
There are some related foundation degrees available in community development and geography and society.

## Relevance to other subjects?
You will find world/global development options in some other degrees, such as business studies, economics and geography and on modular degrees. There is a degree in international business and globalisation you could consider and another option would be human rights.

## Important advice
Start finding out about global issues from the media. Keep up-to-date with current issues and events. Find out what is going on in your local community; for example, is there a pressure group against a local development such as a new road, airport, railway, wind farm or housing?

Be aware of national and global campaigns by aid agencies. Take note of leaflets and adverts that come through your door. A gap year could be useful to you, and you might like to investigate the many opportunities available for putting your concerns and understanding into practice. Be active. World development is for the sort of people who want to make a difference. Think about volunteering, joining a campaign group or doing something for a local charity.

# Future careers

## ▷After A levels

Although world development doesn't prepare you for a specific career, knowledge of world development issues would be invaluable in careers in local government or the Civil Service, and in financial services such as banks. Working for a global company would be another option, as would work with charities or voluntary organisations.

## ▷After a degree

### Working in world development

You will have an understanding of the forces that drive modern societies and of global issues. This knowledge will prove useful in careers in government, law, public administration, commerce, financial services and public relations. You may be inspired to get involved in local or even national politics or work for a political party or campaign group. There could also be careers in the development field with government and voluntary organisations, charities, aid agencies and transnational bodies, and you would be well placed to work anywhere in the world. If you want to work for a voluntary organisation (often called non-governmental organisations, or NGOs) as a field worker you will need overseas experience in development work. Look for internships and four- to six-month placements abroad. Many agencies look for specialists people with particular expertise such as logistics, language skills, advocacy skills and fundraising skills. This is where a combined degree can be a definite advantage.

### Working outside world development

World development gives you knowledge and skills that could be applied to many different careers. Local or national government are possibilities and you might also wish to consider training in social work or teaching. You could also consider a range of other graduate-level jobs in finance, retail management or administration.

## Sources of information

United Nations
www.un.org

World Development Movement
www.wdm.org.uk

Development in Action
www.developmentinaction.org

Drop the Debt
www.jubileedebtcampaign.org.uk

GreenNet
www.gn.apc.org

One World
http://oneworld.org

Restless Development
www.restlessdevelopment.org

Bond (British Overseas NGOs for Development)
www.bond.org.uk

Department for International Development (has free publications)
www.gov.uk/government/organisations/department-for-international-development

---

'Be willing to take stepping-stone jobs to get where you want to be. I started out as a volunteer with a charity and ended up with an internship, which helped me a lot.' Daniel, emergency response officer with a leading charity

## Useful information

Joint Council for Qualifications (publish national exam results)
www.jcq.org.uk

AQA
www.aqa.org.uk

Cambridge Pre-U
www.cie.org.uk

CCEA
www.ccea.org.uk

Edexcel
www.edexcel.org.uk

International Baccalaureate Organisation
www.ibo.org

OCR
www.ocr.org.uk

Scottish Baccalaureate
www.sqa.org.uk/baccalaureates

Welsh Baccalaureate
www.welshbaccalaureate.org.uk

WJEC
www.wjec.co.uk

Lightning Source UK Ltd.
Milton Keynes UK
UKOW04f1713120814

236838UK00003B/132/P